Islam on Trial

Chawkat Moucarry addresses as a sincere friend, but without detours, the reasons for the crisis which is shaking the Muslim world. Taking them into consideration, examining them and getting involved in the vast undertaking of re-founding Islamic theological thought is a way of salvation for Muslim societies. The huge issues that need rethinking include: freedom of conscience, ontological and legal equality between people regardless of gender and metaphysical preference, de-sacralazation of violence, and the autonomy of knowledge in connection with revelation and belief. The work on these key issues must be carried out with boldness and determination. The support of people such as Chawkat Moucarry is really precious.

Adhering to the principle of otherness, especially confessional, getting familiar with diverse lifestyles and appreciating cultural differences are a requirement and a priority in order to understand the human experience in its total diversity, in its uniqueness as well as in its concrete universality.

Fair exchange and inter-religious dialogue, based on mutual understanding and respect and the equal dignity of human beings, are the prerequisites for building social cohesion, reconciliation between peoples and peace between nations. Chawkat Moucarry contributes masterfully to this with heart intelligence. As a faithful Christian, he states in his conclusion that unconditional love is the only adequate response to Islamist violence and a secularized society. We are all grateful to him for this response which is also ours. We take the liberty of simply putting forward the idea – which is in no way incongruous with the exemplary reasoning of our author – that prior to this, justice must be done and the law laid down.

Ghaleb Bencheikh El Hocine
President of Fondation de l'Islam de France

Moucarry's writing about Muslims and Islam is unique for several reasons. Having grown up among Muslims in Syria and with Arabic as his mother tongue, he has no difficulty in relating to Muslims and reading the Qur'an and Hadith in their original language. Having lived in France and the UK for many years, he understands very well all the complex questions about being a Muslim in secular Europe. Because of his academic study of Islam, he appreciates Islam at its very best and recognizes the diversity among Muslims. His work with an international NGO in many Majority World countries has enabled him to understand the sensitivities and opportunities involved in Christian-Muslim relations. This book therefore deserves to be read widely by Christians and Muslims all over the world.

Colin Chapman
Former Lecturer in Islamic Studies,
Near East School of Theology and Arab Baptist Theological Seminary,
Beirut, Lebanon

Despite his normal reticence, Moucarry begins his book with a fascinating self-introduction. This is no mere self-indulgence. His background in Syria, France and Britain determines the book's content and tone. Moucarry developed close friendships with Muslim boys and their families in his school in Syria. Later, throughout his life, he has enjoyed strong relationships with Muslims of varying backgrounds, including scholars and leaders. We note therefore his warm empathy with Islam and Muslims. Through doctoral studies at the Sorbonne and years of careful qur'anic and Hadith study, a thorough academic approach undergirds the whole book. Moucarry works brilliantly and relevantly through aspects of Islam in Part 1 and Christian-Muslim debate in Part 2. I strongly recommend this book and hope it will be widely distributed.

Martin Goldsmith
Former Lecturer and Overseas Representative,
All Nations Christian College, Ware, UK
Author of *Beyond Beards and Burqas, What about other Faiths?*,
Get a grip on Mission

This is a very helpful, informative and satisfying book to read. Satisfying because of the high level of integrity that Chawkat demonstrates throughout. This integrity has developed because of his background and experience, including Arabic being his mother tongue, his close involvement with Muslims from his teenage years, his serious study of Islam to PhD level, his close association with the breadth of the Christian church from Catholic to evangelical, his many close Muslim friends and his critical but never judgemental character and approach. The autobiographical chapter at the beginning was both fascinating and significant. Chawkat thinks widely, researches carefully, analyses deeply and then writes clearly. Not only was it clear that he knew what he was talking about, but the way he writes gave me a growing confidence to take seriously the challenges that Islam faces and the challenges we face as we engage with Muslims. I wholeheartedly welcome and recommend this book to all those who are building friendships with Muslims.

Bryan Knell
Former UK Director of Arab World Ministries
Founding Convenor of Christian Responses to Islam in Britain
Advisor for the Global Connections Muslim World Forum
Trustee of Mahabba UK

Chawkat's voice in the field of Muslim-Christian relations is more needed today than ever. His background as a committed Christian with deep roots in the historic Catholic church of the Middle East positions him well for the task. His upbringing in Syria provides a view of Islam from the inside. A wide-ranging and multilingual experience of student ministry (France's IFES), scholarship and teaching (All Nations Christian College, UK) and global relief and development (World Vision) produce a unique perspective on Christian engagement with Muslims. Chawkat achieves the rare balance of a scholarly pursuit of truth and a Christlike heart of empathy. He walks the way of Jesus among the Samaritans as he opened the possibility of worship in spirit and truth to a stunned Samaritan woman. Chawkat models the value of deep listening to our Muslim friends. This book can take us further down the road of incarnational living.

Mike Kuhn, PhD
Former Lecturer in Biblical Theology and Discipleship,
Arab Baptist Theological Seminary, Beirut, Lebanon

Chawkat Moucarry comes from a background where engagement and friendship between Muslim and Christian was possible. Everything he writes is coloured by this experience. It is a matter of concern to him and to all people of goodwill that such relations are now widely vitiated by extremism. Moucarry ably rehearses the long history of Muslim-Christian encounter. He is aware of both the collaboration, for example, in learning and the systemic discrimination of the Dhimma against Christians and Jews. There have been centuries of conflict but also periods of peaceful co-existence. Sometimes even seemingly common ground, like family values, reveal different anthropologies and worldviews. Moucarry is a powerful advocate for peace but knows that true peace is not appeasement of extremism. Because of his knowledge of Islam from the "inside," he is an effective apologist of the Christian faith in his dialogue with Muslims in our world today, we need more Chawkat Moucarrys.

Michael Nazir-Ali, PhD
President of Oxford Centre for Training, Research, Advocacy and Dialogue,
London, UK

This is a mature reflection, based on long experience of inter-faith dialogue, on how to build bridges between Christians and Muslims in the West, avoiding both hostility and naivete. Chawkat Moucarry begins with his personal story of growing up in Syria and then brings together illuminating historical summaries of Muslim and Christian beliefs and practices, irenic but incisive theological interrogation of both and judicious political proposals. Hopefully, this book will educate Christians and Muslims alike, and move us beyond caricatures or blanket slogans such as "Islamophobia" and "jihadists" to addressing seriously the very real challenges that all of us share while also respecting the significant differences among us.

Vinoth Ramachandra, PhD
IFES Secretary for Dialogue and Social Engagement,
Columbo, Sri Lanka

Islam on Trial

Globalization, Islamism, and Christianity

Chawkat Moucarry

GLOBAL LIBRARY

© 2022 Chawkat Moucarry

Published 2022 by Langham Global Library
An imprint of Langham Publishing
www.langhampublishing.org

Langham Publishing and its imprints are a ministry of Langham Partnership

Langham Partnership
PO Box 296, Carlisle, Cumbria, CA3 9WZ, UK
www.langham.org

ISBNs:
978-1-83973-581-3 Print
978-1-83973-582-0 ePub
978-1-83973-583-7 Mobi
978-1-83973-584-4 PDF

Chawkat Moucarry has asserted his right under the Copyright, Designs and Patents Act, 1988 to be identified as the Author of this work.

All rights reserved. No part of this publication may be reproduced, stored in a retrieval system or transmitted, in any form or by any means, electronic, mechanical, photocopying, recording or otherwise, without the prior written permission of the publisher or the Copyright Licensing Agency.

Requests to reuse content from Langham Publishing are processed through PLSclear. Please visit www.plsclear.com to complete your request.

All Scripture quotations, unless otherwise indicated, are taken from the Holy Bible, New International Version®, NIV®. Copyright ©1973, 1978, 1984, 2011 by Biblica, Inc.™ Used by permission of Zondervan.

Scripture quotations marked (NLT) are taken from the Holy Bible, New Living Translation, copyright © 1996, 2004, 2007, 2013, 2015 by Tyndale House Foundation. Used by permission of Tyndale House Publishers, Inc., Carol Stream, Illinois 60188. All rights reserved.

Quotations of Qur'anic texts are the author's own translation.

British Library Cataloguing-in-Publication Data
A catalogue record for this book is available from the British Library

ISBN: 978-1-83973-581-3

Cover & Book Design: projectluz.com

Langham Partnership actively supports theological dialogue and an author's right to publish but does not necessarily endorse the views and opinions set forth here or in works referenced within this publication, nor can we guarantee technical and grammatical correctness. Langham Partnership does not accept any responsibility or liability to persons or property as a consequence of the reading, use or interpretation of its published content.

In loving memory of my parents
To my sisters: Nour, Leyla and Nayla
To my wife, our son and three daughters
May our heavenly Father fill you with his redemptive love!

Contents

Foreword xi
Preface xvii
Introduction: My Spiritual Journey 1

Part One: Islam: A Religion with Many Faces

1 Islam as Religion.. 15
2 Islam as Community 33
3 Islam as Law 55
4 Radical Islam.. 75
5 Islam: Current Issues 97

Part Two: Islam and Christianity

6 The Corruption of the Bible: Myth or Reality?............. 119
7 Jesus Christ 137
8 One God in Three Persons 153
9 Forgiveness in Islam and Christianity 171
10 Shared Beliefs and Values 183
   Conclusion: Unconditional Love as a Response to Islamist Violence and Secular Society........................ 199
   Select Bibliography.. 207

Foreword

The relationship between Islam and other religions in general, and Christianity in particular, has been the subject of countless works from the Middle Ages to the present day. We shall dismiss those written by the two partisans of unintelligent simplification, namely, polemicists and apologists, and retain only scientific works. Given my area of expertise, I will only refer here to Islamic studies. These, until recently, often echoed accounts from mostly Sunni Muslim sources regarding the life of Muhammad, the history of the Qur'an, or the origins of Islam. In other words, as there is an "orthodox Islam," there also existed, and still exists, an "orthodox Islamology." In recent decades, things have partially evolved thanks in particular to the critical study of non-Islamic sources contemporary to the advent of the Qur'an (*The Secrets of Rabbi Shimôn ben Yoḥai*, several Syriac apocalypses, *Doctrina Jacobi*, etc.) and to the findings of what might be called material history – archeology, epigraphy, codicology, etc. Since the 1970s, and even more intensely since the 2000s, numerous and fruitful collaborations between specialists in Islam, Judaism, different groups of Eastern Christianity, and Manichaeism, as well as researchers in material history, have completely renewed our interrogations on the genesis and the first developments of the Arab religion. Many gray areas and questions without final answers remain, but a few points now seem established.

Contrary to what Islamic sources and the catechism of Islamic "orthodoxy" report, pre-Islamic Arabia was not a land of dark ignorance, steeped in paganism and barbarism. These traditional Islamic claims, undermined by archeology and epigraphy, are part of the apologetics and hagiography found in many religions: before us nothing, after us everything! The Qur'an itself contradicts these data on every page. Alongside rather rare material on paganism and idolatry in Arabia – some vestiges of which would have existed in a fragmentary way – and real Arab prophets (Hūd, Ṣāliḥ, Shu'ayb), the qur'anic corpus contains hundreds of references to figures and biblical themes: from Adam and Eve to Jesus, Mary and John the Baptist, including Noah, Abraham, Moses, Solomon, David, Jonas or Job; from strict monotheism to the resurrection of the dead and the last judgment through prophets and the centrality of Holy Scriptures. Constantly presenting itself as the extension and the fulfillment of the messages of Moses and Jesus, the Qur'an fully claims its belonging to what one might call "the biblical monotheistic milieu." The significant presence of terms from Syriac (*qur'ān, āya, salāt, zakāt*, etc.), Ethiopian (*injīl, jahannam, ḥawāriyy*, etc.) and Hebrew origin (*yawm al-dīn, jannat 'adn, ḥajj, 'umra*, etc.), liturgical languages of Christian groups and Judaism, or even the allusive nature of biblical data, corroborate this fact. The stories of Abraham or Moses are not fully told from beginning to end. Only certain episodes are taken from them and in a certain way interpreted and glossed upon. Jesus is called Christ, Word of God, and Spirit of God with no explanation whatsoever of these complex christological expressions. All this seems to indicate that the early listeners or readers of the core message of Islam were familiar with this material and that mere allusions were enough for them to grasp their meanings. The things found in the Qur'an about Mary are more numerous than in the synoptic Gospels. Recent research, taking up and supplementing the previous work of people like Alphonse Mingana or Tor Andrea, has brought to light in a convincing way what was hardly recognizable in the Holy Scriptures of Muslims, namely clear traces of hymns and homilies of saints and wise Syriac-speaking Christians like Ephrem of Nisibis, Aphraates the Persian, Narsai of Nisibis and Jacob of Serugh, so-called apocryphal gospels and Arabic paraphrase of Judeo-Christian legal texts such as *the Didascalia of the Apostles*.

In several passages, the Qur'an declares its admiration for the Jews, the chosen people descended from Israel (e.g. 2:122; 5:12; 45:16), and for Christians, especially monks (e.g. 5:82; 21:90–92; 57:27). But in other places the tone changes. The message becomes harsh against the "Peoples of the Scripture," accusing them, among other things, of falsifying the books of Moses and of Jesus as well as forgetting and betraying their missions. Sometimes severity turns into aggressiveness, leaving Christians only the choice between conversion, paying the protection tax as a sign of submission, or death. Why are there contradictions like these and others in the qur'anic text? Are we dealing with one author? Should we look for the answer in the traditional division of Muhammad's life between a Meccan period, when he was orientated towards transcendence and spirituality, and a Medinan period, when he became a military and political leader and was confronted with the complex, contradictory and tragic realities associated with this role in a context marked by numerous hostilities?

Historical criticism has seriously challenged the correctness of this division as well as many other so-called "biographies" of Muhammad. Some specialists raise the question of the plurality of authors of the qur'anic corpus and the different dating of the multiple layers of the text, some of which would be prior to the time of the Prophet, others contemporary, and still others not only after him but after the conquests and the formation of the Arab Empire.

We know that the Qur'an is a corpus, a compound and composite text. Some scholars see in it a text of compromise between opposing groups, drawn up at a time when the community of the faithful needed unity more than ever. Through numerous and very erudite studies, Karl-Friedrich Pohlmann detects the presence of at least two groups among Muhammad's followers, divergent in their faith and in permanent tension against each other: (1) an early, faithful group that would have had eschatological and apocalyptic beliefs, and spiritual and ascetic leanings, close to the Christian monachism of late antiquity. These non-political and non-militant devotees advocated repentance, prayer, fasting, almsgiving, kindness and non-violence in order to prepare for the imminent end of the world and to be saved from the wrath of God. (2) a later, opportunistic group – those whom the Qur'an frequently calls "the hypocrites" – would have been made up of militant men who believed that the world should be prepared for the last judgment through fighting, conquest and looting. For them, just war (*jihād*) was superior to any other form of piety. According to Pohlmann, the texts characterizing the two groups are simultaneously present in the qur'anic text where their religious visions are sometimes inextricably mixed. Can we see in the first group those that Fred Donner presents as the early followers of Muhammad called "the Believers" (*mu'minūn*) including the monotheists of previous religions who were not even asked to convert? And in the second group, the converted pagan Arabs, or even the partisans of the conquests and of the caliphate called "the Submitted" (*muslimūn*)? What about the hypothesis according to which the production of this compromise text, marked by its enigmatic "voluntary disorder," would be the work of the Caliph 'Abd al-Malik, fifth Umayyad ruler, who reigned in the second half of the first century of the Islamic era, who built in blood a certain unity of Islamic territories and whom many consider to be the founder of Islam, the religion of "submission" to God, as the institutional and collective religion of the empire?

From John Wansbrough to Chase Robinson and Stephen Shoemaker, including Michael Cook, Patricia Crone and Alfred-Louis de Prémare, 'Abd al-Malik was considered the master builder of the official, imperial version of the Qur'an, the one that we know. Other versions, different in content and form, belonging to other factions often in open conflict with the caliphal power, would have circulated for several centuries before being permanently done away with. If we consider these hypotheses, which are increasingly supported by current multidisciplinary research, we can assume that there is no split between the initial message of the Qur'an and previous monotheisms. On the contrary, despite its distinctiveness and adaptations, it is a certain continuity that is striking. The break-up will come later, for primarily historical and political reasons, when the Caliphal Empire wanted to impose its domination and demonstrate its superiority over the conquered peoples.

If I insist a little on these issues, which are as little known as they are crucial, it is because the work by Chawkat Moucarry, without being a scientific study, reflects them admirably. Moucarry is a believing Christian, a seeker of peace between individuals and communities, and deeply concerned by violence and fanaticism – he has been personally affected by the terrible civil wars in his region and country. He seeks to shed light on what brings together, and what differentiates, Christianity and Islam. A scholar, equipped with a solid knowledge of both religions in their historical reality as well as in their current situation, he devotes a good part of his book to the presentation of the theological and doctrinal foundations of these. This can be useful to students and to those interested in knowing more about Christianity and Islam. This book is an excellent introduction, simple, accessible and well documented, of the two main religions of the Levant, Chawkat's native region. The author also reminds us of a striking reality which is unfortunately often ignored: "In a sense, Islam does not exist, only Muslims do. They are, like everyone else, very different from each other. Many are kind and friendly, some are less so." (page 109)

The same can be said (with respective differences being considered) about Christians. And what matters to Moucarry is the way in which these two religions are embodied, lived out, and practiced by their respective followers and their mutual relationships. This is why in order to overcome disagreements – sometimes sources of intolerance and violence that he does not hide in any way – he implicitly assumes the traditional and wise division between faith (in Arabic *īmān*) and belief (*'aqīda*). Faith, an unfathomable spiritual mystery comparable to love, is all about what is essential and foundational; based on freedom and lived out by individuals and their moral conscience, faith applies to universal truths. As for belief, it is determined by the environment, history, geography, education, culture and society; it has to do with contingencies, auxiliaries, circumstances, and is subject to time and place. It is therefore intimately linked to collective norms and constraints, to Law and orthopraxy, to certain conditions that can be explained in a specific time and context but which become dangerous, because they are archaic, if we try to apply them always and everywhere.

Having presented and explored the sometimes profound doctrinal differences between Christians and Muslims, Chawkat Moucarry suggests a certain number of points they have in common, those which transcend the divisions and can serve as a bedrock for peaceful living together. These points all relate to faith and not to belief: the recognition of a unique and merciful God, the crucial importance of godly people and of the Scriptures, the dignity and fundamental unity of humankind, solidarity between human beings and the duty to protect life, the centrality of the individual, the family, the child, the awareness of responsibility for actions through faith in the last judgment, the power of love in action, etc.

Thus, Moucarry's approach coincides with certain aspects of the work of the historian: discerning what is essential and what is not, challenging what appears as self-evident and pseudo-certainties, revisiting the past as a living, active entity, which has something to say to the present to enrich it and make it move forward in an intelligent way. He seems to go back to the time of the qur'anic "Believers," to the time of one faith in God, his messengers, his Scriptures and the last judgment; before the time of the "Submitted," those following the empire's conquests, its standards, its constraints, its violence. One may disagree with some of Chawkat Moucarry's arguments, but one cannot doubt his humanism, his sincerity, his rational quest for brotherhood and peace. The same can be said of the responsible historian.

Mohammad Ali Amir-Moezzi
Professor, École Pratique des Hautes Études, Sorbonne, France

Preface

In August 2020, I had the pleasure of spending a week-long vacation in Ardèche at the invitation of a friend from Lyon, Dr. Raphaël Nogier. We first met in Besançon in the mid-1970s when we were both medical students. Raphaël, after reading the French edition of my book on forgiveness in Islam and Christianity (published in February 2020), gave me advice: "Chawkat, you should write a book on Islam accessible to a wide readership in which you would also deal with some specific questions French people are asking about this religion, and you should share in this book something of your personal journey to help the reader understand some of your unusual positions." Raphaël's suggestion struck me as a very good one, so it wasn't long before I picked up my pen again. This book is the outcome of that suggestion made during a simple conversation between two longstanding friends.

Many scholars agree that Islam is in crisis though they diverge on its root causes. This crisis is not recent, but it is accentuated by the cumulative effect of several phenomena characteristic of our time. First, Islamic extremism, which in its ideological and militant expression is often called "radical Islam," "political Islam" or "Islamism." It has taken on alarming dimensions since some radical (albeit very few) Muslims decided some forty years ago to use violence to assert their demands. The word "jihadism" refers now to this minority trend which is very active within the Muslim community. This trend puts a strain on all Muslims who are expected to speak out on their religion's relationship to violence.

The second phenomenon is globalization which has made secularization much more widely spread in the world. Globalization brings people out of their centuries-old isolation and exposes them to ideologies, systems of thought, religions and cultures that remained geographically circumscribed until recent times. Muslims living in predominantly non-Muslim countries are at the forefront of this confrontation. Muslims in Europe, and in France in particular, live under secular regimes, declared or de facto. This reality leads many of them to take a fresh look at their religion and to understand it in terms unexplored by Islamic tradition. This movement, well underway among Muslims living in the West, is likely to trigger a real reformation of

Islam, comparable in some ways to what Protestant reformation of the sixteenth century was for Christianity.

The third phenomenon is the dialogue between Islam and Christianity. Of course, this dialogue is very old. In fact, the Prophet of Islam initiated it himself when he met the Christian community of Najran (south of the Arabian Peninsula). Numerous qur'anic texts encourage Muslims to engage in this dialogue in a way faithful to the monotheistic message and respectful of other monotheistic people such as Jews and Christians (e.g. 3:64; 29:46). What is new, however, is that never before in history have Muslims been confronted with the gospel message in such numbers. At no time have there been so many Muslims all over the world who recognize Jesus Christ not only as a great prophet but as their Lord and Savior. Arab radio and television stations, such as al-Jazeera, regularly report on this unprecedented phenomenon.

The title and subtitle of this book refer to this triple questioning of Islam due to Islamism, globalization and Christianity. Here are a few examples that illustrate the reality of this questioning. Historically, mosques have always been run by male leaders or imams. However, there are now several Muslim women who claim this role; for example, Kahina Bahloul and Eva Janadin in Paris, and Sherin Khankan in Copenhagen. On 31 January 2021, the Muslim Council of Britain elected a young woman as General Secretary, Ms. Zara Mohammed, which represents a significant step in the development of the Muslim community in Europe, namely in terms of women leadership.

On a personal note, and to illustrate what globalization means nowadays, I was recently invited to supervise two master's dissertations prepared by Yemeni female students who had chosen a topic directly related to Christianity. These dissertations were defended at the University of Sanaa (17 July 2019 and 14 September 2020). Thanks to Zoom, I took part in the two defenses from my home in France. A close friend of mine, a young man who is a citizen of the Islamic Republic of Mauritania, has just completed his master's dissertation in Christian theology at a French seminary. His studies came after his decision to follow Christ, a decision he made alone in his homeland seven years ago after a web-based search for the truth. I am regularly invited (by Forum Veritas France) to dialogue with Muslim leaders on various subjects. Thanks to YouTube, these debates are accessible to everyone, no matter what country they live in.

The internet offers unprecedented means of communication, but it is a double-edged sword. Personally, I regret that many Christians and Muslims who use social networks often do so in a confrontational style. Polemics produce "more heat than light." I believe in the virtues of Islamic-Christian dialogue, provided it is conducted with mutual respect and concern for the truth. This legitimately gives this dialogue an apologetic, even missional, dimension.[1]

This book therefore begins with an introductory chapter tracing the main stages of my spiritual journey from Aleppo, my hometown in Syria, to Paris via England, the country where I lived for twenty-three years. Some readers may be surprised to learn that there is an indigenous Christian community in Syria, which was sizeable but has declined dramatically over the past decade due to war. It pleases me that Syria played a decisive role in the spread of Christianity in the first centuries.

It was on his way to Damascus, the capital of Syria, to arrest the leaders of the church in this city, that Saul of Tarsus met the risen Christ and became the apostle Paul (Acts 9:1–19). Likewise, it was in Antioch in Syria (not to be confused with Antioch in Pisidia) that Christ's disciples were called "Christians" for the first time (Acts 11:26). It was also in Antioch that the first international church was born, made up of Christians from Jewish and pagan background (Acts 11:19–21). No wonder that within a few years, this same church became the first missionary church, which consecrated Paul and Barnabas and sent them on mission to evangelize the surrounding peoples (Acts 13:1–3).

After this very personal introductory chapter, I approach Islam from different angles (religion, community, law), then I deal with radical Islam, emphasizing the religious and non-religious roots of Islamist ideology. In the last chapter of this first section, I attempt to answer topical questions that were put to me by my friend from Lyon.

The second part of the book is devoted to the main theological questions that divide Christianity and Islam concerning the Bible, God, Jesus Christ and salvation. This part sums up certain themes that I investigated in my last three books (mentioned in the bibliography). Islam, a post-Christian religion, scrutinizes the Christian faith and questions the reliability of the Bible, the doctrine of the divine Trinity and the historicity of the crucifixion of Christ. The first four chapters of this section of the book respond to Islamic critiques of Christianity and examine the merits of arguments put forward by Muslim theologians on issues that go to the heart of the monotheistic faith. The last chapter of the book emphasizes that despite their theological differences,

---

1. In 1998 I was invited to teach a course on Christianity for a whole week at an Islamic theological seminary in Trabzon (Turkey). The invitation was sent to me by one of the professors in this seminary who had spent a month at All Nations Christian College (Ware, England) where I was teaching.

Christians and Muslims have in common a significant number of religious beliefs and ethical values that enable them to work hand in hand in the service of their society.

I am an Arab and I am in no way ashamed of my cultural heritage though I have a critical perspective on Arab civilization. I am also a committed Christian and I claim no neutrality when it comes to faith issues. Yet, I strive to deal with them with impartiality as much as I can. To be fair one needs to compare what is comparable, namely the teaching of the Scriptures – Islamic Scriptures and Christian Scriptures. We should avoid comparing extremists in one religion with moderates in the other, or Islamic reality with Christian ideal. I am critical of parts of church teaching and history as well as Islamic traditional teaching. I am aware that a growing number of reformist Muslims are themselves very critical of their own tradition. I had the privilege of engaging with some of them, such as Sheikh Mohammed Abu Zaid, Mr. Ghaleb Bencheikh and Imam Tareq Oubrou to name but a few.[2]

I hope this book, which is written primarily for Christians, will provide answers to some questions they have about Islam, will give them insight into this religion, and will enrich their relationships with Muslims. The book has been written with Muslim readers in mind as well so that they may find food for thought about Christianity. Christians can no longer ignore "Islam, [become] a French Religion" (to use the title of a recent book). Likewise, truth-seeking Muslims have easily nowadays the possibility to access a Bible-based information about Christ, in addition to the qur'anic presentation which is, it must be admitted, both incomplete and biased.

To make this book easy to read, I have chosen to limit the number of footnotes to what is strictly necessary. References to the Hadith (or Prophetic Tradition) are however essential, as it represents the second foundation of Islam after the Qur'an. They are given in an abridged form indicating the name of the compiler, the title of the book in Arabic (and its translation) as well as the chapter number, for example, "Bukhari, *Iman* (Faith), 4." This allows the interested reader to identify the source of the quoted text. In the chapters of the second part, I refer in the footnotes to the sections of my

---

2. Sheikh Abu Zaid is the president of the Sunni Islamic Tribunal in Saïda (Lebanon). Following his first visit to the USA in 2014, he wrote a book (in Arabic) entitled *The America I Have Seen*, a title first used by Sayyid Qutb (1906–1966, known as the spiritual father of modern Islamism) for the book he wrote upon his return to Egypt in 1950. In their respective books, these two men take radically opposite perspectives on the USA. G. Bencheikh is a broadcaster and the President of the 'Fondation de l'Islam de France'. T. Oubrou is a theologian and the Imam of Bordeaux mosque. These two leading figures of Islam in France tirelessly advocate, including in their writings, an Islamic reformation in France and beyond.

previous books where the same subject receives a more in-depth treatment. My translation of the qur'anic texts benefited from several French and English translations. Biblical quotations come from the New International Version (NIV). References include the name of the abbreviated book followed by the chapter and verse number(s). Qur'anic references include the number of the sūra (chapter), without giving its title, followed by the verse number(s). When two dates separated by a forward slash (/) appear, the first refers to the Islamic calendar, the second to the calendar in use in the West. Quotes from Arabic or French sources not available in English are my own translation.

I would like to express my deep gratitude to Dr. Raphaël Nogier, to Dr. Michael Kuhn and to Rev. Colin Chapman. They were kind enough to read the whole manuscript and share with me their very perceptive comments.

May the reading of this book encourage those who seek, beyond a rapprochement between Christians and Muslims, to advance the kingdom of God amongst us.

Ch. Moucarry

Introduction

My Spiritual Journey

"To Me, to Live Is Christ" (Phil 1:21)

I do not usually like to speak openly about my life since I am quite reserved. However, my friend from Lyon, who gave me the idea for this book, managed to convince me that it would be useful for readers to have a glimpse of my background. He said that it would help them better understand my interests and the (sometimes unexpected) opinions I express on some topics. It therefore seemed fitting to me to outline at the beginning of this book my personal journey from Syria, my home country, to France where I currently reside, including a rather long detour via England.

Aleppo: My Childhood

I was born in Aleppo, a city in northern Syria, of Christian parents of the Greek-Catholic (Melkite) rite. I have an Arab-Turkish first name, which was my paternal grandfather's name. He died a few years before I was born. I was given the name Georges when I was baptized because the name Chawkat (which means "strength") is not Christian. My last name, Moucarry, is a nickname, probably due to the profession of one of my ancestors. It has the same root as "Qur'an" and means "the one who teaches to read." At the start of my stay in France, many people had difficulty pronouncing (or remembering) my first name (Chawkat). I told them they could call me Georges (which is also written on my identity papers). Several friends in France continue to call me Georges.

My father had a biblical name, that of a high Syrian officer, Naaman. Naaman was cured of his leprosy by the prophet Elisha, which led him to follow the God of Israel before he returned to Damascus (2 Kgs 5). My father was not a practicing Christian – he displayed values I would call humanistic.

He was a game hunter and my best memories are of the hunting parties I spent with him. He worked at the post office and had several Muslim friends. One of them, Abou Ziad, was a close friend. Our families were also very close. Abou Ziad once confided in me: "If I had to take a long trip, I would entrust my family to your father."

My dad loved his children dearly, but he was a rather reserved man who did not easily show his feelings. The greatest influence he had on me, without even realizing it, was simply to teach me by his example that Christians and Muslims can be true friends. This was not the case of all Christians in Aleppo, nor of Muslims. The Muslim and Christian communities lived in separate districts and hardly mingled. They lived alongside rather than with each other. The buildings were also inhabited either by Christians or by Muslims, but not both. Things have changed a lot since then, but social segregation has not completely disappeared.

My mother (Angèle was her first name) was a multilingual woman. In addition to Arabic and French, she had learned Turkish from her father and Armenian at the school of the Armenian Sisters of the Immaculate Conception. She spoke in Armenian with our Armenian neighbors. She was pious and wanted to become a religious sister (she had spent three years in a convent in Belgium), but she had to give up her vocation due to health issues.

I have a few memories of my maternal grandfather. He was an ethnic Armenian (his last name was Meguerdidjian), and he was born in Killiz, not far from the Syrian-Turkish border, where he lived for a long time. His mother tongue was not Armenian, though, but Turkish. He was one of many Armenians who had migrated to Aleppo to flee the 1915 genocide. He barely spoke Arabic. He used to wake up early in the morning to say his prayers. I was very impressed with the way he prayed, as his words were accompanied by bodily postures, a bit like Muslims.

Mum was keen to send her children to private Catholic schools so that we could have a good religious education. These schools had a very good reputation for the quality of their teaching in general, hence they attracted several Muslim students from rather well-off families. My three sisters attended the Joan of Arc school run by the Sisters of St. Joseph of the Apparition; I went to the school of the Marist Brothers of Champagnat.

As a child, undoubtedly under the influence of my mother, I became an altar servant (we no longer say "choir boy"). Among my tasks, which I enjoyed doing at mass several times each Sunday, was the reading of an epistle (usually of St. Paul) just before the reading of the gospel by the priest. An Old Testament text was not read at mass, presumably to prevent the faithful from confusing the Israel of the Bible with the contemporary State of Israel with which Syria is still at war. This is how I gradually became familiar with the texts of the New Testament.

Aleppo: My Teen Years

I was twelve or thirteen when I first felt the desire to become a priest. One day, at the end of mass, I confided my desire to one of the parish priests. He asked me: "How many brothers and sisters do you have?" I answered that I have three sisters and no brother. He went on: "Go ask your Mum to give you a brother." "But my Mum is not like Elizabeth to have a child at her age!" When I got home, I told my Mum about my conversation with the priest. She was furious: "I'm not that old. It's your Dad who doesn't want to have any more children."

My father, who was not a wealthy man by any means, believed he was not financially capable of raising a large family. Years later, I learned that he had pressured Mum to have an abortion, but she resisted him. My parents were rewarded with a big surprise no one had anticipated, not even my mother's gynecologist. When Mum was taken to hospital, she gave birth to twins – my sister Nayla and me! In the Eastern Catholic Church, an only son was not admitted to the priesthood because he was responsible for looking after his parents when they got old. For the same reason, he was exempt from military service. If there were two sons in a family, the two did not serve in the army at the same time.

I was thirteen in 1967 when the Six-Day War broke out between Israel and its Arab neighbors. One of the indirect consequences of the war was the nationalization of most Christian schools, many of which had been founded by Western religious orders. Indeed, the Syrian regime was led by the Baath nationalist party and the government was leftist and anti-Western.[1] The government wanted to more closely control the teaching given in private schools by appointing one of its representatives on each school's board of directors. The principals of these schools, influenced by the bishops of Aleppo, refused what they considered to be unacceptable government interference. The government then decided to nationalize these schools, which resulted in most foreign teachers leaving the country. The education standard dropped immediately.

---

1. The word "baath" means "rebirth" or "resurrection" and refers in this context to the renewal of the Arab nation. Two Syrians founded this socialist and secular party, an (Orthodox) Christian and a (Sunni) Muslim, to promote unity in the Arab nation based on national sentiment so that Arabs could transcend the many religious and ethnic loyalties that divided them.

One day my father approached me with a suggestion: "Now that the schools are nationalized, there is no reason you should continue paying to attend a supposedly private school. [These schools maintained a special status.] So I suggest you enroll in a government public school next year. This has the advantage of having students who are more representative of the society in which you live, as they are mostly Muslim students from all walks of life." My Dad's proposal made a lot of sense to me and I accepted it immediately.

A year later, I became a student of the al-Ma'moun school (named after the famous Abbasid caliph), the most prestigious of Aleppo's public high schools. I then began to discover a world that was totally foreign to me. The vast majority of students were indeed Muslim. We were a handful of Christians in a class of sixty students, and most were from working-class backgrounds. When they learned that I had attended a private secondary school, some students asked me if I could help them improve their French. I thus became a volunteer French teacher in the classes that took place at the end of the day.

Many of my friends, on hearing I was a Christian, began asking me questions about Christianity and Christians. In turn, I was curious to learn more about Islam and Muslims. One day the idea occurred to me to ask the Islamic religious education teacher if I could attend his class. He was very surprised because Christian students were exempt from these classes; they had their own religious education class at another time of the week. He replied, "If your parents agree, you're welcome." Not only was I allowed to attend the Islamic religious education class, but I was a keen and interactive student. Regularly, the teacher would ask me what Christians thought of the subject he was teaching, and I tried to give him an answer as best as I could. Gradually, I formed deep friendships with my Muslim classmates. Several invited me to visit them, and I in turn invited them to come to my home. More than one shared with me that it was the first time in his life that he had a Christian at home or visited a Christian family.

I still vividly remember the only day when my whole class was taken to a cinema in town to watch an important film. The film described the epic story of Salah al-Din al-Ayyoubi, known in the West as Saladin, a Muslim of Kurdish background (born in Tikrit, Iraq) who defeated the Crusaders in 1187, reclaimed Jerusalem from their hands, and destroyed its Latin kingdom. The vanquished invaders had the cross on their banners and waged their wars in the name of "the Prince of Peace" (Isa 9:6). What a contradiction! Even today this glorious and somewhat mystified past continues to be taught systematically in public schools, and both nationalist governments and Islamists keep it in the forefront of their shared ideological struggle against Western countries.

In high school, it was not long before I joined the JEC (Christian Student Youth). I quickly became responsible for my high school group, which numbered five to six students. We met weekly, and our meetings always began with a gospel reading followed by prayer and a discussion of a topic prepared beforehand. We were fully aware that as Christian students in a predominantly Muslim public high school, we had a specific witness to share with our Muslim friends, through our lives as well as through our words.

We organized cultural activities to attract our school friends, for example, a weekend excursion to discover a historic site not far from the city. We were well served as Aleppo, being one of the oldest inhabited cities in the world, had no shortage of historic sites. One day a Muslim friend of mine who was also a member of the youth section of the Baath party, gave me this warning: "Chawkat, be careful. You are being watched because of your activism in school." The JEC chaplain at the time was a young priest from Aleppo, until last year the Greek-Catholic Archbishop of Aleppo, Mgr. Jean-Clément Jeanbart, whom I have the honor to count among my friends. Looking back, I realize that my call to serve the Lord among Muslims in particular, dates to my high school years. It was there that I started learning to engage in a missional dialogue with Muslim friends from whom nothing really separated me except Christ, whom they certainly venerated but only as a prophet.

I was sixteen when my father died (aged 54) in Beirut at St. Joseph Hospital where he had been hospitalized for surgery. This event turned my life upside down and made me discover, in a very personal way, the reality of divine fatherhood. This realization kept me from sinking into loneliness and distress, aggravated by the wild passions specific to some teenagers. Ten days after Dad died, another of my heroes passed away: the Egyptian leader, Gamal Abdel Nasser, champion of pan-Arab nationalism. Less than two months later, another heroic figure died, General de Gaulle, who alone symbolized all that France represented in terms of greatness, particularly for the Christians of Syria (and Lebanon), a country which was under French mandate between the two World Wars.

Of all the authors (Arab and foreigner) that I read in those years, Gibran Khalil Gibran was undoubtedly the one that marked me most. In the West, he is best known for his book "The Prophet," but we owe him many other works including "Jesus, the Son of Man," made of a long series of very beautiful meditations on gospel characters and texts. I still have all of Gibran's writings in my library, divided into two volumes, the ones in Arabic in one volume and the ones translated from English into Arabic in the other.

Besançon: Spiritual Renewal

Since the priesthood was not an option for me, I decided, for lack of a better alternative, to choose another humanitarian profession, that of physician (very prized by Syrian families for their children). I was also very keen to discover new horizons. France was my first choice because of the influence French culture had on the environment where I grew up.

My choice fell on Besançon simply because the son of one of our neighbors was already there. I could count on him to help me during the first months. The reality of life abroad for an eighteen-year-old was not easy. My French was not as good as I thought; I had never spoken it in Syria, though I had a solid foundation from school. Lectures were given in a large hall where I was one anonymous student among a few hundreds. I was far away from family, friends and country. Student life was much politicized following the May 1968 civil unrest in France.

Every day there were political book tables outside the university restaurant. One day I noticed that one of them offered literature in Arabic! I was overjoyed when I discovered that the displayed literature was mainly Bibles and Bible-related brochures. The person who ran the book table was a medical student. Through him I was introduced to the GBU (Groupes Bibliques Universitaires), a movement of Christian evangelical students whose mission is to encourage students to read the Bible. Students were also invited to take part in Bible study groups and prayer meetings. I quickly joined the GBU of Besançon, which I attended diligently for three years.[2]

I learned quite a lot from GBU students, in particular, the centrality of God's word in the life and faith of believers, the importance of prayer and fellowship, and the significance of the cross of Jesus Christ in the redemption of humankind. My situation as a recently arrived foreign student undoubtedly made me more open and sensitive to the gospel message. I experienced a spiritual renewal that can be equated with conversion. I had an overwhelming desire to testify about Christ to my fellow students. To my surprise, several students came to Christ and their number kept growing. One of the first new believers once said to me (before his conversion): "You know I love everyone, except maybe Arabs." Having pointed out to him that being Syrian, I am one of them, he replied: "Oh no, you're not Arab, for me Arabs are people from North Africa."

---

2. The GBU is a founding member of the International Fellowship of Evangelical Students (IFES), to which UCCF is affiliated in Britain and InterVarsity in the US.

Within two years, the GBU grew in number and included more than fifty students. We were very grateful to the (Catholic) Grand Séminaire (where several students lived, including myself) for allowing us to meet in the chapel. Gradually I became convinced that God was calling me to serve him as a layperson and that I needed to prepare myself for it. One day I made the decision to interrupt my studies and go to the Paris region to begin theological training.

This decision was not an easy one because I knew that my family would not understand it. When I told my mother, she immediately stopped her financial support, without even telling me, so deep was her disappointment. But the compelling love of Christ left me with little choice (cf. Matt 10:34–38). I had to hastily find odd jobs to support myself. I accepted the first one that came my way, joining the washing-up team at the Besançon University restaurant where I used to go daily as a student.

Paris: Theological Training and Student Ministry

In Paris, I intended to take a part-time job to finance my studies, but I couldn't find any. Seeing me in an impasse, a staff member from the seminary offered to contact a local church to see if they would support me. I was extremely happy when I learned a few days later that the church (located not far from Saint-Etienne) had agreed to finance my studies, with no conditions!

This is how I was able to follow the master's program in Christian theology at the Faculté Libre de Théologie Évangélique of Vaux-sur-Seine. At the same time, I attended courses at the Centre Sèvres (Jesuit training school) in Paris and at the École Pratique des Hautes Études (Sorbonne). Throughout my studies, I was involved in the GBU and held Bible book tables first at Paris III University (Censier), then at the Cité Universitaire Internationale de Paris where I resided for more than three years. At the end of my studies, the GBU offered me the national position of special staff for relations with foreign students. I gladly accepted this offer, which was fully in line with my own aspirations. This job was an opportunity for me to help GBU students in their relations with Muslim students and to take part in Muslim-Christian dialogues in university towns in France and elsewhere.

At the end of my master's degree in Christian theology, I felt a strong desire to pursue Islamic studies in order to better position myself as an Arab Christian in connection with the religion of the majority of my people. This desire was reinforced by the fact that in my work with the GBU, Muslim students sometimes asked me theological questions I had not necessarily thought about (e.g. about the reliability of the Bible, the reality of Jesus's crucifixion, the prophecy of Muhammad). I decided, in parallel with my work, to start studying Islam at EPHE (religious sciences department). My DEA (Diplôme d'Études Approfondies) dissertation was titled: "The Alteration of the Judeo-Christian Scriptures According to the Qur'an and Islamic Tradition." Twelve years later (in 1994), I defended a PhD thesis entitled: "Pardon, Repentance, Conversion: Study of These Concepts in Islam and Their Biblical Equivalents."

The twelve years between the two degrees were due to my full-time job and the fact that I got married in the meantime. Within seven and a half years of marriage, Hanne-Lis, my Danish wife, and I became the happy parents of four children (Christophe, Marie, Sophie and Irène). My studies and my writings have always been closely linked to my origins and my work. In June 1982 I had the joy of learning that my application for French citizenship had been accepted. I will always be Syrian, but in addition, I am now a French citizen by adoption.

I am very grateful for the theological training I received in the various institutions I attended. Theological training allowed me to deepen my knowledge of the Scriptures and to strengthen my faith, even to purify it. My Islamic studies enabled me to better understand Islam and Muslims, and to examine closely the Christian faith. Having come under the scrutiny of Islamic theology, my faith grew as did my appreciation for what makes it unique; namely, God's universal grace and unconditional love manifested in Jesus Christ. I pay particular tribute to Prof. Daniel Gimaret, who kindly directed all my research work in Islamics. When I re-read his books, I am always impressed with the extent of his knowledge, his academic rigor and the impartiality of his teaching.

I have already mentioned the debt I owe to the evangelical students I knew in Besançon. I am sure they will not mind me expressing a few criticisms about them, which apply by no means to all evangelical Christians. These people (many of whom have remained friends) were what one might call pietistic Christians. Their faith had an anti-intellectual bias and was marked with a certain degree of legalism. They were also inclined to judge other Christian traditions, Catholics for example. Finally, there were many "Zionist Christians" among them who saw a theological legitimacy for the State of Israel in the promises and prophecies of the Bible.[3] Many believed that the creation of the State of Israel in 1948 was the forerunner of Jesus Christ's return.

---

3. The expression "Christian Zionists" refers to Christians (including evangelicals) who support Zionist ideology. I prefer the expression "Zionist Christians," since the primary motive of these Christians is not political but religious.

For several years, despite my fully acknowledged Arabness, I adhered to this dispensationalist theology, believing that Bible teaching took priority over all other considerations. It was only after my enrollment at the theological seminary of Vaux-sur-Seine that I learned that not all evangelical Christians accept this theology. Far from it. I pay tribute here to one of the lecturers of this seminary, Prof. Henri Blocher, who stood out for his admirable theological expertise combined with an exemplary life of faith. I greatly appreciated his teaching as well as his supervision of my master's dissertation, which was titled: "The Mystery of the History of Salvation of Jews and Gentiles in Romans 11." This dissertation provided the opportunity for me to take a thorough look into the Bible teaching, to break once and for all with dispensationalist theology, and to adopt a perspective I believe is more in line with Jesus's teaching on Israel.

To prevent any suspicion of anti-Semitism, I am pleased to mention here what to me remains one of the most telling signs of the Holy Spirit's action in my life. Growing up in Syria under a nationalist regime, I had not realized how much I had absorbed the anti-Jewish sentiment conveyed in the education system and the media. This sentiment had developed among all Arabs due to the successive wars between Israel and Arab countries (especially in 1948, 1956, 1967 and 1973). The spiritual renewal I experienced in Besançon impacted my whole being, in particular by setting me free from the deep animosity I had towards not only Israelis but Jews in general. I still remember the day when I first met a Jewish woman face to face in a Christian event. When we realized which countries we were from, we spontaneously fell into each other's arms and cried bitter tears. I knew at that precise moment that these tears were the clear signs of an inner, real and powerful liberation.

England: Theological Teaching and Humanitarian Work

Having worked among students for twelve years, I thought the time had come for me to pass on the baton. With the strong encouragement of my wife, and in part thanks to her paid job, I made the decision to give myself two years off to complete my PhD thesis. It was the right time to make this decision. A Tunisian friend had converted to Jesus Christ in his native country upon his return from a two-year study stay in Paris where we had met. A few months later, he had no choice but to return to France because of persecution from his family. He had just completed his theological training and was ready to take over the student work. The journey of this dear friend is quite remarkable; having worked for several years for the GBU in France, he was entrusted with the leadership of the IFES ministry in the Arab world, a position he still holds with great competence.

A few months before my thesis defense, I began looking for a job. I had no desire to pursue an academic career in a French university as I would have had to accept the constraints of neutrality. I was hoping to find work in a Christian organization that would allow me to carry out the mission to which I was called. In May 1994 I received letters from two Christian colleges in England asking me to consider joining them. After much thought, prayer and job interviews, my wife and I decided to accept the job offer from All Nations Christian College in Ware, Hertfordshire. ANCC students (of whom almost half were non-British) attended the college to prepare for mission work abroad or among ethnic minorities in the UK. These students were all professionals who were preparing to get involved in mission work using their professional skills (engineer, doctor, teacher, nurse, Bible translator, etc.). Some had already served for several years and wanted to upgrade their training.

Our four young children perfectly adapted to England, faster and arguably easier than their parents. For twelve years, I had the joy of teaching Islamic studies, a course on the Middle East, and another one on "prejudice and discrimination" (religious, ethnic, sexual, cultural, etc.). Among the highlights of the academic year was an intensive ten-day Introduction to Islam course held in December. This course, also open to outsiders, was given by several speakers, including a Muslim lecturer. Another highlight was the yearly debate I had with another lecturer, a Messianic Jew, who taught "the Hebrew Bible" among other subjects. Students were delighted to attend this debate which shed light on two very different approaches to the Israeli-Palestinian conflict. My colleague often stressed the need to make peace between the two peoples. I insisted on justice as the required path to achieve true and lasting peace.

I was starting to feel a bit confined in England even though I had made several trips to Asia (South Korea, Dubai, India, Thailand, Turkey), Europe and the US. I also felt the need to go to the field myself to translate what I was teaching into reality. So I successfully applied for a post that had been recently created by a well-known NGO in the English-speaking world, World Vision International, a development, relief and advocacy organization with forty thousand employees spread over five continents. Three things attracted me to WVI. First, it seeks to put into practice in developing countries the gospel commandment to love our neighbors. Second, it is a global organization operating in around eighty countries, including twenty predominantly Muslim countries. Third, it is a non-denominational Christian organization that takes seriously the witness to Jesus Christ "by life, deed, word and sign that encourage people to respond to the Gospel."

My job as director of interfaith relations was to train staff of all faiths (using a course I created for this purpose) to enhance their collaboration. In other words, without ignoring the real differences existing between different religions, it is critical for us all to take the full measure of what brings people together (on the spiritual, moral and human level) so as to work together for the service of the common good. The ten years spent at WVI were a very fulfilling and learning experience. I had the opportunity to discover men and women from all walks of life, from all over the world, who were committed to advance justice, solidarity and equality in their communities. I especially enjoyed working with Muslim staff and religious leaders in the countries I visited. The challenges we face are not only economic, they are humanitarian and spiritual. It is urgent that churches in the West and Christian organizations invest more in the Majority World to jointly meet these challenges. They are global, as the COVID-19 pandemic reminds us.

Back to France

After twenty-three years in England, having reached retirement age (according to French legislation), my wife and I returned to France (in 2017). It is not that we disliked life in England, but we feel much closer to French culture. Three of our children have stayed in England, and our oldest daughter, Marie, has been living in Montreal for ten years with her family.

Looking back on my journey so far, I see three red threads in the fabric of my life. The first is Islam, with which I have been engaging in different ways since my childhood. For me, Muslims are my closest neighbors. I regret that Christians in Europe do not make more efforts to welcome them and engage with them in a missional dialogue.

The second thread is the question of migration, a highly sensitive issue to deal with, especially in the context of Islamist terrorism. One of my very first published articles was entitled: "The Alien according to the Torah."[4] In this article, I highlighted the remarkable divine teaching given to the Israelites regarding their attitude towards non-Israelites living amongst them. I drew out some present-day conclusions about the behavior of Israelis towards Palestinians on one hand, and on the other, Christian attitudes towards

---

4. Moucarry, "The Alien," 17–20.

immigrants in France. We will not meet the challenge of migration without making deliberate efforts to adapt on both sides.

The third thread is Israel and the discriminatory treatment that the Jewish State reserves for Palestinians, in particular in the Occupied Territories (notably in the West Bank). Due to their anti-Semitic past, European countries appear to be paralyzed by a nagging and deep sense of guilt towards Jews. The question of human rights is strangely kept out of the Israeli-Palestinian conflict by the international community. Zionist Christians, despite their good intentions, only make the situation worse. They forget fundamental gospel values such as justice, peace, solidarity with the poor, and liberation of the oppressed.

I would like to bring the story of my personal journey to a close with a thanksgiving prayer to the One to whom I owe everything:

> I praise you, God, for your powerful and gentle action in my life at each stage and through each event, happy or unhappy. Among the unhappy ones was the death of my father when I was still a teenager, and the untimely death of Christine, my daughter and Christophe's twin sister.
>
> I praise you for the family I grew up in, and in particular for my parents.
>
> I praise you for the friends I have met on my journey, Christians, Muslims and all the others.
>
> I praise you for the tremendous spiritual and theological heritage of the Catholic church, of which I am the happy heir, and for the very significant role evangelical Christians have played in the formation of my faith.
>
> I praise you for having given me the grace to know your Son Jesus Christ in all his splendor.
>
> I praise you for calling me to be a disciple and witness of Christ, especially to many Arab and Muslim friends.
>
> I praise you for this life despite its brokenness and for the tremendous hope of life eternal.
>
> I praise you, my God and my Lord, for the meaning you give to my life. Together with apostle Paul I confess that "to me, to live is Christ" (Phil 1:21). Amen.

Part One

Islam: A Religion with Many Faces

1

Islam as Religion

The vast majority of Muslim writers are convinced of the superiority of Islam over Judaism and Christianity. Islam is not simply a spiritual religion concerned only with life after death as, they believe, the case is with Christianity. Nor is it a religion centered on life on earth as with Judaism. Islam is as concerned with this life as it is with the next.

This chapter will approach Islam mainly from the perspective of its religious teaching. The following two chapters will be devoted to Islam as a community, united but diverse, and to Islam as a source for legislation. The fourth chapter will deal with radical Islam, which puts the entire Muslim community to the test as their religion is in fact associated with violence in the minds of many people. They are expected to explain how Islam relates to violence perpetrated by people self-identified as Muslims. The last chapter of this part will look at current issues concerning the life of the Muslim community in France and farther afield.

Conversion, Submission, Peace

What exactly does the word *islam* mean? For a long time, the meaning of this term did not raise any questions. Muslims agreed it meant "submission" (to God) and "surrender." Today some Muslims voices, like Muhammad Shahrour, challenge this traditional meaning and seek to replace it with "trust," "abandonment," or "surrender of oneself" (to God). Some Muslims go so far as to say that the word actually means "peace." These suggestions come either from Muslims with mystical leanings living in Western countries where the concept of submission is not particularly popular, or from humanist Muslims who seek to correct the image of Islam seriously damaged by the violence committed in its name.

It is true that the Arabic words for "submission" and "peace" have the same three-letter root, S-L-M, hence the connection between them, but they do not mean the same thing. In the qur'anic context, the verb *aslama* is used repeatedly in the general sense of conversion to the one God as well as in the particular sense of conversion to the new religion proclaimed by Muhammad (5:3; 6:125). In the general sense, the prophets were all Muslims, like Abraham (3:67), as were the patriarchs (2:133) and the disciples of Jesus (5:111). The expression often used in connection with conversion to God is "to submit one's face to God" (2:112; 3:20; 31:22).

The same verb is used in the context of a confrontation between Muslims and polytheists. The polytheists had to choose between fighting and submitting (48:16). Some Arab tribes who chose to join Islam claimed to have embraced the faith, but in reality, they simply surrendered to the Muslim army (49:14). However, since they had submitted, Muslims had to cease the fight and make peace with them (4:90–91).

According to Islamic tradition, the Prophet addressed letters to the main political leaders in the region surrounding Arabia. In the letter sent to Heraclius, the Byzantine emperor, Muhammad invites him to convert to the new religion in thinly veiled terms: "Convert to Islam and you will be safe" (*aslim taslam*).[1] As a matter of fact, the Prophet himself led an army against the Byzantines in northern Arabia on two occasions (in 630 and 631). The outcomes of both battles were inconclusive.

The connection between Islam and peace or well-being within the Muslim community is reflected in a famous prophetic saying: "The Muslim is the one whose words and deeds pose no threat to other Muslims."[2] Thus, conversion to God results in peace with the Creator and integration into the Muslim community. Submission, willingly or by force, to Islamic leadership ensures peace with the Muslim community. True submission to God is sincere, free and trusting submission. It is an act of faith and total surrender to the good and sovereign Creator.

From a Christian perspective, the concept of submission has more than one meaning. Servile submission to the commandments of the law, even divine law, has nothing to do with the freedom brought by the gospel (Gal 3:23–

---

1. Bukhari, *Bad' al-Wahi* (Beginning of Revelation), 1.
2. Bukhari, *Iman* (Faith), 4.

25).³ However, our filial and voluntary submission to our heavenly Father is our fitting response to his love for us. Even Christ learned as a human being to submit to his Father in order to do his will (Heb 5:7–8). Like Muslims, Christians readily call themselves servants of God (see, for example, Titus 1:1). Far from being synonymous with servitude, servanthood in the sense of serving God and neighbor, not by constraint but by love, is paradoxically a source of liberation from what can enslave us inwardly, starting with our preoccupation with ourselves.

The Islamic Creed

The shortest and simplest Islamic creed is expressed in one sentence and two parts: "I bear witness that there is no god (*ilah*) but God (*Allah*) and that Muhammad is the Messenger of God" (*ashhadu an la ilaha illa-llah wa anna Muhammadan rasulu-llah*). This creed is sometimes called the double witness (i.e. about God and Muhammad). People who utter these words sincerely, in Arabic, in the presence of at least two Muslim witnesses, demonstrate their conversion to Islam.

The Arabic word *ilah* refers to the divinity. Most linguists consider that the word *allah* results from the contraction of the definite article *al* and the word *ilah*. However, some believe it is the proper name of God, hence it is untranslatable. The words for God in Semitic languages are very similar. In Hebrew, for example, we have *El*, *Elohim* and *Eloah*. The controversial form of the Islamic confession of faith (there *is no god but* God) is due to the fact that Islam was born in a predominantly polytheistic environment. Arabs believed in a supreme god, *Allah*, with whom they associated many deities. The name of Muhammad's father was "Abdullah," servant of God. The Prophet's mission was precisely to convince them that God is one, has no partners and is the only one to be worshipped.

The affirmation of God's oneness is in line with the biblical message, but how are we to know this one God? This is an important question to which we will return in the second part of this book.

Muhammad is described in the Islamic creed as *rasul*, a messenger (or apostle). Arabs of his time demanded evidence that would authenticate his apostolate. Later, Muslim theologians developed a whole apologetic to

---

3. In this book, the word "Gospel," with capital *G*, refers to the gospel as a written document, with a small *g* to the gospel as a message. In the qur'anic context the word always designates the holy Book revealed by God and preached by Jesus.

demonstrate the divine origin of Muhammad's mission. There are four main components of this apologetic.

Miracles

Muhammad's greatest miracle, if not the only one, is the Qur'an itself, considered to be an inimitable book.[4] The qur'anic miracle consists in the outstanding and unsurpassable quality of this book. This quality, considered supernatural, is primarily literary, but it also concerns the content of the book, in that it records very ancient events as well as predictions of the end times. The qur'anic message is said to be superior to those of the Torah and the Gospel as it strikes a balance between two extremes represented by Judaism and Christianity. The qur'anic miracle is enhanced by the traditional belief that Muhammad was an illiterate man who could neither read nor write.

Even if Muhammad was illiterate, which is far from certain, in ancient times oral tradition played a very important role in the transmission of knowledge. It is fair to assume that he interacted with Jews and Christians who lived in Arabia, including Waraqa bin Nawfal, the paternal cousin of Khadija, Muhammad's first wife. His knowledge of the Bible literature is the result of this interaction. The criterion of literary perfection is very subjective and difficult to assess for non-Arabic speakers. From a biblical point of view, miracles are not enough to demonstrate divine inspiration (Deut 13:1–4; Matt 24:23–25). It is the content of the allegedly revealed message that needs to be examined: does it agree with what God has already revealed?

Biblical Prophecies

According to Muslim writers, Muhammad was predicted in the Bible, namely the Torah and the Gospel. This assertion is impossible to verify since the two qur'anic texts on which it is based do not offer any supporting biblical evidence from the Torah or the Gospels (7:157; 61:6). Chapter 6, which deals with the falsification of the Bible in Islamic thought, will come back to this claim and Muhammad's presumed illiteracy.

---

4. The Prophetic Tradition ascribes several miracles to the Prophet. The reliability of these accounts, hence the historicity of the miracles, is difficult to establish.

Perfection of Islamic Law

According to Muslim thinkers, Islamic law is perfect, unlike both Jewish law and gospel teaching. This explains, on the one hand, that God sent Muhammad to bring to perfection the already revealed divine Scriptures and, on the other hand, that Muhammad was the last prophet (33:40).

For some Muslim authors (like Ibn Taymiyya, F. Razi, I. Faruqi), Jewish law and Christian doctrine are deficient on religious, moral and penal grounds. Here are some examples that illustrate the Islamic perspective and a brief response where necessary:

- The Torah does not speak openly of paradise. In Jesus's time the party of Sadducees, unlike the Pharisees, did not believe in the resurrection of the dead (cf. Matt 22:23). The Qur'an is much more explicit about the reality of heaven and hell.
- Muslim theologians associate the Torah with justice and the Gospel with love. However, the Torah insists on God's mercy and not only on his justice (cf. Exod 34:6–7), and the Gospel highlights God's love without glossing over his justice (Luke 13:1–5; John 3:16–18).
- For Muslims, the penal code of the Jewish law seems overly strict compared to the Islamic code. The first prescribes the death penalty for many crimes while the second does it only in three cases (murder, adultery, apostasy).[5] The gospel does not have a criminal law for the simple reason that it is good news based on God's redemptive love. Instead of condemning us because of our sins, God decided to suspend his judgment and save us. However, the New Testament recognizes the right of civil authorities to administer justice in society and to try people who commit crimes (Rom 13:1–7).
- The Jewish moral law is exemplary in that it instructs the Israelites to love God (Deut 6:5) and their neighbor (Lev 19:18), including the non-Israelite who lives among them (Lev 19:33–34). Jesus summed up the teaching of the Torah with this remarkable twofold command (Matt 22:37–40). Jesus required his disciples to love their enemies to reflect God's love for all human creatures (Matt 5:43–48). This

---

5. The Mosaic code prescribes the death penalty for the following crimes: murder (Lev 24:17), idolatry (Exod 22:20), blasphemy (Lev 24:16), adultery (Lev 20:10), illicit sexual relations (Lev 20:11–14), kidnapping (Exod 21:16), cursing one's parents (Lev 20:9), witchcraft (Exod 22:18), and bestiality (Exod 22:19). For the Islamic penal code, see Bukhari, *Diyat* (Blood-Money), 6.

- goes much further than qur'anic teaching which makes no mention of loving one's enemies.
- In terms of family ethics, the Torah says practically nothing about polygamy and very little about divorce (Deut 24:1–4). In Islam, marriage is limited to four wives and conditioned by the fair treatment of each of them (4:3). As for divorce, it is strongly discouraged without being formally prohibited.[6] Jesus reminds the Pharisees (who belonged to a strict religious party) of God's initial plan for marriage and in doing so he rules out divorce (and polygamy) "except for marital unfaithfulness" (Matt 19:1–9; 5:32).
- Islam accepts Jesus as a prophet, contrary to Judaism, but rejects his divinity. The Islamic perspective on Jesus falls dramatically short of acknowledging his full identity.
- The gospel does pay attention to life on earth but not (as in Islam) in the form of law. Instead life on earth is viewed in the context of a relationship with the Christian's heavenly father, so that in the prayer Jesus taught his disciples, Christians make the following request to their heavenly Father: "Give us today our daily bread" (Matt 6:11).
- Contrary to Islamic perception of Christianity, there is a Christian law. The law of Christ, like his kingdom, is a spiritual law inscribed in the hearts of believers. Unlike Jewish and Islamic laws, it does not consist in external rules such as the food code (Mark 7:18–19), or religious rites (e.g. circumcision, pilgrimage, festivals). It calls us to worship God "the Father in spirit and in truth" (John 4:23) and to love our Creator as well as our neighbor (Matt 22:34–40).
- The moral law brought by Christ is a perfect law like the Creator himself, hence the end of polygamy and divorce. Just because its implementation is beyond our natural capacities does not make it idealistic. If we rely on God, he will enable us to live up to his standards, and the Holy Spirit will transform us to live in a Christ-like manner (Gal 5:22–25).

In light of all of this, it appears that Islamic law and Jewish law are not fundamentally different. They both belong to an old order that the coming of Christ made obsolete. The kingdom of Christ is radically different from the kingdoms of this world (John 18:36–37). It goes beyond the theocratic regime which prevailed in Israel as well as the reign of the Sharīʿa (Islamic law) which

---

6. Ibn Majah, *Talaq* (Divorce), 1.

inspires, to a greater or lesser degree, the constitution and the laws in most of the Muslim world.

Political Success

The final proof of Muhammad's apostolate according to Muslim writers is his victory over his enemies – the polytheistic Arabs and the Medinan Jews who are accused of having conspired together against him. This victory was crowned with the triumphal entry of the Muslim army into Mecca in AD 630 (110:1–3), followed shortly by the conversion to Islam of all Arab tribes two years before the Prophet's death. This entry was mostly peaceful as Meccans agreed to surrender to the Muslim army. One hundred years after Muhammad's death, the progress of the Muslim army was stopped near Poitiers (France) in AD 732 when it was defeated by the troops of Charles Martel (Charlemagne's grandfather). Today the Muslim community has more than 1.8 billion adherents and comes second just after the Christian community.

Is military success really a proof of divine approval? From a Christian perspective, real success is not achieved through the subjugation of human beings. Jesus did not liberate his country from Roman occupation as some of his disciples had hoped (Luke 24:21). The purpose of his mission was a liberation of a completely different order. He was put to death on a cross, an ordeal which apparently signaled the failure of his mission. Yet, by his voluntary and sacrificial death, he routed our real enemies: sin, evil and death. His resurrection from the dead on the third day, and his ascension to heaven forty days later, demonstrate his victory. God attests by these events that Jesus perfectly fulfilled his mission.

Can the Christian faith be summed up in a single sentence, parallel in structure to the Islamic creed? The following statement of the apostle Paul looks very much like a double confession of faith: "There is one God and one mediator between God and mankind, the man Christ Jesus, who gave himself as a ransom for all people" (1 Tim 2:5–6).

The Five Articles of Faith and the Five Pillars

In Islam, there are two key concepts: *iman* (faith) and *islam* (trusting submission). The Islamic faith is summed up in five articles (cf. 4:136).

1. God

God is one, creator, good, righteous, powerful, holy, merciful, faithful, patient, truthful, sovereign, etc.

2. God's angels

They are God's servants. Their mission is to worship God, to communicate his word, and to do his will in this life and the next. Muslims also believe in *jinns*, invisible earthly creatures who are neither humans nor angels. It is believed that Satan and demons were good *jinns* before they disobeyed God.

3. God's books

These are the Holy Scriptures revealed throughout history: the Torah given to Moses, the Psalms to David, the Gospel to Jesus and finally the Qur'an, transmitted by Muhammad. The Qur'an confirms the earlier Scriptures but is superior to them as it is the ultimate and perfect Scripture.

4. God's apostles

These are the prophets sent to humankind, in particular to the Arab and Jewish peoples. The Qur'an refers by name to more than twenty prophetic figures, most of whom are also found in the Bible. The most prominent of these apostles are Moses, David, Jesus and Muhammad, whose respective messages have been delivered in a holy book. Adam, Noah and Abraham are also very important prophets.

5. The last day

Following the resurrection of the dead, God will judge all human creatures. Believers whose lives were marked by good deeds will enjoy eternal bliss in paradise; unbelievers and evil doers will be sent to hell. On judgment day, God will decide who to forgive and who not to forgive. Those who ascribe partners to God will never be forgiven (4:48). They will be punished in hell forever.

Some prophetic sayings add a sixth article, namely the divine "decree" (*al-qadar*), which points out God's sovereignty.[7] God is the ultimate author of

---

7. Muslim, *Iman* (Faith), 1.

human deeds, good and bad. God destines some people to heaven, others to hell.

If we wanted to summarize the heart of the Christian faith in five articles, we could start with the five articles of the Islamic faith. The most important thing about the one and only God is that he is Father (see ch. 8 "One God in Three Persons"). Angels are not as important for Christians as is the fact that humankind was created in God's image. Holy Scripture, both the Old and New Testaments, is the word of God that guides our faith and our lives. As for God's messengers, Jesus Christ holds a unique place among all prophets because of his redemptive work. He will represent God as judge on the last day.

The so-called "Pillars of Religion" represent the practice by which Muslims demonstrate that their faith is genuine. These are five acts of worship that translate faith into practice.[8]

1. Recitation of the Confession of Faith (Shahada)

Muslims proclaim their faith by reciting the Islamic creed: "I bear witness that there is no god (*ilah*) but God (*Allah*), and that Muhammad is the Messenger of God." Reciting the confession is what makes the difference between Muslims and non-Muslims. It is used to formalize a person's conversion to Islam.

The association of God and the Prophet Muhammad in the Islamic creed is highly significant. Although Muhammad is in theory no more than a human being, for Muslims he is the last and the greatest prophet. He is revered (not only by mystics) in a way that may suggest that for Muslims he is much more than a prophet and his status is far above humankind as evidenced by the demonstrations provoked by the publication of the cartoons of the Prophet.

2. Ritual Prayer (Salat)

Salat is a formal act of worship, repeated five times a day in the direction of Mecca. These prayers are preceded by ritual ablutions to make oneself pure and worthy to worship God (4:103; 5:6). Prayer sustains the Muslim's relationship with God and makes up for their bad deeds. At the center of this prayer is the recitation of the first sūra (chapter) of the Qur'an, hence its name, *al-Fatiha*,

---

8. Bukhari, *Iman* (Faith), 1.

meaning the *opening* sūra. Informal and personal prayer (*du'a*) can be said with the formal prayer and at other times.

3. Legal Almsgiving (Zakat)

Almsgiving, as the root of the word suggests, "purifies" the material goods believers possess. It consists of paying 2.5 percent of a person's income to help the poor and to provide for their needs. It is also used for building mosques and other religious duties.

4. Annual Fasting (Sawm)

The month of Ramadan, the ninth month in the Islamic calendar, is the month of fasting (2:183–187). Muslims abstain from food, drink, and sexual activities from sunrise to sunset. They focus on their spiritual needs and seek to develop their moral virtues. Fasting is not an obligation for children, pregnant and nursing mothers, travelers and sick people.

5. Pilgrimage (Hajj)

The pilgrimage is to Mecca (in Saudi Arabia), the first holy city of Islam where the Ka'ba temple is located. It is required at least once in a lifetime, for those who are physically able to afford it (3:97). Muslims from all over the world come to worship God in the very place where his final revelation came down. According to the Qur'an, Abraham and his son Ishmael built the Ka'ba temple.

Some prophetic sayings add *jihad* (i.e. fighting in the cause of God) to these five pillars.[9] Islamic law has many other prescriptions. Muslims are instructed to commit themselves entirely to God. This includes obeying the commandments against idolatry, murder, lying and sexual immorality. Certain foods (e.g. pork, blood and dead animals) are prohibited for consumption (5:3). Fermented drinks, gambling (2:219), usury and loans with interest (2:275) are also forbidden.

Jesus commissioned his disciples to be his witnesses among the nations and to baptize those who accept the gospel. He taught them how to pray and instructed them to remember him and his work of redemption by celebrating the Eucharist (Holy Communion). He summed up the moral requirements

---

9. Bukhari, *Iman* (Faith), 27.

of the Mosaic law with the double commandment about loving God and neighbor, which includes helping those in need, material or otherwise. Fasting is one means of drawing near to God (provided it is done in all humility). Reading diligently God's word is also very important in the Christian life. As for pilgrimage, there is no geographic location where Christians are required to gather to worship God. Since the risen Christ is the new temple (John 2:19–22), his disciples can meet anywhere to worship God through Christ. Pilgrimages to specific places are therefore optional and of low importance.

Considering these data, Christianity and Islam are both theocentric religions (i.e. God is at the center), but for Christians, Jesus Christ in person is God's ultimate revelation. Indeed, Muhammad, although he is the last and greatest prophet for Muslims, is (at least in theory) just a human being. For Christians, Jesus Christ is God made man, the one who reveals God in the fullness of his being.

The Two Sources of Islam: Qur'an and Hadith

The doctrine and practice of Islam are based on two main sources: the Qur'an and the Hadith (or Prophetic Tradition), but only the Qur'an is the inerrant word of God.

The Qur'an

Islamic tradition tells us that Muhammad used to pray regularly in a cave near Mecca. The angel Gabriel appeared to him for the first time when he was forty years old. The contents of the first revelation can be found in Sūra 96, verses 1 to 8. Gabriel ordered: *iqra'*, "proclaim" or "recite." This verb is from the same root as the word *qur'an* which means "proclamation" (of God's word). Surprised and afraid, Muhammad initially refused to comply with the angel's order, but he ended up agreeing to receive what Gabriel wanted to convey to him. He returned home very disturbed by this experience. His wife Khadija took him to her cousin Waraqa bin Nawfal, who had embraced Christianity before the rise of Islam. He was a learned man, "able to write in Hebrew and he wrote in Hebrew those portions of the Gospel that God wanted him to write."[10] Waraqa saw in Muhammad's experience a divine call to serve God as a prophet among his people.

---

10. Bukhari, *Bad' al-Wahy* (Beginning of the Revelation), 3.

The revelation spanned twenty-two years, first in Mecca (610–622) and then in Medina (623–632). All the revelations were collected and put into writing a few decades after the Prophet's death when Muslims realized that those who had learned the Qur'an by heart were dying in large numbers, some on the battlefield. The Qur'an is therefore composed of 114 chapters called sūras, classified roughly in decreasing order of length: the shortest at the end and the longest at the beginning (except Sūra 1). This order is not at all chronological because the shortest sūras were chronologically the first. Each sūra has a title that relates to one of its subjects. The size of the Qur'an is comparable to that of the New Testament, around seven thousand verses. The shortest sūras have just three verses (103, 108 and 110) and the longest (Sūra 2) has 286 verses.

For Muslims, the Qur'an is God's *word* in the full sense of the term. Thus the qur'anic text is the words spoken by God without any human or angelic intervention. The Prophet did not contribute in any way to the message, which was dictated to him verbatim. The result of this literal revelation is that the text is God's word only in the Arabic language. There are many translations available, but they are all considered to be paraphrases or interpretations of the divine word, in no way comparable to the original text, which is unique and inimitable.

The first sūra (*al-Fatiha*) is placed at the head of the Qur'an although it contains only seven verses. It is recited seventeen times a day by practicing Muslims, who pray five times a day. It is considered the greatest of all sūras, the one that sums up the entire qur'anic message:

> In the name of God, the All-Merciful, the Ever-Merciful,
> Praise be to God, the Lord of the worlds.
> The All-Merciful, the Ever-Merciful.
> King on the Day of Judgment.
> You alone we worship, and You alone we ask for help.
> Show us the straight way.
> The way of those upon whom You have bestowed Your grace,
> Those whose portion is not wrath, and who do not go astray.
> Amen.

According to a well-known Muslim scholar, Muhammad 'Abduh, qur'anic revelation covers five main topics all outlined in the first sūra:[11]

(1) Monotheism (*tawhid*) is emphasized in the words:

---

11. 'Abduh, *Tafsir al-Manar*, vol. 1, 36–38.

Praise be to God, Lord of the worlds.

(2) The double promise about eternal reward and punishment (*al-waʿd wa l-waʿid*) is indicated in these verses:
In the name of the Ever-Merciful, the All-Merciful.
King on the Day of Judgment.

(3) Worship (*ʿibada*) is mentioned in the verse:
You alone we worship, and You alone we ask for help.

(4) The path to eternal happiness is designated in the sentence:
Show us the straight way.

(5) The narratives about those who obey God and those who do not are noted in the verse:
The way of those upon whom You have bestowed Your grace,
Those whose portion is not wrath, and who do not go astray.

The Prophet is not a central figure in the Qur'an, unlike Jesus in the four Gospels. At the heart of the Qur'an, there is the discourse of God which takes many forms: rule of law, warnings about the coming judgment, accounts concerning the people of Israel and the prophets, promises of heaven for believers and of hell for unbelievers, prayers, calls to repentance and submission to God, etc.

The Hadith (Prophetic Tradition)

The Prophet is presented in the Qur'an as a model for all Muslims (33:21), hence, Muslims aspire to follow his example. The Qur'an speaks very little of Muhammad who is known mainly through stories in the Hadith (the word literally means a saying, a word, an account). This abundant literature compiles all the words and actions of the Prophet, his way of doing things and his habits (*sunna*), as well as his teachings reported by his companions and his wife Aisha.

In addition to the Prophet, the Hadith records the teaching of his close companions. Some sayings are in fact words uttered by God – they are holy (hadiths *qudsi*), for example, the saying where God declares, "Verily, My mercy will always prevail over My anger."[12] There are also verses that should have been in the Qur'an but for some reason have only been kept in the Hadith, for example, the text prescribing the stoning of married people who have

---

12. Bukhari, *Tawhid* (Monotheism), 15.

committed adultery.¹³ The Hadith is the second source of Islamic faith – its authority comes after the Qur'an.

Islamic law contains beliefs, practices and rules based exclusively on the narratives of the Hadith, for example:

> Circumcision (Bukhari, *Libas* [Clothing], 64).
> The five canonical prayers (Bukhari, *Salat* [Prayer], 1).
> Muhammad's intercession on the last day (Bukhari, *Tawhid* [Monotheism], 19).
> Muhammad's nightly journey to heaven (Bukhari, *Manaqib al-Ansar* [Merits of the *Ansar*], 42).
> Muhammad's miracles (Bukhari, *Manaqib* [Merits], 25).
> God's ninety-nine names known as his most beautiful names (Bukhari, *Tawhid* [Monotheism], 12).
> The death penalty for apostasy (Bukhari, *Jihad* [Combat], 149).
> The return of Jesus to earth (Bukhari, *Anbiya'* [Prophets], 52).

There are nine canonical Hadith compilations for Sunni Muslims, all written in Arabic. Shiʻa Muslims have their own collections. With one exception, all Sunni compilations were written in the third century AH (Islamic era, which begins in 622 when the Prophet migrated to Medina). Muslim scholars have classified Hadith accounts in four categories according to their degree of reliability: authentic, fair, weak, inauthentic. While there is consensus on the reliability of some accounts, many other accounts are accepted by some scholars and rejected by others.¹⁴

Muhammad's teaching is therefore found mainly in the collections of the Hadith; however, well-known sayings are attributed to the Prophet although they are not found in any of these collections. These so-called non-canonical hadiths have been transmitted in qur'anic commentaries and other works of theology, mysticism and jurisprudence, such as this one: "The [true] Lord of the people is the one who puts himself at their service." Unlike the Qur'an,

---

13. Muslim, *Hudud* (Penal Sanctions), 4.

14. Here are two surprising examples of sayings attributed to the Prophet. He is believed to have said that most people in hell will be women (Bukhari, *Nikah* [Marriage], 88). He also said: "When a fly falls into the bowl of one of you, let him immerse the whole insect in the liquid and remove it, because one of the two wings contains a remedy and the other a disease" (Bukhari, *Tibb* [Medicine], 58). How much credit can be given to these statements (both found in Bukhari's highly regarded compilation)? Western scholarship takes a very critical approach to Hadith literature and challenges its historical reliability altogether. We have deliberately chosen to follow the traditional Islamic perspective on this literature which accepts that not all Hadith narratives are authentic.

the Hadith compilations can be translated without their authority being affected. The collections by Bukhari and Muslim, both of which are titled *Sahih* (authentic), are available in many languages.

Seven Characteristics of Islam

We will conclude this chapter by giving a list of seven characteristics which seem to define Islam as well as Christianity: Abrahamic, holistic, rational, universal, missionary, final and saving.

1. Abrahamic

Abraham is one of the greatest figures in Islam. For Muslims he represents the prototype of the Prophet Muhammad. He is the spiritual father of all Muslims (22:78) and a good example for all believers (60:4). He was a passionate monotheistic believer although he grew up in a polytheistic society (6:74–82). He had two sons, Isaac and Ishmael, from two different wives, Sarah and Hagar. Both sons were prophets (2:136). With his son Ishmael, Abraham built the Kaʿba temple in Mecca and implored God to send a prophet to their offspring to show them how to worship their Creator (2:122–129). In response to Abraham's prayer, God sent Muhammad to teach God's religion to Arabs and non-Arabs.

2. Holistic

Islam recognizes that Judaism and Christianity are both revealed religions but neither is perfect. Unlike these two religions, Islam is concerned with both life on earth and in the hereafter. This double concern is summed up by a contemporary famous motto whose author is unknown: "Islam is religion and state" (*al-islam din wa dawla*). The Hadith collections deal with a very wide range of topics. Bukhari's collection has ninety-seven titles relating to almost all aspects of life. Sharīʿa is a set of laws of a religious, economic, family, social, political, and even military nature, dealing with individual matters as well as with social life. The four schools of Islamic law differ on many issues but they all agree that Islam is a holistic religion. Thus, Islam has always been understood and experienced as a religion for believers as well as a system of government for society. The word *umma* means both a community of believers and a political nation.

Without denying that Islam is all-embracing, Muslim reformers challenge the traditional alliance in Islam between religion and state. They argue that the Prophet played no political role in Mecca. In Medina he became a political leader simply because he was the best man for the job.

3. Rational

To the extent that Islam is based on divine revelation, it is not a rationalistic religion. It recognizes that there is a spiritual realm that transcends the physical world. In Islam, revelation is not seen as disclosing *who* God is, but rather as disclosing God's *will* for humankind. It is designed to show us how to worship our Creator and live in a way that pleases him. In other words, what we need to know for our eternal destiny is within the scope of our understanding. In this sense Islam is a rational religion (it makes sense) but not a rationalistic one (it acknowledges the reality of what is supernatural which cannot be fully comprehended with our limited minds).

The great mysteries of the Christian faith (trinity, incarnation, redemption) do not make much sense to the Muslim mind for at least three reasons:

(1) If God revealed himself, he would no longer be transcendent. He would be accessible to us, subject to our investigation and therefore not so fundamentally different from us.

(2) As humans we are both unworthy and unable to comprehend God's self-revelation.

(3) There is no need for us to know God in person; all we need to know is God's will for us in order to achieve success in this life and the next.

4. Universal

The Prophet Muhammad was an Arab and preached the Qur'an to the Arab people. However, the Qur'an makes it clear that the message Muhammad was given was not only for Arabs but for all peoples on earth: "We (God) sent you (Muhammad) only as a mercy for the worlds" (21:107; cf. 7:158). Islam is therefore a universal religion which Muslims have been mandated to spread amongst all nations.

5. Missionary

The Arabic word for "mission" (*da'wa*) derives from a verb which literally means "to invite" or "to call." Muslim preachers should follow the Prophet's example, who was instructed to preach the message persuasively and courteously: "Call to the way of your Lord, with wisdom and good exhortation; and argue with them in the best possible way" (16:125).

Jews and Christians also are invited to convert to Islam (3:20). Muslims should be respectful when debating with them: "Do not argue with the People of the Book but in the best possible way, except in the case of those amongst them who have been unjust" (29:46; cf. 3:64). If Muslims are prevented from carrying out their mission, then they have the right to fight their opponents, militarily if necessary (9:29).

6. Final

Islam teaches that Christianity and Judaism are both revealed religions. However, Muslim scholars point out that these two religions were valid only until Islam was revealed. Just as Christianity superseded Judaism, Islam supersedes both Judaism and Christianity. Not all Muslim scholars accept this traditional teaching. Some, especially those who live in contact with Western countries, argue that Judaism and Christianity remain legitimate religions.

7. Saving

Salvation in Islam is understood mainly in an eschatological sense; namely, the forgiveness of sins on the day of judgment which will result in access to paradise. Muslims believe that Islam is God's perfect revelation, unlike Judaism and Christianity, hence they see it as God's final and only saving religion. The Qur'an asserts that "the [only] religion [that is acceptable] in the sight of God is Islam" (3:19). This is usually interpreted to mean that only Muslims will be saved: "If anyone follows a religion other than Islam, never will it be accepted of him, and in the afterlife he will be among the losers" (3:85).

However, we do find in the Qur'an some more inclusive texts. These texts suggest that all monotheistic believers will go to paradise together with Muslims: "Those who believe (Muslims), those who are Jews, Christians and Sabeans – whoever believes in God and the last day and works righteousness – surely their reward is with their Lord. They have neither to fear nor to grieve"

(2:62; cf. 5:69).[15] We have seen that the general meaning of the word *islam* is about believing, obeying and worshipping the one and only God. Muslim reformers take this word in Sūra 3 verses 19 and 85 in this sense. They consider that all monotheistic faiths, especially Judaism and Christianity, preach Islam, understood in the general sense of the word, which does not necessarily include faith in the Prophet of Islam.

Readers familiar with Christian doctrine will have noticed that the seven characteristics of Islamic religion just reviewed could equally be applied to Christianity, which partly explains the historic rivalry between the two largest monotheistic religions in the world. This fact can serve to fuel conflict between Christians and Muslims, but it can equally serve to stimulate a real dialogue between them.

The space for freedom of expression that has been limited in some countries is now considerably enlarged thanks to social networks. This space provides an unprecedented opportunity to engage in fruitful dialogue between the two communities. Unfortunately, Christians and Muslims do not always use this space wisely. Some people even wage a verbal war against those they see as their adversaries. Examples of contemporary polemicists include the Coptic priest Zakaria Boutros and the Indian propagandist Zakir Naik. Polemicists (from the Greek word *polemos*, "war") do not honor the God whom they claim to serve. In their dealings with Muslims, Christians should keep in mind this recommendation of the apostle Peter: "Always be prepared to give an answer to everyone who asks you to give the reason for the hope that you have. But do this with *gentleness and respect*" (1 Pet 3:15; emphasis added).

---

15. The origin of Sabeans (still found in small number in Iraq) is not known. For some they represent a group of Jewish followers of John the Baptist.

2

Islam as Community

So far we have looked at the tenets of Islam, the scriptural sources of this religion and its main characteristics. All this draws Muslims together, providing a focus for unity and cohesion. The Muslim community is certainly monotheistic, but it is by no means a unified community. It is very diverse, just like any other world religion.

This chapter will first underline this diversity from several angles (ethnic, denominational, legal, theological, economic, political and individual). It will then list some prominent Islamic customs before concluding with important characteristics of Islamic societies and cultures.

Diversity of the Muslim Community
Ethnic Diversity

We have noted that Islam is a universal religion. Although it started amongst the Arab people, it was not a religion intended only for Arabs. The Muslim community comprises Arabs and non-Arabs. In 2015, the Muslim community numbered 1.8 billion people, which represents about 24 percent of the global population, estimated at 7.5 billion. Arab Muslims represent only about 20 percent of the number of Muslims worldwide.[1]

Thus, not all Muslims are Arab and not all Arabs are Muslim. Amongst the 330 million Arabs there are about fifteen million who are Christian, distributed mainly in the Middle East, especially in Egypt. Most Arabs speak Arabic as their first language; many continue to define themselves as Arabs (culturally, sociologically) even if they no longer speak Arabic.

---

1. See Pew Research Center's Forum on Religion & Public Life, *Mapping the Global Muslim Population*. https://www.pewresearch.org/fact-tank/2017/08/09/muslims-and-islam-key-findings-in-the-u-s-and-around-the-world/.

The Muslim community is spread over all the continents and Muslims are found in most nations. Over 61 percent of Muslims live in Asia. The regions of South and Southeast Asia are home to a high proportion of Muslims. The Indian subcontinent (Pakistan, India and Bangladesh) is also a region where Muslims are found in great numbers.

The fact that the Muslim community comprises many peoples means it is culturally very diverse. Like any religion, Islam shapes the cultures of the people and is shaped by them. Interaction between religion and society is the mark of a living and growing faith. Thus Muslims in Southeast Asia are different from Muslims in sub-Saharan Africa; Muslims in Central Asia are unlike Muslims in the Arab world; and in the Arab world, Muslims in the Middle East are not exactly the same as their fellow Muslims in North Africa or in the Gulf States. Muslims in secular countries (e.g. Western Europe, North America, Australia) understand and live out their faith in ways significantly different from Muslim-majority countries.

Denominational Diversity

Muslims are divided into two main groups, Sunnis and Shi'ites (or Shi'a).[2] The division between Sunnis and Shi'ites goes back to the time of the Prophet's death. Some Muslims, later called Sunnis, agreed that Abu Bakr (Muhammad's father-in-law) should be Muhammad's first successor, whereas the Shi'ites believed that Ali (Muhammad's cousin and son-in-law) had been designated by the Prophet as his successor. Sunni Muslims later acknowledged Ali as the fourth caliph, but his assassination revived the division between Sunnis and Shi'ites. These two groups fought one another mercilessly.[3] They have evolved separately from each other and have developed two very different traditions. The Shi'ite imam is both a religious and political leader whereas the role of Sunni caliph is mainly political. For Shi'ite Muslims, the authority of the clergy (*wilayat al-faqih*) is superior to political power and is not subject to election. In Iran, this rule by the clergy is represented today by the Supreme Leader of the Revolution, Ayatollah Ali Khamene'i, himself a former president of the Republic (1981–1989). According to A. Amir-Moezzi, one of the best experts

---

2. The word *shi'a* means a "group" or a "party" (28:15; 37:83). This word is sometimes used in a derogatory way to emphasize the sectarian character of the group.

3. The bloody conflicts that opposed fellow Muslims in the aftermath of the Prophet death are documented in H. Ouardi, *Les Califes maudits*, vol. 1, *La Déchirure*, vol. 2, *À l'ombre des sabres*, vol. 3, *Meurtre à la mosquée*. Paris: Albin Michel, 2019-2021.

in Shi'a Islam, if Sunni Islam can be described as the religion of the Book (the Qur'an), Shi'ism is the religion of the imam who is the interpreter and the embodiment of the Qur'an.

Another major difference between the two main branches of Islam concerns the authenticity of the Qur'an. The Shi'ites blame the first Sunni caliphs for having seriously undermined the integrity of qur'anic revelation by destroying and replacing the authentic text with a very different one in which we no longer find the passages where the Prophet would have designated Ali as his successor. In addition, the Shi'ites have their own collections of the Prophetic Tradition which are not part of the Sunni nine official Hadith compilations (Bukhari, Muslim, etc.).

The vast majority of Muslims are Sunni. The word *sunni* derives from the Prophet's *sunna*, meaning custom or practice. Sunni Muslims are very keen to point out they believe in the Qur'an and they walk in the Prophet's footsteps. They represent over 80 percent of the Muslim population worldwide.

Shi'a Muslims make up 15 percent of the Muslim community. The Shi'ites are sometimes called "Imamites" because they believe that the imams, not the caliphs, are the legitimate successors of the Prophet. The word *imam* means "guide" or "leader." Most Shi'ites (up to 80 percent) live in just four countries: Iran, Pakistan, India and Iraq. They outnumber Sunni Muslims in only five countries: Iran, Iraq, Azerbaijan, Bahrain and Lebanon. The main group of Shi'a Muslims are the Twelvers, who believe in twelve legitimate imams having succeeded the Prophet as leaders of the Muslim community.

The age-long opposition between Sunni and Shi'a Muslims, coupled with the antagonism between Arabs and Persians, is growing increasingly violent. On one side, we have Shi'ite Iran and its regional allies in Iraq (ruled by a Shi'a-majority government), Syria (Alawite regime), Lebanon (Hezbullah powerful party) and Yemen (Houthi opposition). On the other side, we have Sunni Saudi Arabia and its regional allies in Egypt (where the leading Islamic university of al-Azhar is located), in the Arab-Persian Gulf (UAE, Bahrain) and in Lebanon (al-Mustaqbal party led by the al-Hariri Saudi-Lebanese family).

Other Shi'a Muslims are the Ismailis, or Seveners, represented today by the followers of the Agha Khan, who accept only the first seven imams, and the Zaydis, or Fivers, who accept only the first five imams. The 'Ibadis are yet another group of non-Sunni Muslims; they are found mostly in Oman, Zanzibar, Algeria, and Djerba (Tunisia).

Other Muslim groups include the Druze (Syria, Lebanon, Israel) and the Nusayris, or Alawites (Turkey, Syria, Lebanon). Recently, other groups have emerged such as the Ahmadis (originally from Pakistan and very active in the

UK and other parts of the world) and the Nation of Islam (United States). These groups do not exceed 5 percent of the global Muslim population.

Legal Diversity

Islamic law is very comprehensive. It includes religious doctrine, social and family regulations, economic and political legislation, etc. *Fiqh*, the science of law or jurisprudence, deals with the interpretation of Islamic sources. The Qur'an and the Hadith are interpreted in light of two main principles: the consensus (*ijma'*) of the community represented by its scholars and the principle of analogy (*qiyas*). This principle relies on revealed data (in the Qur'an and Hadith) to draw a conclusion about an issue not addressed in the sources. For example, drug use is prohibited because it has adverse effects similar to the consumption of wine (forbidden in the Qur'an). Community consensus is based on the belief that God, since he is faithful, does not mislead the community of believers represented by its scholars.

Muslim jurists have understood Islamic sources in different ways. This has resulted in a diversity of schools, each claiming to have correctly interpreted divine revelation and prophetic teaching. Shi'a Muslims have their own school of jurisprudence: the Jaafarite school, linked to the sixth Imam Jaafar al-Sadiq. Sunni Muslims have four schools, all considered legitimate schools. These schools of jurisprudence (*madhahib*) are named after their respective founders who lived in the first three centuries of Islamic era: Hanafi (Turkey, Middle East, Pakistan, India, Afghanistan), Maliki (North and West Africa, Egypt, Sudan, Kuwait), Shafi'i (Middle East, Yemen, UAE, East Africa, Indonesia, Malaysia), and Hanbali (Kuwait, Bahrain, Oman, Qatar). The regime in Saudi Arabia follows the Wahhabi school founded by Muhammad Ibn 'Abd al-Wahhab (1703–1792) which derives from the Hanbali school, the strictest of the four.

Islamic law groups human acts in five categories: mandatory, recommended, permissible, reprehensible, and forbidden. While the status of many actions is not disputed (e.g. prayer is mandatory, divorce reprehensible, murder forbidden), on other actions there is difference of opinions amongst Muslim jurists. At the popular level, Muslims tend to think of human acts simply in terms of either *halal* (lawful) or *haram* (unlawful).

Theological Diversity

Several theological schools exist in mainstream Islam. The most significant is the Ash'ari school, founded by Abu al-Hasan al-Ash'ari (AH 324/AD 935), and its rival, the Mu'tazili school (lit. "dissident"). Both represent mainstream Islam and are found amongst Muslims everywhere.

Historically, Ash'ari theology prevailed amongst Sunni Muslims and Mu'tazili theology amongst the Shi'a. However, Mu'tazili theology seems to be increasingly popular today including among Sunni Muslims. The reason has to do with the respective characteristics of the two schools. Ash'ari thought emphasizes God's sovereignty and his freedom to act in the world as he sees fit. This can lead to ascribing a certain arbitrariness to God and conceiving submission to him in fatalistic terms. In contrast, Mu'tazili theology emphasizes rationality, justice, responsibility and freedom. As these themes are quite popular in modern and humanist thought, Mu'tazilism attracts more and more Muslims in search of a faith that satisfies human reason.

Economic Diversity

By and large, the majority of Muslims live in the so-called developing world and therefore in rather poor countries. The oil-producing countries of the Gulf, whose population is relatively small, are not typical of Islamic countries. Many Muslims resent the contrasting reality in the Muslim world. The oil-rich countries invest their extravagant wealth in Western nations and not in development projects. On the whole, Muslims are critical of these monarchies who in their eyes pay only lip service to Islam and the Muslim community.

Economic challenges in the Muslim world, as in the developing world in general, make other challenges even more difficult to tackle. In many of these countries the birth rate is relatively high, resulting in huge problems in areas such as housing, climate, education, health care and employment. Many people are tempted to migrate to so-called developed countries to find jobs. Others, who have managed to achieve high-level education, do not find adequate work in their own countries. They too seek better career opportunities abroad, and in doing so perhaps unwittingly contribute to the impoverishment of their countries through what is referred to as "brain drain." Fortunately, many migrants do send money from their host countries to their home country to support their relatives, which helps the economy to certain extent. This aid supports the local economy much more than economic aid received through official channels (e.g. NGOs, governments). Thankfully, economic poverty is often counterbalanced with greater solidarity, stronger resilience, respect for the values of life and family, and a deeper spirituality.

Political Diversity

Islam is more than a religion – it is a major political force. Because Islamic law is comprehensive, and because the Prophet was also a political leader, Islam has always been closely associated with politics and governance. In many Muslim-majority countries, Islam is the state religion. This association of political and religious powers represents a double-edged sword. On one hand, it gives Islam political and other advantages, on the other, Islam is often used and abused by political leaders whose main concern is to protect their position. It is perhaps no accident that some self-proclaimed Islamic regimes are authoritarian and corrupt. Islamic regimes, including those who overtly claim Islam as their foundation, are different from each other. Some are royalist while others follow a republican model.

Countries typically pursue their own political interests, and conflicting national interests can be the cause of opposition amongst nations. When the same religion is the state religion in opposing countries, it is likely to become a divisive force instead of a force for good. Instead of transcending political rivalries, the religious community becomes divided along political lines. This can only have adverse repercussions on the religion and its followers.

Many Muslims are aware that the Muslim community is far from presenting itself as one united community (or nation), as it should do in line with qur'anic teaching (21:92); however, they profoundly disagree over how to address this problem. Radical Muslims believe division amongst Muslims is caused by the fact that Islamic law is not fully implemented in Islamic nations. They call for more vigorous enforcement of Sharīʿa law, including restoration of the caliphate (abolished in 1924). The Caliph would then preside over the Muslim community worldwide and represent it as a major player in world politics.

Other Muslims take a completely different view. Reformist Muslims (like Rachid Benzine and Abdennour Bidar) believe the weakness of Islam is due partly to its association with the political establishment, resulting in worldliness, self-indulgent attitudes amongst Muslims, oppression of Muslims by fellow Muslims, stifling of Islamic creativity and ossification of Islamic teaching. These Muslims call for an Islamic reformation whose objectives include disentangling Islam from political power, recovering Islam as a great spirituality, and establishing a just society within the Muslim community and beyond. It is significant that a number of reformers as well as radical Muslims live in non-Muslim countries. Some have come to these countries as political refugees after being persecuted in their own countries. Professor Nasr Hamid Abu Zayd is one of them.[4]

Individual Diversity

Muslims are first and foremost human beings with their own journeys in life that shape their personalities. Individual character determines the way they understand and live out their faith. Thus, the Muslim community is diverse also because the members who compose it are different due to backgrounds, upbringing, education, family and social contexts, and perhaps even their genes. Broadly speaking, there are seven types of Muslims.

Liberal Muslims (some Muslim hard-liners may consider them nominal Muslims) are at one end of the spectrum. Their version of Islam at times may have little to do with Islamic tradition and dogma. Islam gives them a social and cultural identity, rather than a religious imperative. Emotionally they feel part of the community, although they do not adhere to all tenets of Islamic faith. Some militant and provocative people amongst them openly challenge Islamic faith and practice. Professor Mohammed Arkoun is definitely one of the most thought-provoking liberal Muslims.[5]

Secular Muslims see Islam as essentially a private religion just like any other religion. They strongly believe that Islam should be completely dissociated from political parties and government agendas, and that, provided Muslims have freedom to practice their religion, they should not force their faith on others. They observe that we live in a pluralist world where commitment to Islamic faith represents only one legitimate option among many other options, in Muslim as well as non-Muslim societies. Secular Muslims in Islamic nations

---

4. Nasr Hamid Abu Zayd (1943–2010) is a Muslim scholar from Egypt who taught Arabic literature and Islamic studies at several Cairo universities. Because of his critical perspective on Islamic tradition, he was charged with apostasy and his marriage annulled under Sharīʿa law (according to which a Muslim woman cannot be the wife of a non-Muslim). He had to take refuge (with his wife) in the Netherlands where he resumed his teaching at the University of Leiden. Some of his works have been translated into English including *Reformation of Islamic Thought: A Critical Historical Analysis* (Amsterdam: Amsterdam University Press, 2006).

5. Mohammed Arkoun (1928–2010), originally from Algeria, was a (critical) historian of Islamic thought. He taught at numerous universities in France (notably at Paris III-Sorbonne Nouvelle) and abroad. Some of his writings are available in English including *The Unthought in Contemporary Islamic Thought* (London: Saqi Books, 2002).

such as Egypt, face staunch opposition which can lead to their assassination as it did with Faraj Fuda.[6]

Mystical Muslims (known as "Sufis") are drawn to Islam because of its deep spirituality. They find in the mystical tradition a fulfilling response to their spiritual search (e.g. Jawdat Saïd and Abd Al-Haqq Guiderdoni). They long for a close relationship with God, who is seen as a loving, caring and personal God. Mystical Muslims are practicing Muslims, but their practice is not limited to the Five Pillars. They often meet in small fellowships with like-minded Muslims to worship God with their own rituals. Islam offers them an alternative way of living in a world dominated by materialism, consumerism, individualism and hedonism.

Reformist Muslims (e.g. Mohamed Bajrafil and Hakim El Karoui) question aspects of Islamic tradition they consider to be primarily cultural and alien to the core beliefs and practices of Islam. They understand Islam as a dynamic and life-changing movement. They seek to engage the Muslim community in a holistic *jihad*, which includes a constant and determined struggle to fight the ills of society: superstition, bigotry, nominalism, illiteracy, corruption, injustice, etc. For reformers, Islam is essentially a religion and everything else is contextual: culture, civilization, history, even Sharī'a itself. They take a critical look at many narratives found in the Prophetic Tradition, and some reformers are even critical of certain elements of the qur'anic message as well as aspects of the life of Muhammad. Their aim is to see Islam transforming traditional Muslim societies and gaining new relevance and attraction in modern and postmodern societies. Reformist Muslims are often hated by those in power in countries ruled by a despotic regime such as Sudan was until 2019. Mahmoud Mohamed Taha paid with his life for his reforming vision of Islam.[7]

Conservative Muslims are suspicious of their fellow Muslims who want to introduce radical change to Islamic societies. They see themselves as the custodians of the faith, therefore they distance themselves from both reformers and radicals. They acknowledge that the Muslim community does not live

---

6. Faraj Fouda (1945–1992) was an Egyptian writer and journalist. His commitment to human rights and secular regime won him hostility from the highest Islamic authorities at al-Azhar University who accused him of blasphemy. Shortly after, he was assassinated by an Islamist group.

7. Mahmoud Mohamed Taha (1909–1985) was at the same time a politician, a theologian and a Sufi thinker. He denounced the misuse of religion by political power under President Gaafar Nimeiri (1969–1985) of Sudan. After a fake trial in which he refused to participate, he was put to death for apostasy, but his legacy remains notably through one of his disciples, Abdullahi Ahmed An-Naim. Among his most important works is undoubtedly *The Second Message of Islam* (Syracuse: Syracuse University Press, 1996).

up to Islamic virtues (3:110); nonetheless, they point out that Islam is still a fast-growing religion. Their way to reduce the gap between reality and ideal is through thorough religious education enhancing, not jettisoning, Islamic tradition and old-age wisdom.

Radical Muslims, also known as "fundamentalists" or "Islamists," bemoan the decline of the Muslim community and its decreasing role in world affairs. For them the cultural, economic and even political domination of Muslim peoples by non-Muslim nations represents an affront to Islam. They are also critical of political and religious establishments, which they hold responsible for this decline. They dream of a return to a "golden age" when Muslims were (allegedly) united. At that time, they were proud of their religion and committed to spread it as far as possible. Radical Muslims want to bring back this age through full implementation of Sharīʿa. They seek to vindicate the Muslim community by calling Muslim youth to take seriously the claims of their faith and its social and political implications.

Some radical Muslims (e.g. Rachid Rida, Yusuf al-Qaradawi, Tariq Ramadan, Rachid Ghannouchi) see themselves as the true reformers because they seek to rid Islam of the old-age weight of tradition which has ended up stifling the vitality of the prophetic message. In fact, they are revivalist Muslims who, unlike progressive reformers, advocate the application of Sharīʿa in all its rigor, even if it must be done in stages.

Terrorist Muslims, or "jihadists," usually share the ideology of radical Muslims but go a step further. While radicals seek to achieve their objectives through peaceful means (including democratic elections), terrorists engage in violence for the sake of their cause. They justify their actions with a partisan, literal and non-contextual interpretation of the Qur'an and the Hadith. Terrorists are extremists and their actions are spectacular, but their number is very small compared to the size of the Muslim community worldwide. They are not at all representative of the community. They seek to attract the attention of the media, and often succeed, unlike ordinary Muslims who are often their first victims.

Religious Customs

As we have just seen, the Muslim community is very diverse in many respects (ethnically, theologically, politically, economically, etc.). Yet, Muslims are united by faith in God and his last Prophet as well as by their practice of the five religious obligations. The Muslim community is also characterized by several religious customs which help to form its distinctive social identity. Here are some of these customs, starting with the most important one.

Prayer

In the Five Pillars of Islam, ritual prayer (*salat*) comes second after the confession of faith. Prayer is of major importance as, according to a prophetic saying, it represents the dividing line between faith and unbelief.[8] Socially too, prayer is the most public expression of faith in Muslim societies. It marks the rhythm of the day throughout the whole year, whereas fasting affects Islamic social life during only one month (the month of Ramadan).

The call to prayer (*adhan*) is made from the minaret of the mosque by the "prayer caller" (*mu'adhdhin*) whose voice is often broadcast through loud speakers. He calls people to turn to God and worship him. The call to prayer consists in chanting the following words:

> God is the greatest. God is the greatest.
> I bear witness that there is no god but God.
> I bear witness that Muhammad is God's Apostle.
> Come to prayer! Come to prayer!
> Come to bliss! Come to bliss!
> God is the greatest. God is the greatest.
> There is no god but God.

Muslims are expected to pray at least five times a day at a specific time of the day: sunrise (*subh*), noon (*zuhr*), afternoon (*'asr*), sunset (*maghrib*), and evening (*'isha'*). Often the call to prayer is also made at dawn (*fajr*).[9] Daily and regular prayers remind Muslims to dedicate their lives and all their day's activities to the service and worship of the Creator God. They can pray anywhere, but they need to pray towards Mecca where the *Ka'ba* is found.

Islamic prayer involves the soul as well as the body. Physical postures (kneeling, bowing, prostrating) are used to express the worshipper's inner attitude of submission to God. These physical expressions can also be found within Christian and Jewish communities. The prayer's ritual includes taking off one's shoes before entering the mosque to show respect for the sanctity of

---

8. Muslim, *Iman* (Faith), 37.

9. In Christian traditions, monks pray seven times a day. In Jewish tradition, people pray three times a day.

the place, and performing ablutions before praying so as to enter into a state of ritual purity.

There are two words for "mosque" in Arabic: *masjid*, the place of worship, and *jami'*, the place of getting together. These words illustrate the twofold role – religious and social – which the mosque plays in Muslim societies. All Muslims, men and women, can pray in the mosque, although men attend more regularly than women do. They pray at the same time, but usually in different places to enable them to be entirely focused on the worship of almighty God.

Friday prayer (*salat al-jum'a*) is the weekly community prayer. All Muslims are expected to offer corporate prayer during Friday noon prayer. Apart from prayer itself, Friday worship is characterized by the sermon (*khutba*) usually given by the imam. The sermon is generally based on qur'anic texts (always recited in Arabic) and narratives taken from the Hadith (Prophetic Tradition). The preacher uses this teaching opportunity to address topical issues (moral, social, economic, and sometimes political).

Festivals

The Muslim community has two major festivals (*'id*): the Festival of Sacrifice (*'id al-adha*), and the Festival of Fast-breaking (*'id al-fitr*) at end of the month of Ramadan. The dates of these festivals are fixed according to the Islamic lunar calendar (which is eleven days shorter than the Western calendar).

On the Festival of Sacrifice, Muslims remember Abraham's sacrifice of his son whose life God spared thanks to "a great sacrifice" (37:100–111). They celebrate Abraham's obedient faith that enabled him to pass the divine test. The form of the celebration varies from culture to culture, but usually includes dressing in one's best clothes, holding community prayers, slaughtering an animal (usually a sheep), eating plenty of good food, giving to the poor, and spending time with family and friends. Different local names are given to this festival depending on the region; for example *'id al-kabir*, "the Great Festival" in the Arab world, and *Tabaski* in West Africa.

The second feast celebrates the breaking of the fast at the end of the month of Ramadan. Although this is known as "the Smaller Festival," it can be celebrated with greater festivities and social manifestations than the Festival of Sacrifice. Every day, people break their fast with seasonal food in an atmosphere of communal celebration.

Muslims have other less important festivals: the birth of the Prophet, his nocturnal journey to paradise via Jerusalem (17:1), the start of a new year (according to Islamic calendar) and the night the Qur'an was revealed (*laylat al-qadr*).

Circumcision

All Muslims are expected to have their newborn baby boys circumcised. This requirement does not have a religious significance. It is one of five practices taught by nature, according to a prophetic saying: "Five practices are characteristics of *fitra*:[10] circumcision, shaving the pubic hair, trimming the moustache, clipping the nails, and depilating the hair of the armpits." These practices, like burying the dead within twenty-four hours, appear to be based on hygienic rather than religious grounds.

Female circumcision, or FGM (Female Genital Mutilation), is not, strictly speaking, an Islamic custom. It is practiced in many non-Islamic societies, and Arabs practiced it long before the birth of Islam. The Qur'an does not mention either male or female circumcision. It would appear that the Prophet did not object to a less extreme form of female circumcision, neither did he endorse it.[11] Therefore, like so-called honor killings, female circumcision is an ancient cultural practice found in Muslim and non-Muslim societies.

Reciting God's Names

Islamic tradition ascribes ninety-nine names (or attributes) to God, known as God's "most beautiful names" (7:180). Many of these names are found in the Qur'an: the wise, the forgiving, the life-giving, the living, the trustworthy, the generous, the first, the last, the provider, the truth, etc. Others are listed in the Hadith. According to a prophetic saying, paradise is promised to those who know all the divine names by heart.[12] Traditionally, Muslims use a thirty-

---

10. Bukhari, *Libas* (Clothing), 67. The word *fitra* refers to an innate disposition, that is what human beings would do naturally without being guided by any specific divine revelation. Islam is understood as the religion of *fitra* in the sense that people are born with a natural disposition to believe in the Creator and worship one and only God.

11. According to one account, "A woman used to perform [female] circumcision in Medina. The Prophet said to her: 'Do not cut severely as that is better for a woman and more desirable for a husband'"; Abu Dawud, *Adab* (Good Manners), 180. Aisha, the wife of the Prophet, reports a saying by her husband (referring to her own experience) according to which ablution is obligatory when, in the intimate relationship between the spouses, the circumcised parts touch each other; Tirmidhi, *Tahara* (Ritual Cleanness), 80. According to a disputed saying attributed to Muhammad, "circumcision is recommended, *sunna*, for men, and a good thing, *makruma*, for women"; Ibn Hanbal, *Musnad* "Book of the People of Basra", no. 21050.

12. Bukhari, *Tawhid* (Monotheism), 12.

three-bead rosary to help them recite these names. They recite all of them by going three times through the rosary (*subha*).

This religious custom, widespread in the Muslim world, has its secular version. Many Muslims and non-Muslims use the beads for seemingly no other reason than to keep their hands busy.

Memorizing the Qur'an

The Qur'an is Islam's Holy Scripture, highly revered by all Muslims. They regard it as God's final word to humankind. Reciting qur'anic verses is an integral part of the Islamic worship tradition. Paradise is promised to those who are able to recite the whole book. On judgment day, Muslims who have memorized the Qur'an will have the privilege of interceding for ten relatives.[13] Memorizing (*hifz*) the Qur'an is therefore a noble and saving activity. This prompts Muslims to learn God's word and to teach it to their children.

Many Muslims send their young sons and daughters to an Islamic school (*madrasa*) with this purpose. Such schools are usually associated with a local mosque. The school teacher is often the imam himself. In many parts of the Muslim world, these schools offer children the broader educational opportunity of reading and writing. In an oral culture, reciting the Qur'an is of paramount importance, especially in contexts where few people can read.

Many Muslims recite qur'anic verses (or even entire sūras) without having a strong grasp of the Arabic language, hence they recite without a clear understanding of what they are saying. It is believed that reciting the Qur'an represents a powerful virtue, purifying the heart in which it dwells.

Use of Religious Language

Muslims in general, even non-practicing ones, tend to have a deep sense of God being in control of everything in the world, including their daily lives. This awareness of God's undisputed and universal sovereignty has affected the Arabic language and other languages spoken by Muslim peoples. As a result, Muslims across the world use many Arabic expressions referring to God in their greetings and their everyday conversations. Some of these expressions are also used by Christians living in Muslim-majority societies, including those

---

13. Ibn Hanbal, *Musnad* "Book on the Ten People to Whom Paradise Was Promised," no. 1284.

who speak languages other than Arabic. Amongst the most commonly used religious expressions are the following:

Bismi-llahi r-rahmani r-rahim: "In the name of God the All-Merciful, the Ever-Merciful," often reduced to *bismi-llah*, "In the name of God." This expression is used to call upon God's blessing, protection and help at the start of a speech, a meal, a trip, etc., and always before reciting the Qur'an.

Allahu akbar: "God is the greatest." Used in various circumstances, these words can express a whole range of attitudes such as trust, submission, resolve, defiance, exalting God, asking his help, or vindicating his honor.

In sha'a llah: "God willing."

Wa llahi: "I swear by God."

Al-hamdu lillahi: "Praise be to God." These first two words in the Qur'an appear more than thirty times in the holy Book. They are often used in response to the question, "How are you?"

As-salamu 'alaykum: "Peace be upon you." This traditional Islamic greeting is going to be used by people in heaven (7:46). The response is: *wa 'alaykumu s-salam*: "And upon you peace."

Salla llahu 'alayhi wa sallam: "May God's blessing and pleasure rest upon him." This expression (difficult to translate) is used by Muslims every time they mention the Prophet Muhammad to mark their respect for him. It calls God's blessing upon the Prophet as head and representative of the Muslim community.

'Alayhi s-salam: "Peace be upon him." Muslims use these words every time they pronounce the name of any prophet to mark their respect for him.

Ma sha'a llah: "Whatever God's wants!" This is an exclamation of surprise: Amazing!

Subhana llah: This exclamation of surprise can also mean "God forbid" (i.e. God is far above doing this or God being that).

Bi-amani llah: "Under God's protection." This is a farewell expression.

Arguably, people do not always use these expressions with intentionality; however, when meaningfully uttered, they reflect the fear of God in a person's heart. The expressions *as-salamu 'alaykum* and *in sha'a llah* are also found in the Bible (John 20:21; Jas 4:15). The second one is sometimes used in a fatalistic way. Fatalism sets in opposition God's sovereignty and human action and becomes an excuse for doing nothing. Yet, this need not be the case as the Qur'an connects divine power with human responsibility: "God does not change a people unless they decide to change themselves" (13:11).

Popular Practices

Like any religion, Islam has to a greater or lesser degree taken on the cultural and religious traditions of the people where it has spread, hence the diversity of practices in different contexts. Islam, as interpreted by theologians and jurists, does not always meet people's felt needs. This leads many Muslims to seek answers to down-to-earth questions (e.g. on guidance, healing, protection from harm) from alternative and sometimes unorthodox sources.

Sufi brotherhoods (i.e. mystical groups) thrive in traditional societies where ritualistic Islam does not reach deep enough into the human soul. In some countries, these spiritual fellowships represent widespread networks whose influence is greater than official mosques. Through specific exercises, often accompanied by stimulating music and chanting (e.g. whirling dervishes or dances), their members yearn to achieve a personal and experiential relationship with a loving God that is missing in legalistic Islam.

Notwithstanding the belief that the Prophet will intercede for his community on judgment day, Islamic teaching claims no need for human or angelic mediation between God and human beings in this life. Yet because God is transcendent and far above humankind, people feel the need for a mediator. In some places this figure is assumed by holy people such as the prophet Elijah, the Virgin Mary or Jesus himself. These people are revered especially by Muslims who live in contact with Christian communities. Shrines and graveyards are associated with living or dead saints, and people come to pray to them and ask for their assistance.

In some African countries the intermediaries between God and Muslims is a local spiritual leader (a *marabout* or a *pir*) who is believed to possess and dispense *baraka* (divine blessing). People seek his help in times of crisis, sickness or uncertainty. Muslim boys are sent to him by poor parents to learn the recitation of the Qur'an by heart in his *madrasa* (school). Often these children, known in Senegal as *talibés* and in Mali and Niger as *garibous*, are sent as beggars by their master to collect money for him on the streets of the towns and cities.

God is all-powerful, yet some Muslims feel powerless in life's testing circumstances. They live in fear of evil and of the evil one, especially when a person thought to be demon-possessed is known to them. To overcome this fear, they sometimes resort to a power figure (a man or a woman) who has the reputation for working miracles or performing exorcisms. More often than not, this person is involved in witchcraft and magic rituals. Protection from evil is also associated with certain objects such as relics of saints or the blue representation of Fatima's hand (one of the Prophet's daughters). Envy is seen as a particularly powerful and harmful force; hence the use of the eye symbol to ward off bad influence emanating from envious people.

These and other features of Islamic practices are typical of folk or popular Islam. Pristine Islam (and any other religion for this matter) is found hardly anywhere in the world. The degree to which popular Islam diverges from official Islamic teaching varies from place to place. These practices are generally tolerated by Muslim leaders, depending on who they are, how much influence they wield in their community, and the kind of religious training they have received.

Characteristics of Islamic Cultures

So far we have discussed both the unity and the diversity of the Muslim community as a religious community. We also looked at major Islamic practices. But what about Islamic culture, or should we say "cultures"? Whatever society Islam has penetrated, it has gradually but profoundly transformed people's lives. As a result, Muslim societies share many common features. At the risk of oversimplifying a complex and ever-changing reality, the final part of this chapter will consider some of characteristics of Muslim cultures.

Religious Identity

Most Muslim societies have not yet been deeply affected by secularization. They are still traditional and conservative. Religion shapes people's thinking and behaviour, even among non-practicing Muslims.

Because of globalization, Muslim societies are increasingly more open to Western culture through the media, internet, tourism, education, business and migration. Interaction between the Western world and the Muslim world affects Muslim societies much more than in the past. Modern values such as freedom, human rights, democracy and tolerance are attractive to many Muslims, especially young people.

Unfortunately, these values are often associated with social trends that are less attractive to the Muslim mind (e.g. materialism, atheism, individualism and sexual permissiveness). As a result, the religious identity of Muslim societies is being undermined. Some militant Muslims argue that the pervasive influence of Western secular culture represents a very serious threat. They call for a robust response in the form of an Islamic revival to enable Muslims to resist the growing secularization of their community and to protect their own identity and values.

Community, Family, Solidarity

Like other traditional societies, Muslim societies are characterized by a strong sense of belonging. Members of the Muslim community are described in the Qur'an as brothers and sisters because they share the same faith (49:10). Their oneness transcends ethnic and theological diversity. The use of Arabic as a liturgical language provides a solid unifying factor, and the annual pilgrimage to Mecca constitutes a powerful demonstration of this unity.

Muslims feel the same sense of belonging in their family. Islam honors the family and teaches that the family is the place where people fulfil their humanity. Sexual relationships are to be enjoyed only between husband and wife. Leading an unmarried life is not a long-term option for adult Muslim men and women. Children represent a great blessing. Parents have the responsibility of caring for their children, and children must respect and obey their parents.

The Muslim community is likened to one body whose members show compassion, solidarity and support for each other: "Believers are kind, loving, and supportive of one another. They form one body so that when one of its members is in pain all the other members share its insomnia and fever."[14] Community life characterizes Muslim societies, and relationships are strong amongst community members. Solidarity between rich and poor, strong and weak, Arabs and non-Arabs is highly praised. This is best demonstrated in the third pillar, namely, legal almsgiving, whose aim is to support the weak, the oppressed, the poor, the disabled and disadvantaged members of the community. Like any human society, the Muslim community is not immune from internal turmoil and divisions; however, Muslims will all stand up with one voice when they perceive a danger from outside which threatens fellow Muslims.

---

14. Bukhari, *Adab* (Good Manners), 27.

Relationships and Work

In Western societies, work is often at the heart of social life. People's value depends a great deal on their worth as workers. Great emphasis is placed on achievement, effectiveness and performance. Perhaps this is the unavoidable price to be paid by developed, affluent and consumerist societies.

Many Muslims and non-Muslims in the developing world work very hard yet live in a society where relationships rather than work play a vital role in the community. People enjoy spending time socializing with and supporting each other. Health care is provided by family members as much as by medical professionals. In general people work fewer hours, and their working environment is less stressful. They may be less productive, but they have a better quality of life. Because their lives are not driven by work, they feel less need to spend time and money on weekend leisure activities and recreational holidays.

Men and Women

Western societies tend to follow an egalitarian model between men and women, although they are often inconsistent. Men and women basically share the same identity, roles and rights. They have the same job opportunities and have access to all professions, including the army and the police. In many countries same-sex partnerships are legal and viewed as a legitimate alternative to heterosexual marriages.

By contrast, in Muslim and other conservative societies, men and women are seen as equal but do not share the same roles. Traditionally the role of women is a domestic one, while men are responsible for more public roles. The husband is the head of the household, although the wife may have greater influence on the children than her husband.

Sexuality is also seen as a defining difference in humankind, and gender identity is seen as essential to a person's personality. Muslims identify sexual temptation as a major strategy used by the devil. One saying says when a man and a woman are on their own, the devil is always there. To avoid falling into temptation, traditional Muslim societies function in such a way as to minimize sexual immorality: most schools are same-sex schools; dress codes are strict (especially for women); social interaction between men and women is minimal; a Muslim woman cannot freely travel without the company of a close male relative; getting married at a young age is commended contrary to singleness.

Modesty is a core Islamic value; one Muslim scholar compared it with love in Christianity and justice in Judaism. To some extent Muslim societies practice a gender-driven segregation, the purpose of which is to enable them to comply with divine law, especially in the realm of sexual ethics.

Honor and Shame

"Honor and shame" is a key concept in many traditional societies including Muslim societies. It operates at all levels: individual, family, faith community, and nation. It is deeply rooted in people's way of thinking and often determines their behavior. The question people instinctively ask when making a critical decision is, "What will people say if I (or we) do this?" Even religiously minded people will ask this question, which tends to replace, at least in the beginning, the more important question, "What will God say if I (or we) do this?"

The concept of honor and shame is, of course, linked to the concept of right and wrong, but a theological problem arises when honor and shame determines our actions more than do right and wrong. So, what is right becomes what will preserve my social reputation, and what is wrong becomes what brings dishonor to my name in the eyes of others. All human beings seek to save face, but in traditional Muslim societies, saving face is a must.

The prevalence of this concept in Islamic societies explains why people tend to hide evil, rather than confess or acknowledge it. An old adage, almost forgotten now in Western societies, says, "Do not wash your dirty linen in public." It is bad for people to act secretly against social norms and divine law; however, leading an openly sinful life is seen by many Muslims as an affront to public order, arrogant and reprehensible behavior, and an incitement to do more evil. For Muslims, Western culture has become not only sinful but also shamelessly decadent (e.g. sexual immorality, abortion, drunkenness, and media dissemination of less-than-virtuous lifestyles). For many Westerners, turning a blind eye to people's secret wrongdoing is seen as hypocritical as shown regularly in scandals reported by the media.

The sense of family and community solidarity strengthens the concept of honor and dishonor. The combination of feelings of solidarity and dishonor can have very serious consequences within the Muslim community, wherever it is present, including in countries where Islam is a minority. Relationships between men and women and the conversion of Muslims to another religion, namely Christianity, represent two sensitive areas where the feeling of dishonor can manifest itself among many Muslims through acts of rejection or even persecution. Girls and women are most often the victims of this type of persecution. This explains certain practices such as virginity certificates intended to establish the honor of the future bride, or even honor killings committed to wash in blood the scorned honor of a family. The difficulties faced by Muslim converts to Christianity in France is the subject of a report published on 30 March 2021 by the European Centre for Law and Justice.[15] The situation in France is similar to that of other Western countries where the Muslim community represents a strong minority.

Hospitality

In many traditional societies, including Muslim societies, people are very hospitable. They have managed to retain hospitality as one of their key values because they do not live under the same time and work pressures that dominate Western societies. They also value human relationships and are keen on building such relationships, although initially some may show a suspicious attitude towards foreigners.

It can be a very humbling experience to see ordinary people show warm, generous hospitality despite limited resources. Food is closely associated with hospitality, and a meal is often a good opportunity for people to share much more than food. This makes it even more difficult for Muslims to understand why immigrants do not find the same kind of welcome in Western countries.

Arab Influence

Islam was born in the Arab world and was founded through the agency of an Arab prophet. The Qur'an, as we have noted, is God's revealed word in Arabic, Islam's liturgical language (to some extent comparable to what Latin used to be for Western Christianity). The fifth pillar demands that all Muslims go on pilgrimage to Mecca in Saudi Arabia. All this explains why Muslim societies are influenced by the Arabic language, as well as by Arab history and civilization. Languages spoken by non-Arab Muslims often share links with Arabic, and the Arabic word for God, *Allah*, has been adopted and has sometimes replaced traditional names for God in these languages.

Most Muslims are able to recite parts of the Qur'an in Arabic such as the first chapter, *al-Fatiha*, which represents an integral part of their daily prayers. Many Muslims look up to Arab Muslims as their "older brothers" since they belong to the privileged people who received God's revelation in their own

---

15. The report, titled "The Persecution of Ex-Muslim Christians in France," is available (with a supporting video report) on the centre's website: http://media.aclj.org/pdf/The-Persecution-of-Ex-Musulims-Christians-in-France-ECLJ-Report-April-2021.pdf.

language, though some resent what they see as the arrogance of Arab Muslims and point out that Arab Muslims are a minority. Muslim names often have an Arabic origin, and many contain one of God's names preceded by "servant of," *'abd*. For example:

> *'Abdul-Lah*, servant of God.
> *'Abdul-Karim*, servant of the Generous One.
> *'Abdul-Nasir*, servant of the One who gives victory.
> *'Abdul-Basir*, servant of the All-Seeing One.
> *'Abdul-Hamid*, servant of the Praised One.

Arabic continues to play a key role in Islamic sciences (qur'anic exegesis, theology, law, etc.). Although there are reputed Islamic learning institutions on every continent, Islamic universities in the Arab world, especially in Egypt and Saudi Arabia, remain the most prestigious ones. The spiritual center of the Muslim world is in the Middle East, and Islam's holy sites are Mecca, Medina and Jerusalem, as well as in Syria and Iraq for Shi'a Muslims.

3

Islam as Law

Globalization has brought about greater openness of peoples to each other thanks to the revolution in information technology and the development of transport. We now live in a village the size of the world. No religious community can any longer live entirely isolated from other communities, and the Muslim community is no exception. As a result, Islamic law is being tested, in Western countries in particular, by everything that globalization conveys in terms of humanist ideologies, materialist philosophies, and new and old religions.

Muslims respond to this unprecedented challenge in several ways. Some are in favor of revising traditional Islamic teaching, while others feel threatened, withdraw into themselves and become radicalized. A small number engage in violence, especially among young and marginalized people. The majority of Muslims unwillingly endure this challenge without really knowing how to respond.

This chapter will examine this challenge in connection with three themes: politics, women and secularism.

Islam and Politics

In Islam, God is "the Lord of the worlds" (1:4). His limitless sovereignty is to be reflected within the *umma* (community or nation). Sharī'a law expresses the universal lordship of the Creator. Since Islamic law is comprehensive, it can only be fully implemented in a society where the political regime itself acknowledges this law. During his lifetime, the Prophet assumed the role of leader of the community after he migrated to the city of Yathrib, which was then renamed *al-Madinah*, meaning "the city" of the Prophet. On his death, the prophetic function ceased, and political leadership passed into the hands of the caliph for the Sunnis and the imam for the Shi'a. The religious function was passed on to the religious authorities, namely the *'ulemas* (scholars) whose links with the caliph (or the imam) have remained fairly close depending on the period.

Today, these authorities continue to play an important role in Islamic nations. The mufti (chief jurist) of a Sunni country, or the spiritual guide of a Shi'a country, is the person who is responsible for giving authoritative rulings on matters concerning the affairs of the community. The Sharī'a-inspired regime in Islamic countries is reminiscent of the theocratic regime of ancient Israel in which the three offices (royal, priestly and prophetic) were nevertheless separate.

Thus the political and religious powers are not confused but they are both subject to the authority of Sharī'a: "Whoever does not judge according to what God has revealed [in the Qur'an], these are the unbelievers" (5:44). The constitution and laws of Islamic countries are inspired by Sharī'a law, even in countries with a secular regime like Turkey and most of West Africa. In most Muslim-majority countries, Islam is the state religion. Some republics have the title "Islamic" explicitly in their denomination (e.g. Iran, Mauritania, Pakistan). Sharī'a, understood in the broad sense of Islamic teaching, is thus one of the major sources of legislation in terms of political, civil, legal and economic laws. Thus, criminal code is only one aspect of Sharī'a, and like Sharī'a as a whole, its interpretation varies according to different jurisprudence schools.

Religious Minorities: From Dhimmitude to Citizenship

The Qur'an describes Jews and Christians as "the People of the Book," because the Jews received the Torah and the Christians the Gospel, two Scriptures prior to the Qur'an. It is a very positive title that puts them in a group of their own among non-Muslims. Muslims are the unsurpassed community of the Book, since the Qur'an is God's ultimate revelation. Islamic law reserves special treatment for Jews and Christians in that they have the right to live alongside the Muslim community without having to convert to Islam, unlike other non-Muslims. Provided they accept Islamic leadership, they have the right to manage their internal affairs with their own laws. In Islamic law Jews and Christians have the status of *dhimmis*, protected minorities. They have to pay a protection tax (*jizya*) as a sign of their submission to Islamic authorities.

In return, these authorities guarantee them the protection of their lives and possessions (9:29).¹

The status of protected minorities is considered in Islamic law as a privilege exclusive to the "People of the Book." (Other non-Muslims do not enjoy this privilege and therefore do not have the right to live alongside the Muslim community if they decide to keep their religion.) Yet this status has resulted in Jews and Christians being considered second-class citizens. At certain times in history, they have suffered humiliation, discrimination, and even persecution to varying degrees. The status was abolished by a decree issued in 1855 by the Ottoman empire for all countries under its authority. Although it is no longer enforced in Islamic nations, many of its aspects have not disappeared. It still plays a certain role in the legal system in many different Islamic countries which have also been influenced to an extent by European laws. Thus Jews and Christians cannot occupy positions of high responsibility in predominantly Islamic countries as, according to Sharī'a, Muslims cannot be ruled by non-Muslims.

We must recognize that in Christendom, the Jews were not treated any better as they were accused of having killed God in the person of Jesus Christ. For centuries, Jewish communities living in "Christian" Europe have suffered greatly, arguably more than in the Muslim world.

Many Jews from Europe and most Jews from Islamic countries migrated to Israel after the Jewish State was created in 1948. Likewise, many Christians reluctantly continue to migrate to non-Muslim countries but rarely for religious reasons. The economic and political situations play an important role in their decision. Many Muslims make the same choice and for the same reasons.

Increasingly, Muslim citizens are challenging their countries' oppressive regimes which use religion to reinforce their power. They criticize these regimes for corruption and bad governance that have caused economic decline. Thus, among the challenges facing many Islamic nations, political freedom, equality for all citizens and economic development figure prominently. The "Arab Spring" demonstrations in the last decade testified to the deep political and economic frustrations felt especially by young people.

In January 2016, more than 300 academics and Muslim leaders from 120 countries gathered in the Moroccan city of Marrakesh to speak out on the situation in the Muslim world severely affected by Islamist terrorism. They issued what is called the "Marrakesh Declaration on the Rights of Religious

---

1. People subject to this tax are exempt from *zakat*, the legal almsgiving paid only by Muslims.

Minorities in the Muslim World." In this relatively short document, they condemn the use of violence to settle conflicts in different parts of the Muslim world. They deplore the suffering that religious minorities have endured as a result of "criminal groups" acting in the name of Islam.

The first part of the document highlights qur'anic (and universal) values such as: human dignity (17:70), religious freedom (2:256), human fraternity (49:13), justice (16:90), peace (2:208; 8:61), mercy (21:107), fairness (60:8), and respect for commitments and agreements (5:1; 16:91). The second part considers that "the Constitution of Medina," issued by the Prophet shortly after his migration from Mecca to Medina in AD 622, provides a solid foundation for the formation of a nation (*umma*) in which all citizens enjoy the same rights and have the same obligations, regardless of their religion, ethnicity and language. This Constitution, says the Declaration, has not been abrogated and is in full accord with the principles of the United Nations and the Universal Declaration of Human Rights. The third part of the document calls for a contextual implementation of Islamic law that considers the new environment in which Muslims live in different parts of the world.

The text invites Muslims to work with all other religious communities based on a "common word" (*kalima sawa'*; cf. Qur'an 3:64). They are not to just respect and tolerate each other, but commit to protecting the rights and freedoms of all members of society, which the law must guarantee. The Declaration mentions practical implications of this commitment and issues an urgent appeal to all Muslim scholars and leaders to strengthen the concept of "citizenship" (*muwatana*) in predominantly Muslim societies.

At the end of the paper, politicians and decision-makers as well as civil society activists and religious communities are all urged to take full part in eradicating anything that could harm the peaceful coexistence of citizens. This requires a change in education programs that incite hostility and extremism. All religious leaders are called upon to resist attacks on religions and incitement to hatred and racism. The Declaration concludes with this solemn statement: "It is not allowed to use religion to justify a violation of the rights of religious minorities living in Islamic countries."[2]

The concept of citizenship that the Declaration promotes will help Arab-Muslim societies make a significant step forward on the path toward freedom,

---

2. This summary is based on the official Arabic version of this text in which the arguments are more elaborated than in the English version. The statement (released on 27 January 2016) is available online in Arabic. A summary is given in English: http://www.marrakeshdeclaration.org.

equality and fraternity between believers (whoever they are) and non-believers. The question remains as to what extent political and religious authorities are prepared to embark on this path which will undoubtedly challenge the interests of many and require a fresh look at Islam in order to have the same rules for Muslims and non-Muslims, for men and women, etc.

Religious Freedom

The Sharī'a penal code provides for physical punishment for certain crimes, for example, cutting off the thief's hand (5:38–39) and flogging with eighty lashes the person who has given false witness against a married Muslim woman accusing her of immorality (24:4). The death penalty is required for three crimes: murder, marital infidelity and apostasy.[3] The sanction for murder is based on a qur'anic text which gives the victim's family the possibility of forgiving the murderer (2:178–179). The punishment for adultery, for a man or a woman, and for apostasy, is not found in the Qur'an but in Hadith narratives.[4]

The legal penalty prescribed by Sharī'a for apostasy is based on several prophetic accounts, including this one: "Those who replace their religion for another one, put them to death."[5] This punishment, also found in the Mosaic law (Exod 22:20), goes against religious freedom as stated in article 18 of the UN Universal Declaration of Human Rights (1948): "Everyone has the right to freedom of thought, conscience and religion; this right includes freedom to change his religion or belief, and freedom, either alone or in community with others and in public or private, to manifest his religion or belief in teaching, practice, worship and observance."[6]

The Islamic Council of Europe in Paris published an article on 19 September 1981 entitled "A Universal Islamic Declaration of Human Rights." Article 12 is about freedom of religion: "Every person has the right to express his thoughts and beliefs so long as he remains within the limits prescribed by the Law." Article 13 entitled "Right to Freedom of Religion" simply says: "Every person has the right to freedom of conscience and worship in accordance with his religious beliefs." Compared to the UN Declaration, the Islamic Declaration does not specify that the right to religious freedom includes the freedom to

---

3. Bukhari, *Diyat* (Blood-Money), 6.
4. Muslim, *Hudud* (Penal Sanctions), 4.
5. Bukhari, *Jihad* (Struggle), 149.
6. https://www.birmingham.ac.uk/schools/ptr/departments/theologyandreligion/research/ciforb/news/2017/forb-in-international-law.aspx.

convert to a religion other than Islam. This right to religious freedom is clearly framed "within the limits prescribed by the Law," meaning Sharī'a law (as specified in the Arabic version of the text), which does not grant Muslims the right to give up their religion. Moreover, all the rights in this Declaration are to be interpreted "within the limits set by the Sharī'a."[7]

Muslim reformers highlight several qur'anic texts which they interpret in a non-restrictive manner contrary to Islamic tradition:

> There is no coercion in religion (2:256).
>
> If your Lord [O Muhammad] had willed, all who live on earth would have believed. Are you going to force people to become believers? (10:99).
>
> Say [O Muhammad]: The truth is from your Lord. Believe who wants, therefore, and disbelieve who wants (18:29).
>
> To you your religion, to me [Muhammad] mine (109:6).

Today, many Muslims convert to another religion, or simply become atheists or agnostics. If they are in Muslim societies, they live constantly under the "sword of Damocles,"[8] especially if they express their opinions freely. They are tolerated in some countries on condition that they keep their new faith to themselves so as not to disturb "public order." To escape these restrictions that can easily lead to persecution, many leave their home countries and take refuge in places where religious freedom is guaranteed.

Democracy

Democracy is usually thought of as a government of the people by the people, whereas Islam seeks to govern the Muslim community according to Sharī'a law, hence its incompatibility in principle with democracy. Democracy, in the modern sense of the term, is a relatively recent concept. In Athens, slaves were not allowed to freely express their views. The Bible does not speak about democracy. What the prophets demand of the Israelites is that they practice righteousness, obey the law, and show compassion to the weakest members of the community (Isa 1:17; Jas 5:1–6).

---

7. See the website of the Arab Center for Education in International Humanitarian Law and Human Rights. https://acihl.org/articles.htm?article_id=5#note6. See also: http://www.marrakeshdeclaration.org/.

8. https://www.history.com/news/what-was-the-sword-of-damocles.

Conservative Muslims make several arguments to vilify Western-style democracy:

- The key role of money in the financing of electoral campaigns. In the United States in particular, the successful candidate is the one who benefits from the most expensive campaign and is supported by powerful pressure groups.
- People vote for candidates who make them promises that promote national interests. Policies based on ethical and humanitarian values are often overlooked. Aid to developing countries does not reach 0.7 percent of GDP, a figure set by developed countries themselves.
- It is common for small parties to play a disproportionate role in coalition governments resulting from democratic elections (e.g. Israel).
- The very high abstention rate in many countries casts serious doubt on the democratic nature of elections.
- Democracy does not guarantee an equitable policy, national or international. It is common for democratic elections to bring to power populist candidates with little concern for the common good.
- Democracy brings to power governments that have little respect for the religious and ethical values promoted by monotheistic religions. The laws on abortion and on same-sex marriage were passed after a democratic process – it is not difficult to see that democracy combined with freedom leads to moral laxity.

These criticisms are not without merit. They highlight that democracy produces laws made by humans, whereas Sharī'a is the law that has been given by God. But is there a credible alternative to democracy if we rule out an authoritarian or despotic regime? Winston Churchill is believed to have given his assessment of democracy in a famous quote: "No one pretends that democracy is perfect or all-wise. Indeed, it has been said that democracy is the worst form of Government except for all those other forms that have been tried from time to time . . ."[9]

In this area too, Muslim voices are raised to stress that the seeds of democracy can be found in the Qur'an. A whole sūra is called *al-shura* (consultation or deliberation), a title taken from a verse which describes Muslims in these terms: "They (Muslims) manage their affairs by consultation" (42:38). God ordered the Prophet himself to make decisions only after consulting his community

---

9. https://winstonchurchill.org/resources/quotes/the-worst-form-of-government/.

(3:159). Thus, democracy is compatible with a new understanding of Islamic sources which, without denying the foundations of Islam as a religion, would call into question Islam as the main source of legislation. It took the church in Western Europe a long time before it accepted living under a secular regime in which it had no political power.

Today, an estimated 20 percent of Muslims live in predominantly non-Muslim countries (nearly 350 million). India alone has around 200 million Muslims and as such is the third largest Muslim nation (after Indonesia and Pakistan). What if these Muslim minorities, in the UK or any other non-Muslim country, lived under authoritarian and dictatorial regimes? This does not mean, of course, that Muslims (or other minorities) living in democratic countries do not have problems, but their problems would be much more serious if they were to live under an undemocratic and arbitrary regime.

It is up to Muslims, as well as Christians, to advance the values (religious, ethical and humanitarian) in which they believe through their local and national representatives. We should not underestimate the influence that charities and other associations can have, especially when there is government encouragement.

The Status of Women

This is an extremely sensitive subject. We must therefore strive to be fair to Islamic teaching without ignoring some of its controversial aspects. One of the ways for a Christian to minimize the risk of presenting things in a biased manner is to follow the teaching of Christ who demands impartiality and self-examination of his followers (Matt 7:1–5). I will endeavor to look at some difficult issues of Islamic teaching without being judgmental. What this section proposes to do is not an exhaustive study of the status of women, but a simple reminder of the main texts of the Scriptures – the Qur'an and the Hadith for Islam, and the Bible (especially the New Testament) for Christianity. I will only make a few comments, leaving readers to form their own opinions of what the texts teach, even if it means interpreting them in the way they deem most appropriate.

Men and Women Are Equal before God

Men and women will receive the same retribution as a reward for their faith and good works:

> For Muslim men and women, for believing men and women, for devout men and women, for righteous men and women, for men and women who are patient, for men and women who fear [God], for men and women who make offerings, for men and women who fast, for men and women who are chaste, for men and women who call upon God a lot, for them all God has prepared forgiveness and a very great reward. (33:38)

> Then God said, "Let us make mankind in our image, in our likeness, so that they may rule over the fish in the sea and the birds in the sky, over the livestock and all the wild animals, and over all the creatures that move along the ground." So God created mankind in his own image, in the image of God he created them; male and female he created them. (Gen 1:26–27)

Men and women are equal before divine law:

> As for the thief, male and female, cut off his or her hands, a retribution from God for their crime, by way of example, God is Almighty and Wise. (5:38)

> There is neither Jew nor Gentile, neither slave nor free, nor is there male and female, for you are all one in Christ Jesus. (Gal 3:28)

However, the relationship between husband and wife is not reciprocal:

> Women shall have rights similar to the rights against them in a just manner. But men have a degree [of advantage] over them. God is Almighty and Wise. (2:228)

> Men are in charge of women, because God has made the one of them to excel the other, and because they spend of their property [for the support of women]. (4:34)

> Submit to one another out of reverence for Christ. Wives, submit yourselves to your own husbands as you do to the Lord. For the husband is the head of the wife as Christ is the head of the church, his body, of which he is the Savior. Now as the church submits to Christ, so also wives should submit to their husbands in everything. Husbands, love your wives, just as Christ loved the church and gave himself up for her. (Eph 5:21–25; cf. Col 3:18)

Discrimination against Women?

There are several qur'anic texts which, at first glance, seem unfavorable to women. The same is true of many narratives found in the Prophetic Tradition.

(1) In the distribution of inheritance, the male's share is twice that of the female's (4:11). In his French translation of the Qur'an, Muhammad Hamidullah explains this disparity in these terms:

> This provision which would appear to us to be marked by partiality is in no way biased. It is justified by several reasons: (i) The woman is maintained by law at the expense of her father, brother, etc., then of her husband, son, etc., with regard to housing, food, clothing, etc.; (ii) She also receives the "honorary wages" of the marriage, the dowry and the dower, over which neither her husband, nor her father or her other relatives have any rights; (iii) She has no obligation to men, not even to feed her infant (to whom the father must find a nanny who he pays). Despite everything, she inherits from her father, her husband, her children and other relatives.

(2) The testimony of two women is equivalent to that of a man (2:282). One day the Prophet gave his companions his explanation of this disparity:

> "Isn't a woman's testimony half the testimony of a man?"
> "Yes, indeed," we answered.
> "This," he continued, "is due to the inferiority of her intelligence."[10]

(3) A Muslim man can marry a monotheistic woman, Jewish or Christian, without the latter having to convert to Islam (5:5). However, a Muslim woman cannot marry a Jewish or Christian man. The husband is the head of the family, so he must always be a Muslim.[11] This provision of Sharī'a law creates very serious problems in many Islamic countries, because a man who has converted to Christianity and subsequently married a Christian woman is still considered a Muslim. Their children are also treated, especially in the education system, as Muslims. These difficulties explain why some couples decide to emigrate to protect the future of their children.

---

10. Bukhari, *Shahadat* (Witnesses), 12.

11. In Tunisia, the government and parliament are reviewing the laws concerning the status of Tunisian women. A Muslim woman can now marry a non-Muslim man.

(4) The husband is allowed in certain cases to discipline his wife, even to hit her:

> As for those from whom you fear disobedience, admonish them and banish them to beds apart, and scourge them. Then if they obey you, seek not a way against them. God is Most High and Great. (4:34)

Many Muslim authors are somewhat embarrassed by this text, and understandably so. They try to interpret it in a way that minimizes its scope. For some, the physical correction must be very light and do no harm to the woman. Others try to find a totally implausible meaning for the verb *daraba*, which in the context of this verse cannot mean anything other than "to strike" or "to beat."

In the Hadith we have many stories about women, some of which are openly misogynistic. Here is a selection of words that are all found in Bukhari's collection, considered the most trustworthy by Muslim scholars. In one of the accounts, the Prophet recounts a vision he had of heaven and hell: "I visited heaven and saw that it was mostly inhabited by the poor; I visited hell and saw that it was mostly inhabited by women."[12] Another story explains that the majority of women will be in hell because they curse a lot and are ungrateful to their husbands.[13] A third prophetic saying asks men to show compassion for women as their nature is flawed:

> Recommend that you be kind to women. They were created from a rib, and in a rib the upper part is the most curved. If you try to straighten it, you break it, and if you leave it, it continues to stay curled. So recommend being kind to women.[14]

The wife must always be ready to fulfill her marital duty: "When a husband calls his wife to come to his bed and she refuses to come, the angels curse her until the morning."[15] The prophet warned his community of a danger to which they should beware: "I will not leave behind me any cause of trouble more fatal to men than women."[16] We learn from the very mouth of Aisha, the beloved wife of the Prophet, that she was six years old when she was given in marriage

---

12. Bukhari, *Nikah* (Marriage), 88.
13. Bukhari, *Zakat* (Legal Almsgiving), 45.
14. Bukhari, *Nikah* (Marriage), 80.
15. Bukhari, *Nikah* (Marriage), 85. According to another version, the angels will keep cursing the woman until she consents to join her husband.
16. Bukhari, *Nikah* (Marriage), 18.

to Muhammad and "nine years old when she was placed in his hands."[17] The latter, "in one night had relations with all his wives, and they were, at that time, nine in number."[18] The Prophet therefore had at least nine wives unlike Muslims who are only allowed to have four and on condition of being fair to each of them (4:3).

Jesus did not utter any derogatory words towards women. He himself chose not to marry in order to devote himself entirely to his mission (Matt 19:11–12). The Gospel of Luke tells us that among Jesus's disciples there were several wealthy women who took part in the maintenance of the group (Luke 8:1–3). One day when Jesus was teaching in the temple in Jerusalem, a group of Jewish leaders brought him an adulterous woman in the hope that he would condemn her to death in accordance with Mosaic law, or else be himself accused of undermining this law. To their surprise, Jesus stood up for the woman and challenged her accusers: "Let any one of you who is without sin be the first to throw a stone at her." After her accusers all slowly left, Jesus took the initiative to offer forgiveness to the woman while calling her to a new life:

> "Woman, where are [your accusers]? Has no one condemned you?"
> "No one, sir."
> "Then neither do I condemn you. Go now and leave your life of sin." (John 8:10–11).

Muhammad once stood before a woman, from the tribe of Ghamid, who had committed adultery. Having repented, she introduced herself to him and asked him to "purify" her by applying the legal sanction for adultery, namely the death penalty. When the Prophet knew that the woman was pregnant, he asked her to go and give birth to her baby and to feed it until the child was weaned. Sometime later, the woman returned with her weaned child and made the same request. Muhammad then took the child from the mother's arms, gave it to a Muslim next to him, and ordered those around him to stone the woman. The Prophet praised the woman for her sincere repentance which led her to ask for God's law to be carried out against her.[19]

In their letters to churches, the apostles Paul and Peter teach about women and how husbands should behave towards them. Here is a significant selection of their recommendations.

---

17. Bukhari, *Manaqib* (Merits), 44.
18. Bukhari, *Ghusl* (Ablution), 4.
19. Muslim, *Hudud* (Legal Sanctions), 5.

A man ought not to cover his head, since he is the image and glory of God; but the woman is the glory of man. For man did not come from woman, but woman from man; neither was man created for woman, but woman for man. It is for this reason that a woman ought to have authority over her own head, because of the angels. Nevertheless, in the Lord woman is not independent of man, nor is man independent of woman. For as woman came from man, so also man is born of woman. But everything comes from God. (1 Cor 11:7–12)

A woman should learn in quietness and full submission. I do not permit a woman to teach or to assume authority over a man; she must be quiet. For Adam was formed first, then Eve. And Adam was not the one deceived; it was the woman who was deceived and became a sinner. But women will be saved through childbearing – if they continue in faith, love and holiness with propriety. (1 Tim 2:11–15)

Wives, in the same way submit yourselves to your own husbands so that, if any of them do not believe the word, they may be won over without words by the behavior of their wives, when they see the purity and reverence of your lives. Your beauty should not come from outward adornment, such as elaborate hairstyles and the wearing of gold jewelry or fine clothes. Rather, it should be that of your inner self, the unfading beauty of a gentle and quiet spirit, which is of great worth in God's sight. For this is the way the holy women of the past who put their hope in God used to adorn themselves. They submitted themselves to their own husbands, like Sarah, who obeyed Abraham and called him her lord. You are her daughters if you do what is right and do not give way to fear.
  Husbands, in the same way be considerate as you live with your wives, and treat them with respect as the weaker partner and as heirs with you of the gracious gift of life, so that nothing will hinder your prayers. (1 Pet 3:1–7)

Among Muslim reformers there are many feminists (e.g. Ayesha Chaudry, Asma Lamrabet, Amina Wadud). Some Muslim feminists make a threefold criticism of the biblical text: the woman was taken from the man, she was deceived by the devil and she led Adam into disobedience (cf. Gen 2:21–23; 3:1–6).

According to the qur'anic text, the man and the woman were both deceived by the devil who brought about their fall (cf. 2:35–36; 7:19–24; 20:117–121). But the qur'anic accounts are shorter than the Genesis narrative and they do not go into detail. Besides, the woman's name, Eve, is not even mentioned. However, most Muslim scholars understand the qur'anic texts in question (4:1; 7:189) in the sense of the creation of the woman from the man, which is confirmed by several prophetic accounts (the one cited above specifies that the woman was taken from the rib of the man). One way in which Muslim writers, especially feminists, respond to the misogyny of the Hadith narratives is to simply say that these narratives, like many others, are fabricated despite being selected by Bukhari as authentic. Generally speaking, reforming Muslims give little or no credit to the Hadith narratives.

Christians recognize the difficulties that exist in some texts of the New Testament, especially those cited above. They give these texts a historical and contextual interpretation which eliminates a good part of their roughness. When dealing with texts that pose a problem, it is important to keep in mind the foundational texts (such as Gen 1:26–27) and not to forget the exemplary attitude of Jesus towards women. There are also some difficult texts in the Old Testament. Here is one:

> I find more bitter than death the woman who is a snare, whose heart is a trap and whose hands are chains. The man who pleases God will escape her, but the sinner she will ensnare. . . .
> I found one upright man among a thousand, but not one upright woman among them all. (Eccl 7:26–28)

The Christian conception of revelation, which consists in recognizing the Scriptures as God's word as well as a human word, may explain such sexist statements. There are other such sayings in some "deuterocanonical" books. These books do not enjoy divine authority among all Christians, and we are not completely surprised to find in these books, considered "apocryphal" (or inauthentic) by Protestant churches, texts unfriendly towards women (e.g. Ecclesiasticus 25:13–26; 26:5–12; 42:9–14).

Muslim societies have a reputation in Western countries as societies where women are abused. Some (perhaps a lot of) Muslim men oppress women, but they are not the only ones in this situation. Many non-Muslim men (including Christians, followers of other religions, and atheists) do the same. The oppression of women is unfortunately a cultural and even spiritual problem, for it is one of the many manifestations of sin in the world. In Muslim societies, this phenomenon does not necessarily reflect a sound interpretation of Islamic law. The oppression of women is by men who, in Islam as in other religions, have interpreted the Holy Scriptures to their own advantage. Women are also abused in Western countries, as evidenced by the #MeToo movement which has highlighted this very sad reality. Their exploitation takes various forms (e.g. domestic violence, murder, prostitution, human trafficking, sexual trafficking). Should we accuse Christianity of these abuses?

Progressive Muslim reformers argue that the world we live in presents the Muslim community with new challenges. According to them, the four traditional law schools (*fiqh*) are not well equipped to meet these challenges. Hence the urgent need to re-examine Sharīʿa, to take a fresh look at its rules and teachings, and to update them whenever necessary. This revision would undoubtedly have a considerable impact on the penal code, the status of women, the role of non-Muslim minorities, as well as on relations between Islam and the state. For some years now, Muslim intellectuals have been looking afresh at Islamic teaching, calling for a critical review of Sharīʿa, and a contextualized approach to Islamic laws. Some Muslim-majority countries have taken steps in the same direction (e.g. polygamy is prohibited in Turkey and Tunisia; female genital cutting is illegal in Mali, Niger, Senegal and Sudan). For them, it is imperative to take a critical look at Sharīʿa law in order to reform traditional Islam, especially since no Islamic country applies Islamic law to the letter.

Islam and the Secular State

Sharīʿa law as a source of legislation for the entire Muslim community makes no room for the concept of secularity (Fr. *laïcité*), which implies the separation of politics and religion. But Sharīʿa is itself a human construct, though it claims to be based on qur'anic and prophetic prescriptions. Almost a thousand years have passed since the days when theologians and jurists developed Sharīʿa. The world has changed a lot since then, including the Muslim world. Can we keep this law intact and continue to claim that Islam is a religion for all peoples and that its teaching remains relevant in the twenty-first century, including for hundreds of millions of Muslims who live in secular countries?

For three hundred years the gospel spread peacefully, from Jerusalem to Egypt and Ethiopia in the south, to Mesopotamia and India in the east, and to Syria, Asia Minor and Europe to the north. During this time, the Christian community lived in pluralistic and polytheistic societies and was regularly persecuted by the Roman empire. The beginning of the fourth century marked a turning point in the history of the church when the emperor Constantine published the edict of Milan on religious tolerance in 313. Then in 380,

Christianity was declared the official religion of the empire. Gradually, the church aligned itself with the political power of the empire and ended up abusing its dominant position. This ill-conceived alliance between spiritual and temporal leadership has proven to be the source of much trouble for Christians.

In France, the reaction against the abusive power of the church led, through the twists and turns of history, to the concept of secularity. The first article of the Constitution of the fifth Republic (1958) states that "France shall be an indivisible, secular, democratic and social Republic. It shall ensure equality of all citizens before the law, without distinction of origin, race or religion. It shall respect all beliefs. It shall be organized on a decentralized basis."[20]

The 1905 law on secularity (the word itself is not there) emphasizes the principle of separation of church and state. The first article stipulates that "the Republic ensures freedom of conscience. It guarantees the free exercise of worship." This law therefore aims to protect religious freedom for believers of all faiths as well as the freedom not to believe. The second article aims to guarantee the equality of all religions before the law as "the Republic does not recognize, pay or finance any religion."[21] In other words, Islam, Christianity and other religions are on the same footing, at least in theory. Separation of state and religion also means state neutrality and non-interference by public authorities in the affairs of religious communities.

Secularity, provided it is properly understood, has many advantages for both believers and the state, as it gives everyone the freedom and the responsibility to fulfil their mission in their own realm. It is perfectly compatible with the famous saying of Christ: "So give back to Caesar what is Caesar's, and to God what is God's" (Matt 22:21). This statement does not mean that divine sovereignty is limited to the spiritual realm or that we can divide our allegiance between the Creator and the state. What it implies is that divine lordship does not exclude acknowledging the legitimacy of human authority and that our loyalty to God transcends but does not suppress our loyalty to secular organizations such as the state.

The problem arises as soon as one seeks to apply secularity in a multiethnic, multicultural and multireligious context. This is the case with twenty-first-century French society which, like many societies, faces the phenomenon of terrorism carried out in the name of Islam.

---

20. https://www.assemblee-nationale.fr/connaissance/constitution.asp#titre_.1

21. https://www.vie-publique.fr/fiches/271400-la-loi-du-9-decembre-1905-de-separation-des-eglises-et-de-letat.

French authorities are entitled to take difficult decisions to ensure the cohesion of society. These decisions are not easy to make because they can be interpreted as limiting individual freedoms in a country that prides itself on being at the forefront of the defense of human rights. The law "regulating the wearing of signs or clothing showing religious affiliation in public schools, colleges and high schools," sometimes called "law on the Islamic veil," was declared in March 2004 in application of the principle of secularity. The law against concealing one's face in public space was adopted in October 2010 to ensure the safety of society. These laws, although formulated in general terms, implicitly target Muslims before any other community. They aim to safeguard national unity at a time when this unity seems threatened. It is likely that more laws will be enacted in the coming years, as the challenges posed by Islamist ideology are not about to go away. A bill aimed at "reinforcing respect for the principles of the Republic" was passed on 24 August 2021. Its purpose is to enable the French government to exert a tougher control of religious organizations that seem to pursue hidden agendas.

Muslims, and Christians, demand that the principle of secularity not be diverted from its primary meaning. For some fundamentalist secularists, secularism has become a true religion.[22] Their militant secularism has the unspoken aim of marginalizing religion and excluding believers from the public realm as if faith were simply a private matter. An exclusivist secularism is unlikely to win the support of Muslims. On the contrary, it risks reinforcing the idea that secularism is being used to prevent them from freely exercising their rights. An inclusive and open secularity is likely to promote their integration into society and encourage them to reconsider the principles of Sharīʿa.

To illustrate this point, let us take as an example two tragic events in 2020 which deeply moved public opinion in France. On 16 October 2020, a horrific murder took place when a young radicalized Muslim (from Chechen background) killed a history and geography professor in Conflans-Sainte-Honorine. The motive for the murder was apparently that the teacher, Mr. Samuel Paty, showed in his civic education class cartoons of the Prophet as part of a discussion about freedom. These cartoons, initially published in 2006 in a

---

22. The case of Mr. Matthieu Faucher is a good illustration of what one might call state secularism. In March 2017, this (agnostic) teacher from Malicornay (Indre) was accused of religious proselytism and sanctioned by the Ministry of National Education for having included biblical texts in a course about religion in its social and cultural dimensions. He was cleared of any suspicion of proselytism by the Limoges court (in 2019). The Ministry of National Education appealed, and it was not until December 2020 that Mr. Faucher was fully vindicated by the Bordeaux Administrative Court of Appeal.

Danish newspaper and later taken up by Charlie Hebdo (a satirical newspaper), aroused a great stir in the Muslim world, which unfortunately resulted in numerous assassinations in various countries of the world.

The murder (by beheading) of Mr. Paty is and remains inexcusable and unjustifiable. The question is whether it was appropriate to use these cartoons as a tool to encourage debate in a class where there were a number of Muslim teenagers. In the days following the murder, nearly all politicians defended tooth and nail the right to publish and use these cartoons in the name of the sacrosanct freedom of expression, which must include the right to blaspheme. The question remains whether it was appropriate to illustrate this debate with potentially offensive cartoons in a class of teenagers from diverse backgrounds. In a letter he addressed to teachers in 1883, Jules Ferry, who played a key role in defining the role of public and secular schools in France, warned teachers against improper exercise of their profession. He recommended that they fulfill their mission with extreme caution:

> You are the helper and, in some respects, the deputy of the father of the family: therefore speak to his child as you would like others to speak to yours; with force and authority, whenever it is an undisputed truth, a precept of common morality; with the greatest reserve, if you risk touching a religious sentiment of which you are not the judge.
>
> If at times you are not sure as to how far you are allowed to go in your moral teaching, here is a rule of thumb you can stick to. When offering students any precept, any maxim, ask yourself if there is a single honest man that you know of who could be offended by what you are about to say. Ask yourself if a father, I say only one, present in your class and listening to you could in good faith refuse his assent to what he hears you say. If so, refrain from saying it; otherwise speak boldly: for what you are going to communicate to the child is not your own wisdom; it is the wisdom of humankind, it is one of those ideas of universal dimension that several centuries have made part of the heritage of humankind.[23]

---

23. Author's translation. The full text of this document is available online. https://enseignement-moral-civique-pedagogie.web.ac-grenoble.fr/content/jules-ferry-1832-1893-lettre-aux-instituteurs.

The startling motto of the French republic "Liberty, Equality, Fraternity" sometimes seems to be reduced to the first word whereas the other two are just as important. The third is all the more to be taken on board in a multicultural society, yet it appears to come last in the Republican discourse.[24] If we want to preserve social cohesion, fight effectively against Islamist ideology and terrorism, and encourage more Muslims to resolutely engage in an understanding of their religion that is compatible with secularity, the latter must be an inclusive secularity, open and sensitive to all schools of thought and all religions.

Shortly after the terrorist attack of 16 October there was another one, on 29 October 2020, in the Basilica of Nice. The perpetrator was a young Tunisian (an illegal migrant arrived in France a few days earlier) who killed two women and a man inside the church itself. Less than ten days later, the bishops of France issued a press release which has great insight. Here is the gist of it:

> By joining the national tribute paid today to Simone, Nadine and Vincent, the bishops of France call on all their compatriots:
>
> What if we started with respect and brotherhood?
>
> Freedom must be defended, without weakness. Does this mean that freedom of expression should have no limits with regards to others and ignore the need for debate and dialogue?
>
> Yes, believers, like all citizens, can be hurt by name-calling, mocking and also by offensive cartoons.
>
> More than additional laws, we invite everyone, in conscience, to respect each other.
>
> "Liberty, Equality, Fraternity": fraternity is a republican value. Our exercise of freedom cannot ignore it. We must take this into account in our individual and collective, personal and institutional, behavior.
>
> We share with you our deep conviction: freedom grows when it goes hand in hand with fraternity.
>
> As Saint Paul says: "'Everything is permitted,' they say, but everything is not beneficial. 'Everything is permitted,' but not

---

24. On 6 July 2018, the Constitutional Council issued an opinion upholding the "principle of fraternity," which had the effect of cancelling the charges against M. Cédric Herrou. The latter, a farmer from the Nice region, came to the aid of thousands of migrants who had crossed the Franco-Italian border in 2016. Mr. Herrou shared his experience in a book (titled *Change Your World*), and in 2019 he created a charity named Emmaüs Roya Community.

everything is constructive. Let no one seek their own interest, but that of others" (1 Cor 10:23–24).

It is time to reflect on the way in which our collective institutions and our individual behaviors should promote respect and uphold fraternity.

This urgent reflection must be initiated by the public authorities.

It concerns each of us. It concerns all of us.[25]

A murder will always be a murder and nothing can excuse the murderers who killed the Charlie Hebdo journalists and Samuel Paty. But the question remains: if freedom of expression is not absolute, what are its limits? The law recognizes that one of these limits is incitement to discrimination, hatred and violence (xenophobia, homophobia, etc.). Can we go further and plead in favor of giving priority to fraternity, which obviously implies freedom and equality? Brotherhood nowadays seems to be the "weakest link" of the Republican motto. Isn't it the value that best promotes peaceful coexistence in a society made up of members of different origins (ethnic, religious, cultural)? We certainly cannot legislate fraternity, but it is up to each one of us to take our responsibilities seriously and to determine consciously what the fraternal behavior would be in each circumstance.

---

25. The bishops of France, meeting in Plenary Assembly on 7 November 2020 (author's translation). The full text can be found on the French Bishops Conference website. https://eglise.catholique.fr/.../2020/.../2020-11-07_-Pas-de-vraie-liberte-sans- respect-et-sans-fraternite.pdf.

4

Radical Islam

Terrorist acts perpetrated in the name of Islam have been regularly in the news over the past two decades, in France as in many other countries. These incidents reached a peak during the short life of the Islamic State in Iraq and Syria, known as ISIS or Daʿesh in Arabic (2014–2019), an organization that was not recognized by any Islamic country. The gradual collapse of the organization has not put an end to its murderous ideology, as evidenced by the multiple attacks that have recently been witnessed in France and elsewhere in the world.

Such acts raise the question of Islam's relationship to politics and violence. For some, Islam has nothing to do with terrorist acts committed in its name by men (and women) who are Muslims in name only. For others, violence is inherent to Islam, and terrorists betray the true face of this religion. Moreover, terrorists consider themselves the only legitimate representatives of Islam.

This chapter sets out to analyze the complex relationship between Islam and violence. It will show that violence is not entirely alien to Islam even though it cannot be reduced to its caricatures of sole extremism. The conclusion will attempt to offer a Christian response to radical Islam and to violence in general.

Definitions

First, a distinction should be made between "force" and "violence," because it sometimes seems that any use of force is equated with violence. Violence can be defined as the illegitimate or disproportionate use of force. Force exerted to apply the law, provided it is measured, is not violence. Violence defined as such can be carried out by individuals, organizations, or the state and its representatives. It manifests itself in different forms, direct or indirect, by people or institutions.

Many people (Muslims and non-Muslims) are reluctant to use expressions such as "Muslim terrorists" or "Islamic terrorism," as they may suggest an intrinsic link between Islam and terrorism. Muslims should not be stigmatized, it is said, by making a close link between Muslims and terrorists claiming to be Muslim. Hence the use of new terms such as "jihadists" or "Islamism." Note that jihadist is a very negative word when used by Westerners, whereas they saw the mujahedeen in Afghanistan as freedom fighters seeking to free the country (in the 1980s) from the yoke of the Soviet army. Yet, these two very similar words derive from the same Arabic root (j-h-d) and, strictly speaking, they have roughly the same meaning. This highlights the potential bias of any moral judgment. Such judgment is always influenced by religion, ideology or personal values – terrorists for some, liberators or martyrs for others.

According to the main Islamic theological school, Ash'arism, Muslims who are misled doctrinally or who disobey divine law, remain Muslims – even believers – as long as they adhere to the shahada (the double confession of faith in God and his last prophet), which is surely the case for jihadists. According to Mu'tazili school, another important school in Islamic theology, Muslims who have committed a major sin (e.g. murder) are neither believers nor non-believers. They have an intermediate status; however, they should be treated by Muslims as fellow Muslims (and therefore should have religious funerals). In other words, it is not theologically wrong, from an Islamic point of view, to speak of "Muslim terrorists," especially when it comes to self-proclaimed Muslims. However, in order not to suggest that Islam is inherently violent, we will avoid expressions such as Islamic terrorism or Muslim terrorists.

It is also important to distinguish between jihadism and Islamism. Islamism refers to the ideology of radical Islam in which the political dimension of religion is dominant. Not all radical Muslims accept the use of violence to achieve their goals. In contrast, jihadists are extremist Muslims who not only adhere to the ideology of radical Islam, but are willing to engage in violence to reach their ends. In other words, the legitimization of the use of violence is what differentiates jihadism from Islamism even if jihadists do not always take action by committing a terrorist attack or fighting within a terrorist organization. Statistics show that over the past decade "non-practicing jihadists" outnumbered jihadists who resorted to violence (77 percent vs. 23 percent).[1]

---

1. A recent study identified 2,500 jihadists in France in the 2010s, 1,400 of whom joined the ranks of Da'esh in Syria (900 for the United Kingdom and Germany, 600 for Belgium), and 1,100 detained in the French prisons. The majority (89 percent) were born in France, although

The ideology of radical Islam is characterized by binary and antagonistic relationships between God and humankind, Islam and other religions, Muslims and non-Muslims, community and individuals, men and women, Islamic and non-Islamic countries.

The danger of stigmatizing Muslims by seeing them as potential terrorists is very real. Indeed, the vast majority of Muslims are not willing to engage in violence, although a sizable minority (among conservative Muslims in particular) feel sympathy, even admiration, for jihadists because of their sacrificial commitment and the perceived greatness of their cause. If, for the sake of argument, the number of jihadists (i.e. Muslims willing to carry out murderous acts) were around eighteen million globally, what would be their percentage? As surprising as it may be, the answer is 1 percent! One jihadist is one too many, therefore one should not be complacent, especially because an active minority can cause considerable devastation. On the other hand, it is important to put things in perspective and not be unduly influenced by the image conveyed by the media. The media distort reality unintentionally as their job is precisely to report on what is exceptional and sensational, and what is likely to sell newspapers and books. Journalists have little interest in peaceful Muslims. Trains, planes and buses that safely reach their destinations don't catch the headlines, only crashes do.

The Muslim Community Is "a Moderate Community"

The Qur'an describes the Muslim community as a balanced community (*ummatan wasatan*): "We (God) have made you a community far from extremes" (2:143). We noted in the chapter "Islam as Religion" that in Islamic thought, Islam is considered superior to Judaism and Christianity in religious, moral and penal terms. On the religious level, Christianity is held to be an idealistic religion as it advocates unconditional forgiveness and has no criminal code (Matt 18:21–22).

Christianity has no political or socio-economic agenda. Christ did not want to be the political leader of his people (John 6:15), and he refused to assume a judicial office (Luke 12:14). He openly declared that his kingship was not of this world (John 18:36), although his peaceful kingdom was called to spread in this world as evidenced in the mission entrusted to his disciples

---

most were of foreign descent. Among the jihadists, women represent 15 percent. See Hakim El Karoui and Benjamin Hodayé, *Les militants du djihad: Portrait d'une génération* (Paris: Fayard, 2021), "Introduction: Le djihadisme au-delà du terrorisme."

(Acts 1:8). Unlike Christianity, Islam is understood by Islamic tradition as a political religion in the sense that this religion has the ambition of extending the rule of Sharīʿa within the Muslim community and beyond its borders. This rule must be exercised by law without ruling out the use of armed force if necessary. For mainstream Muslims, Sharīʿa law is endowed with balanced laws, neither too lenient nor too rigorous on the penal level, neither idealistic nor pragmatic on the religious level, neither permissive nor too strenuous on the moral level.

Sharīʿa law emphasizes that human life is sacred. Believers, namely Muslims, are brothers (49:10). Those who kill a believer should expect to receive eternal punishment, unless they have done so by mistake (4:92–93). Unlike the Mosaic penal code, Islamic penal code (as we have seen in ch. 1) prescribes the death penalty in only three cases: murder, apostasy and sexual immorality involving married people. A qurʾanic text is often quoted, which apparently cites a text from the Torah, emphasizing how precious human life is: "This is why We (God) commanded the children of Israel that whoever kills a person who has not committed murder or sowed corruption on the earth, [is to be seen] as though they had killed all humankind. Anyone who saves a person [is to be seen] as though they saved all humankind" (5.32).[2] Note that the text immediately following this verse promises cruel punishment to unbelievers hostile to God and his Prophet: "The retribution of those who wage war against God and His Prophet and who sow corruption on earth is execution, or crucifixion … a disgrace in this world and a heavy punishment in the Hereafter"(5:33).

Muslim scholars explain that the point in this verse is to respond strongly to non-Muslims who declare war on the Muslim community. Thus, gratuitous violence or offensive warfare is not authorized in Islamic law: "Fight in the way of God those who fight against you, but do not transgress for God does not love transgressors" (2:190; cf. 22:39–40). For most Muslim scholars a legitimate jihad is a defensive one intended to defend Muslims when they are oppressed or persecuted. Jihad must in any case respect certain rules, in particular, sparing civilian populations (especially women, children and the elderly).

The previous chapter has shown that the moderation of Islamic law in criminal matters is not obvious (e.g. punishment for apostasy), and its treatment of non-Muslims is not fair, at least if we consider it in the light of the UN Universal Declaration of Human Rights. The concept of "a middle-way or moderate community" may need to be reinterpreted in secularized

---

2. According to Prof. Pierre Lory, the reference here is to the Jewish Mishna (Sanhedrin 4:5).

societies where many Muslims live. Can the Muslim community be identified in the middle ground between the two extremes – neither part of a godless society (like Western society), nor with minority jihadist groups who disfigure Islam through their violence? Muslims would thus be believers, moderate, yet determined to live their faith fully without resorting to force. For Christians living in Western countries, whose cultures are increasingly moving away from gospel values, moderation means promoting the gospel without seeking to impose it on others.

Can one conceive of Islamic moderation in these terms? This is a question for Muslims to answer. One thing is certain: the concept of jihad in Islamic tradition is not defined only in terms of war. According to a statement by the Prophet, "the true fighter, *mujahid*, is the one who fights against his soul."[3] This is a spiritual fight against the evil that one carries within oneself and which manifests itself in different forms: violence, hatred, revenge, lust, greed, hypocrisy, etc.

According to another saying attributed to the Prophet, "the best jihad is achieved when one speaks a word of truth before an unjust political leader."[4] It is therefore possible to understand jihad in the sense of a spiritual, moral, social, political and even economic commitment. It is in the name of such jihad that, for more than a century, Muslim reformers have been calling their fellow Muslims to fight social evils (illiteracy, despotism, corruption, discrimination against women, etc.). There is a real struggle to be waged against violence perpetrated in the name of Islam, which is causing enormous damage to this religion.

Religious Roots of Islamism

Radical Islam draws on two main sources: religious and non-religious. We need to review these different sources that feed radical ideology of political Islam.

The Qur'an

The word jihad literally means "struggle" or "fight." This struggle, as we have just seen, can take many forms. The word is also a name given to newborn baby boys in Christian as well as Muslim families. Today it refers above all to the

---

3. Tirmidhi, *Fada'il al-Jihad* (Virtues of Jihad), 2.
4. Abu Dawud, *Malahim* (Epic Battles), 17.

armed struggle declared by extremist groups and individuals who justify their fight with references borrowed from the Qur'an and the Prophetic Tradition.

In Mecca, Muhammad was first instructed to ignore his enemies rather than fight them. Shortly after his migration to Medina in AD 622, he received a new revelation authorizing him to fight his enemies: "Fight is prescribed for you though it is hateful to you. You may hate something that is good for you, and you may like something that is bad for you. God knows but you do not know" (2:216). The verb used in this verse, *qaatala* (from *qatala* "to kill"), can only mean one thing: to fight with arms in hand. It has the same meaning as *haaraba,* to make war. The armed struggle against the disbelievers is therefore an obligation for Muslims. This struggle is seen as sacred in some qur'anic texts, such as this one: "Whoever is an enemy of God, of His angels, of His messengers . . . then yes, God is the enemy of the disbelievers" (2:98). In this context of religious conflict, the Prophet had to lead Muslims in the fight against the disbelievers but also against the "People of the Book," some of whom are accused of wickedness (3:110–115). Here are the two main texts mentioned by Muslim writers as an example of what has come to be called "the Verse about the Sword" (*ayat al-sayf*):

> When the sacred months [of truce] are over, then slay the polytheists wherever you find them. Capture them, besiege them, and lie in ambush everywhere. If they repent, perform the prayer-rite (*salat*) and pay the alms-tax (*zakat*), let them go their way. God is Forgiving and Ever-Merciful. (9:5)

> Fight against those who believe neither in God nor in the last day, who do not forbid what God and His Apostle have forbidden, who do not embrace the religion of truth, from among those to whom the Book was given. Do so until they pay the *jizya* tax personally, having been utterly subdued. (9:29)

These two texts are found in the only sūra of the Qur'an which does not begin with the invocation of divine mercy. The first verse enjoins Muslims to fight Arab polytheists and put them to death if they do not convert to Islam. The second calls Muslims not to spare Jews and Christians, referred to as the "People of the Book," as they do not follow the true religion. Polytheists must be fought until they embrace Islam while Jews and Christians are not to be forced to convert to Islam. They are, however, required to recognize the supreme authority of Islam and submit to it by paying the *jizya* (protection tax) as a pledge of their submission.

These two texts are not the only ones that order Muslims to wage war against their enemies until they lay down their arms. There are many more (e.g. 4:88-91; 8:65; 9:73; 25:52; 47:4; 61:11). The promise of paradise is given to Muslims who die as martyrs: "Think not of those who are slain in God's way as dead. No, they live, finding their sustenance in the presence of their Lord, rejoicing in what God has given them out of his bounty" (3:169-170; cf. 3:195; 4:95-96; 61:10-11).

Prophetic Tradition

The Hadith is the second source of Islamic faith and its authority comes second after that of the Qur'an. We find in the nine canonical collections of the Prophetic Tradition many chapters devoted to the war against non-Muslims, for example, jihad, the merits of jihad, military expeditions, *jizya*, and spoils of war. According to a saying attributed to the Prophet, Muhammad enjoyed five privileges which had not been granted to any prophet before him. Among these privileges is the terror he inspired in his enemies long before he faced them on the battlefield, and the right to take the spoils of war.[5]

The Hadith accounts confirm the qur'anic promises made to potential martyrs. One of these accounts lists seven rewards that await the martyr, including: immediate forgiveness of his sins, the right to intercede on the day of judgment for seventy members of his household, and marrying seventy-two *houris* (beautiful women with larges eyes).[6] Islamic doctrine does not offer Muslims certainty about their salvation. Before entering paradise, many will have to spend some time in hell to atone for their sins. The promise of direct access to paradise, through martyrdom, is undoubtedly very attractive to committed believers who feel anxious about their eternal destiny.

The Prophetic Model

For any community of faith, the life of the founder is of great importance. The same applies to the Muslim community. The Qur'an explicitly states that Muhammad is an excellent role model for all Muslims (33:21). He was both a successful prophet and a military leader. The victory he obtained over his enemies is seen by Muslim theologians as one of the main proofs of the divine

---

5. Bukhari, *Salat* (Ritual Prayer), 56.
6. Ibn Majah, *Jihad* (Struggle), 16.

origin of his mission. Among the sayings attributed to him, this one is often quoted in the Hadith in various contexts:

> I have been commanded to wage war against people as long as they do not say: "There is no god but God." As soon as they make this confession, I have no rights over their lives and possessions – unless they commit an offence against God's law. They are accountable only to God.[7]

All Muslims are keen to imitate the Prophet whom they revere with all their hearts. Some seek to imitate him down to the smallest detail (e.g. by growing a beard). The Prophet's military career, which is an integral part of his life, is also likely to appeal to Muslims in certain circumstances as we will see.

Islamic Tradition

In classical Islamic thought, relations between Muslims and non-Muslims are viewed according to the "house" to which the latter belong. The Muslim community lives in "the house of peace" (cf. 10:25) and Muslims have nothing to fear from each other, in theory at least. Non-Muslim nations belong to one of two houses: either to the "house of war" if they are hostile to the *umma*, or to the "house of pact." The signing of a treaty of good understanding with the Muslim community allows non-Muslims to live in peace with Muslims. The division of the world is thus made according to religious criteria.

Islamists have many grievances against their own governments as well as Western countries. They believe that cooperation treaties signed between Muslim countries and Western nations are based on interests that do not serve Muslim peoples. For them these nations belong to the "house of war" and are therefore legitimate targets just as their own governments which they seek to overthrow.

Islamic Theology

Classical Islamic theology defines non-Muslims according to religious criteria. They are disbelievers (*kuffar*) including Jews and Christians. This theology deeply permeates the mentality of Muslims, especially Islamists.

---

7. Bukhari, *Iman* (Faith), 17. As we have seen, according to Islamic law, human life can be taken in the case of murder, apostasy and sexual immorality.

The biblical concept of "neighbor," which defines people according to their common humanity, does not exist in traditional Islamic thought, although there is a prophetic saying that Muslims should wish for their brother what they wish for themselves: "None of you has true faith if you do not desire for your brother what you desire for yourselves."[8] The question is to know who this brother is: the brother in faith or in humanity? In the parallel account found in another canonical compilation, the chapter heading is titled: "Chapter on the characteristics of the faith which consists in desiring for your *Muslim* brother the good which you desire for yourself." In this chapter, the word of the Prophet is recorded in these terms: "No servant has true faith until he desires for his brother, or he said: for his neighbor, what he desires for himself."[9] The Arabic word which is translated here as "neighbor" is *jar*, it actually means "neighbor." The two chapters following this account deal with the obligation to maintain good relations with neighbors. In other words, the neighbor in this prophetic statement is either the brother in the faith or "the neighbor" who lives not far from home.

The fact that people are perceived by Muslim theologians through religious lenses fosters a certain feeling of suspicion towards non-Muslims, nonconformist Muslims or Muslims of another tradition, for example, Sunnis towards Shiʿites and vice versa. In the early centuries of the Islamic era, there was a small group of Muslims called Kharijites, who viewed all other Muslims as non-believers. This group of hardliners excommunicated any Muslim who did not strictly and scrupulously abide by all the obligations of their religious beliefs. This exclusivist theology seems to have resurfaced among contemporary Islamists, who tend to excommunicate all Muslims who do not think like them or do not practice Islam the way they do, and to declare all non-Muslims as enemies.

---

8. Bukhari, *Iman* (Faith), 7. It is not uncommon for well-meaning Muslims to translate this saying in a very loose manner: "None of you will have true faith if you do not love your brother as you love yourselves." (The verb *ahabba* accompanied by the preposition *li* means to desire or to wish, not to love.)

9. Muslim, *Iman* (Faith), 18 (emphasis added). The Arabic translation of the Bible uses, in connection with the command on love of neighbor, not the word *jar* but *qarib* (literally "near"), that is, every human being, especially needy people as illustrated in Jesus's parable of the Good Samaritan (Luke 10:27–35).

Islamic History

After the Prophet's death, Caliph Abu Bakr succeeded him. His two-year rule (632–634) was marked by the "wars of apostasy" whose purpose was to bring back to Islam the Arab tribes who had seceded by declaring that they no longer wanted to follow the religion founded by Muhammad. Sunnis call the four caliphs who succeeded Muhammad "the Righteous Caliphs." During their reign (632–661) the Muslim community experienced very serious internal wars (notably between Sunnis and Shi'ites), as well as remarkable expansion to the north, east and west of Arabia. Exactly a century after the Prophet's death, Muslim armies had reached Poitiers in central France after taking the reins of power throughout the Middle East, North Africa and Spain. They had also conquered vast areas stretching from Iraq to the Indus River in the east.

Islam spread throughout the world by various means such as preaching and trade, but also militarily during the Umayyad, Abbasid and Ottoman empires. Constantinople, the capital of the Byzantine empire, fell to the Ottomans in 1453 and later became the capital of their empire with a new name – Istanbul. The Ottoman army had already invaded and occupied considerable territories in southeastern Europe. They had won the historic battle of Kosovo against the Serbian army in 1389. Vienna itself was besieged twice (in 1529 and 1683), but twice the Ottoman army was repelled. In 1492, the last Islamic kingdom on the Iberian peninsula, Granada, was taken over by the Spaniards. This same year also marks the discovery of the New World by Christopher Columbus. Since then, Islamic civilization seems to be in decline and European influence on the rise.

Islamists recall with nostalgia what they consider to be the golden age of Islam, notably the rule of the first four caliphs, marked by a remarkable expansion of the Islamic empire. They deplore the loss of Andalusia, which was under Islamic rule for almost eight centuries. The glorious and sometimes bloody history of successive Islamic empires remains vivid in the collective memory of Muslims. Islamists want, by the rigorous implementation of Sharī'a, to resuscitate an idealized and long gone past.

Non-Religious Roots of Islamism

The six religious roots of radical Islam we have just reviewed boost Islamist ideology when considered without critical examination. Qur'anic texts and prophetic accounts are understood literally, without taking on board their historical context. Islamic theology and tradition are interpreted as if the world we live in has not changed in the last fourteen centuries. Relying on the prophetic model and drawing inspiration from what Muslims themselves call "the Islamic conquests," which resulted in Islamic occupation of large territories, Islamists dream of restoring the caliphate with the view to unifying a divided Muslim world. This context-free reading of Islamic heritage is greatly influenced by the context in which Muslims live today. This international, regional and national context partly explains why Islamist ideology continues to appeal to a number of ordinary Muslims, especially young people. We need to understand this context which represents the non-religious roots of radical Islam.

Political Protest

Islamism is first of all a protest against the political domination endured by Muslims for several centuries. Between the two World Wars, nearly all Muslim countries were controlled by foreign powers, in particular, Great Britain, France, Italy and the Netherlands, and these European powers were traditionally Christian. There were only three Muslim countries that remained independent: Arabia, Turkey and Afghanistan. This political hegemony also meant, in many countries, the intermittent oppression of the local population and the exploitation of the natural resources in the countries concerned.

The regimes in power in most Islamic countries are authoritarian. This promotes, directly or indirectly, the emergence of radical Islam because the mosque becomes the only place of free expression and opposition. Among the religious opponents to the government, some engage in terrorism and are often imprisoned, tortured and even murdered. Others leave their countries and seek refuge, often in a Western country. Refugee status gives refugees the freedom of opinion and expression that some use, and abuse. This allows some of these Muslim refugees to pursue their ideological battle, which is sometimes reinforced in reaction to what they perceive in Western societies as anti-Islamic. The best-known case in this regard is that of Ayatollah Khomeini who, after taking refuge in Iraq, was expelled by Saddam Hussein before he went to France. From his residence in Neauphle-le-Château, he continued his struggle against the oppressive Shah regime until his triumphant return to Iran in 1979, followed by the establishment of the Islamic Republic of Iran.

Decolonization which started shortly after WWII did not completely sever the ties between European nations and their former colonies. This profoundly displeases Islamists who speak of a new colonialism, economic and military, more subtle than political colonialism but no less harmful. Jihadist groups that are active in sub-Saharan countries, such as AQMI (Al-Qaeda in the

Islamic Maghreb), are angry with France and fight against it, because of its role as neocolonial protector of these secular countries of West Africa. They don't have too much trouble recruiting fighters from jobless youth. Some disempowered young people are attracted to military power attached to jihadist ideology; others give in to the temptation of a better future in Western Europe at the cost of braving death with the perilous crossing of the Sahara and the Mediterranean Sea.

Islamists are also very critical of the ruling regimes in Islamic countries, many of which they see as corrupt and repressive. The GIA (Groupe Islamique Armé – Islamic Armed Group) was born as a reaction to the Algerian government which made the decision to interrupt the democratic process, realizing that the Islamist parties were going to win the 1992 elections. The result was a civil war that spanned an entire decade called the "black decade" (the 1990s).

The Iranian revolution of 1979 was a reaction to the dictatorial regime of the Shah supported by Western countries, particularly the United States. The Shah himself came to power in 1953 in a CIA and MI6 sponsored coup that overthrew the democratically elected government of Mohammad Mossadegh.

Islamists are also very critical of Saudi Arabia and the Gulf States. The country that many consider, not without reason, to be the most conservative and corrupt Islamic country is the United States' best ally (after Israel) in the Middle East. Because of its oil wealth, Western countries are very lenient with its regime, arguably one of the most repressive in the world. The reason is quite simply shared economic interests, especially arms sales by the United States, France and the United Kingdom in particular.

When Islamists seized the Grand Mosque in Mecca (1979) and threatened the Saudi regime, elite units of the French gendarmerie were called in to the rescue. When Saddam Hussein's army invaded Kuwait (1990), an international coalition led by the US, shielded the Saudi regime and liberated Kuwait (1991). What had been unimaginable for Muslims before then actually happened – the occupation of the holy land of Islam by an "army of unbelievers." Saddam's regime had been supported militarily by Western countries in its merciless war against the new Islamic Republic of Iran (1980–1988). The US support for the Mujahedeen of Afghanistan in their fight against the Red Army in the 1980s had far reaching consequences. Many young Arabs went to Afghanistan to support the Mujahedeen – among these future jihadists, called the Afghan Arabs, was Osama bin Laden and his organization, al-Qaeda. They took advantage of the US support before turning their guns on their former ally (eleven Saudi citizens were among the nineteen al-Qaeda terrorists of 11 September 2001).

It is no coincidence that Islamist movements develop in countries where the population feels oppressed. This is the case with Bosnia and Kosovo in the aftermath of the collapse of Yugoslavia. In the early 1990s, the Serbian leaders tried to control the other republics of the Yugoslav Federation, including Bosnia and Herzegovina, where the Muslim population was very large. In Lebanon, Shiʻa Muslims created Hezbollah to liberate southern Lebanon from Israeli occupation (1978–2000). The so-called Islamic State, Daʻesh, was founded by former prisoners of the US military in Iraq, jihadists who allied themselves with members of the Iraqi army, disbanded after the Iraqi invasion in 2003.

In Egypt the Muslim Brotherhood movement, very influential in the Arab-Muslim world, was created in 1928 to resist British colonization. In 1981 a member of an Islamist group assassinated President Sadat, because he had signed a peace treaty with Israel in 1979. In 2012 a Muslim brotherhood leader, Mohamed Morsi, became president of Egypt in its first truly democratic election which came about as a result of the Arab Spring demonstrations. This election followed the dictatorship of President Hosni Moubarak (1981–2012), himself a former army general. Morsi's presidency was short lived as he was overthrown the following year in a coup by his minister of defense, Abdel Fattah al-Sissi, Egypt's current president.

Palestinian jihadist movements (e.g. Hamas, Islamic Jihad) have been strengthened by the failure of negotiations between Israel and the PLO (Palestine Liberation Organization), that initially sought to implement the Oslo accords (1993). The West Bank is still under Israeli occupation despite the presence of the Palestinian Liberation Authority, which is only a symbolic group. The Gaza Strip, evacuated by the Israeli army in 2005, is under a drastic Israeli blockade (by land, air and sea).

Most Muslims (and many Arab Christians) feel a great deal of solidarity with the Palestinian people. Several countries have been forced by military action to comply with UN resolutions (Iraq, Serbia, Indonesia), but because of US backing, Israel has never been forced to implement UN resolutions, especially no. 242 that called Israel to withdraw from the territories it occupied during the 1967 war. Israel continues to enjoy virtually unconditional support from the international community. No wonder the policies of Western countries are seen by many Arab and Muslim people as applying double standards. These policies protect the Jewish State and shield it from sanctions, like those imposed on South Africa when this country was ruled by a racially segregated regime.

Despite the terror caused by terrorist attacks, terrorism is in reality the weapon of the weak. Most of its victims are Muslims living in Islamic countries. The hegemony of Western countries (and of Israel) is not just political, it is also economic, military, scientific and cultural. Terrorism is a protest against a reality that many Muslims, rightly or wrongly, resent bitterly, namely that "might is always right."

Identity Protection

Radical Islam is also a cultural protest. Globalization spares no country in the world, and it reinforces another phenomenon, secularization, which is also a major feature of our time. Countries that have a certain influence on these two phenomena, whether Asian (China, Japan, South Korea) or Western countries (Europe, US), are not Islamic countries. As a result, the latter increasingly face a secular world civilization.

Many Muslims feel threatened in their very identity and fear for the future of their children. Indeed, twenty-first century civilization is marked by atheism (or agnosticism), materialism, individualism, the rule of multinational corporations, and moral and religious relativism. All of this goes against Islamic values and undermines Muslim societies which remain deeply conservative and impregnated with religion, a sense of community and strong moral values.

Thus Islamism represents a protest against secularization, perceived as an antireligious driving force that endangers Muslim identity and faith. This obviously does not stop Muslims from using the most sophisticated technological tools (internet, social networks and the international banking system) to serve their cause.

Boko Haram is a very violent jihadist group operating mainly in the predominantly Muslim northeastern part of Nigeria, which has been economically neglected by the corrupt central government. As its name "education is forbidden" suggests, its objective is to ban Western education in the country which is very rich in natural resources (oil and gas in particular).

Muslims living in Western countries are at the frontline of culture shock and at the center of the conflict between their traditional values and the values of their adopted country. They are part of a minority in a society of freedom which seems to have no religious and moral landmarks. Some Muslims abandon religion and break free from all constraints. Among them are young people who end up falling into criminality in one form or another, especially drug trafficking. Others harden themselves and find in religion the best way to resist a libertarian society. The temptation is then strong to adopt an extremist version of Islam. I have heard many Muslims in France say: "I don't know if I'm French or Algerian (or . . .) – what I know is that I'm a Muslim."

Socio-Economic Marginalization

Authoritarian regimes are also affected, among other evils, by corruption, nepotism and incompetence. These evils largely explain why most Islamic countries have serious economic problems despite the wealth of natural resources of some. Algeria and Nigeria are particularly good examples. Economic challenges make it more difficult to address challenges in other areas such as education, housing and employment. This is why we find asylum seekers among migrants, as well as economic and even climatic migrants (most of whom come from former colonies).

Migrants seek to live in places where they can count on the support of other migrants. In France, these neighborhoods are generally cheaper than others and the only French people who live there do so most often because of their limited financial resources. Islamists have a deep sense of solidarity – they are committed to helping each other and are involved in social work. As a result, a number of young immigrants convert to Islam or become more committed Muslims. The radicalization of these young people is thus greatly facilitated.

Not all Muslims won over by radical Islam are immigrants. Many were born in their adopted country; however, as in France, they may have grown up in a rather disadvantaged environment because of the foreign background of their parents, grandparents or great-grandparents. They encountered difficulties in school, which made their access to employment more difficult as well as their integration into society. Many have experienced discrimination at some point in their lives. School failure often leads to social marginalization creating in the person a deep sense of injustice and frustration. Here again, for some, delinquency becomes an escape route, as evidenced by the fact that the percentage of foreigners or people of foreign background in the prison population is clearly above average. For others, it is religion in its extreme version that offers a lifeline.

Marginalization affects not only immigrants but all people living in precarious conditions, including nationals. The number of young people who convert to Islam is significant. Some, full with the zeal of new converts, end up adopting Islamist ideology and engaging in terrorism. It seems that French converts who joined the ranks of ISIS are overrepresented among young Muslims who went to Syria.

Socio-economic marginalization is aggravated by political marginalization in some countries. In the Philippines, the only large Christian-majority country in all Asia, for many years the government faced a separatist and violent movement in the south of the country. In January 2019, a peace process that began in 2014 was completed. The agreement between Manila and the

Moro Islamic Liberation Front established an autonomous region in the predominantly Muslim part of Mindanao.

In Afghanistan, the war with the Taliban (lit. "students" of Sharīʿa) has been going on for more than twenty years. On 15 August 2021 the Taliban returned to power from which they were ousted in 2001 by an international coalition led by the US. Indeed, much more money was spent on fighting this group militarily than in supporting development projects that would have enabled part of the population to come out of poverty. If anything their victory shows that sheer military force is unable to address deep political, economic and social issues. The new regime is now put to the test: Having won the war and seized power, will Islamist ideology be capable of offering a better future for the country in terms of social justice, economic prosperity and political stability? The decisions made by the Taliban regime so far suggest it is unlikely to meet this challenge. Afghans are among the largest group of asylum seekers in Europe.

Personal Achievement

Secularization in Western societies is in part a reaction to the abuse of power by the church and her clericalism. Having thrown the baby out with the bath water, Western societies find themselves in a spiritual vacuum which favors the growth of sects and the development of certain religions such as Islam, Buddhism and Hinduism. Humans are spiritual beings who need some kind of religious faith. Those who reject faith become overly involved in legitimate human activities (e.g. work, leisure, sport, art) which end up becoming idols. Religion too can become a form of idolatry when it is used to serve our own agendas instead of inspiring believers to humbly serve God and needy neighbors.

We already mentioned the temptation to resort to religion as a protective shield against what is perceived or experienced in Western society as a threat to identity, faith and culture. In some cases, crime is a temporary escape route, which can indirectly lead to religion – many who have passed through prison have been converted to radical Islam by fellow inmates in their search for personal fulfillment. For them, Islam is a way of redemption that offers the opportunity to start a new life free from the burdens of the past. The Muslim community offers them a place of warm welcome where they are fully recognized, respected, and even admired if they come from a non-Muslim background or if they have a serious criminal record.

Islamist ideology therefore attracts people in search of spirituality and meaning for their life as well as a noble cause to serve. Because they often do not have a strong critical mind or an adequate religious education, they can be easily drawn into violence. Moreover, Islam offers its followers an eschatological vision that can fascinate young people seeking a meaningful death by way of martyrdom. According to Islamic eschatology, the end time will be marked by a cosmic battle between good and evil, the battle of "Gog and Magog" as it is called in the Qur'an (18:94; 21:96), the Bible (Ezek 38:2; Rev 20:8) and in the Prophetic Tradition. According to some Hadith narratives, when Jesus returns to earth, he will participate in the apocalyptic struggle against the Antichrist, *al-masih al-dajjal* (lit. "the deceitful messiah"). Some accounts place this battle in Dabiq (name of ISIS periodical) in northern Syria (not far from the city of Aleppo).[10]

People with an adventurous spirit, especially if they are impressionable, are easily recruited to participate in this end-time global battle. Their sacrificial commitment gives meaning to their lives in a society that has left them bitter with a deep sense of disillusion and dissatisfaction. The fact that ISIS claimed to have restored the Islamic caliphate played an important role in winning young people suffering from an existential crisis. For them, the Muslim community was on the verge of recovering its glorious past and putting an end to its age-long humiliation. This triumphalist rhetoric from ISIS included videos depicting the bravery of certain heroes of Islamic history. The crusading movement, despite its initial success, was ultimately defeated by determined Muslims. Saladin is one such legendary figure who represents, to many Arabs and Muslims, the prototype of the rebellious and courageous Muslim leader who, like the Prophet, triumphantly defeated his enemies.

Radical Islam thus feeds on Islamic sources that are understood, perhaps misunderstood, in the light of the national and international context. The suicide bomb as a combat weapon is not part of traditional Islamic teaching. Yet it is a weapon regularly used by jihadists in combat operations. Terrorists who engage in suicide operations see themselves as martyrs and are seen as such by those who share their ideology. However, for the vast majority of Muslim scholars, real martyrs are those killed by the enemy, whether or not

---

10. Muslim, *Fitan* (Trials), 9. This narrative describes the eschatological battle, with the capture of Constantinople by the Muslim army, and the coming of the Antichrist who will be defeated by Jesus Christ when he returns. For a well-documented overview of Islamic eschatology in its Sunni version, see Pierre Lory, "Les signes de la fin des temps dans les traditions musulmanes sunnites," in *Penser la fin du monde*, eds. Emma Aubin-Boltanski and Claudine Gauthier (Paris: CNRS Éditions, 2014), 269–80.

they are soldiers. Traditionally, suicide has been equated with murder against oneself, which is severely sanctioned by Islam since hell awaits murderers. God is described in the Qur'an as the only one who gives life and who takes it back (2:258; 3:156; 10:56; 40:68). Suicide bombings show how far extremist Muslims are from mainstream Islam.

A Christian Perspective on Violence

If we want to assess Islamism and jihadism in the light of the Bible, we must strive to be fair (Deut 1:17), especially towards a religion not our own. As disciples of Christ, we must also be prepared to take a critical look at ourselves, at our own history, and to some extent at our Scriptures (Matt 7:3–5).

Violence is sadly a phenomenon that exists everywhere – in religions, in atheistic ideologies and in all societies. The problem with Islam is that the Qur'an and the Prophetic Tradition seem to justify the use of force if it is done in God's name. Switching from force to violence is not too difficult when sinful people believe they carry out God's will, especially in certain circumstances.

Muslims often remind us that holy war is found in the Bible too, more precisely, in the Old Testament. The Israelites conquered the Promised Land with the sword (cf. Deut 7:1–5). The extermination of the Canaanites is presented in the Bible as a divine judgment executed against them because of their sin and only when their sin "reached its full measure" (Gen 15:16). The great king David conquered the city of Jerusalem and made it the capital of his kingdom by war (1 Chr 11:4–9). However, when David wanted to build a temple, God criticized David's military career and rejected his plan for the following reason: "You are not to build a house for my Name, because you are a warrior and have shed blood" (1 Chr 28:3). The God of peace did not want his name to be associated with that of a man of war, even though he was a great man and a sincere believer (1 Sam 13:14).

With the new covenant made by God in Jesus Christ, the use of force was totally abolished as the kingship of Christ is not of this world. The only legitimate holy war, from a Christian point of view, is the war waged against the forces of evil that enslave our world and ourselves (Eph 6:10–18). Unlike the Prophet of Islam, Jesus taught his disciples not to use force even when they wanted to defend him (Matt 26:52). He fully accepted the implications of his non-violent mission, which allowed his enemies to put him to death. But his life freely given on the cross meant the salvation of the world.[11]

In flagrant contradiction with the teaching of Christ, Christians have not always been able to resist violence. The crusading movement was started and promoted by authorized representatives of the church, including the pope. The only canonized king of France is Louis IX, Saint-Louis, the very pious king who led two crusades.

Christian theologians developed the concept of "just war" which they defined according to very strict criteria. Not all Christian theologians endorse this concept, but all agree that even a just war cannot be a holy war fought under the banner of Christ, unlike armed jihad in Islam.

Many Islamic conquests were not peaceful, but the same could be said of the conquest of the New World, Australia and other territories of the world. While the conquerors did not carry out their colonial enterprises in the name of Christ, many of them were Christian Europeans. It is also in Europe, a land of Christian tradition, that the two World Wars took place, though there was no religious motive behind these wars. European colonialism was the work of predominantly Christian nations with the aim of bringing civilization to so-called uncivilized countries. The Iraq War (2003) was waged, without the authorization of the UN, by American President George W. Bush and British Prime Minister Tony Blair, two political leaders and self-confessed Christians. This war resulted in the destabilization of the entire Middle East with the very serious consequences for the countries of the region. It also dramatically reduced the Christian presence in the region, particularly in Syria and Iraq.

As stated earlier, violence exists in all societies. In authoritarian regimes, the State controls violence, but it also does not hesitate to use it against its opponents. In a democratic regime, ordinary violence manifests itself in the form of criminality of all kinds. In the United States, bearing arms is a constitutional right, and mass killings regularly make headlines.[12] Police violence, particularly against African-Americans, led in 2020 to the "Black Lives Matter" movement. At the very top of the most violent cities in the world

---

11. According to some Muslims, Jesus did not outlaw the use of force. Their interpretation of relevant texts in the Gospels ignores the general teaching of Jesus and his death on the cross. It makes no room for the use of metaphorical language or symbolic gestures (cf. Matt 10:34; Luke 22:36–38; John 2:15).

12. "As of July 31, 2021, 411 mass shootings fit the Mass Shooting Tracker project criterion, leaving 437 people dead and 1,688 injured, for a total of 2,125 total victims, some including the shooter(s)." https://en.wikipedia.org/wiki/List_of_mass_shootings_in_the_United_States_in_2021.

in terms of societal violence are cities in Latin America, a predominantly Christian region.[13] This paradox should encourage us to remain humble and not pass hasty judgments against Muslim societies. By and large, Christians do not behave better than Muslims. The films produced by Hollywood are a fairly accurate mirror of Western societies where money, sex and violence are sadly in daily news and shows. This is the flip side of societies which pride themselves on values such as freedom, democracy and human rights.

We need to unmask the root of violence. Violence lives in every human heart (before being prohibited, authorized or prescribed in the holy books). This is one of the manifestations of evil which is rooted in all of us. One of the ways to combat it is not to sanctify it on religious grounds. It is equally important for believers, Muslim or Christian, to maintain a critical distance from political authorities so that they can criticize them more freely when they make decisions that may generate or justify violence.

Any terrorist act is inexcusable. However, terrorists are still human beings created in God's image and loved by their Creator. Evil disfigures this image but does not erase it. Therefore, terrorists have not lost their human dignity, and God's forgiveness and salvation are available to them too.

Western civilization is as far removed from the kingdom of God as Islamic civilization. The first, defined by philosophical, religious and moral relativism, elevates freedom to the rank of a supreme and unchallenged divinity. The second, characterized by self-confidence, authoritarianism and intolerance, disconnects truth from love. The gospel is at equal distance from these two models of civilization. This message offers love of God and neighbor as a supreme value. Love, of course, has concern for truth, and according to Jesus, only the truth sets us free (John 8:32). Those who love are willing to give up their freedom for the good of others:

> Live as free people, but do not use your freedom as a cover-up for evil; live as God's slaves. Show proper respect to everyone, love the family of believers, fear God, honor the emperor (1 Pet 2:16–17; cf. 1 Cor 10:23; Gal 5:1, 13).

Thus, Christianity with its monotheistic beliefs of the incarnation and redemption is significantly different from the monotheistic belief of pure transcendence in Judaism and Islam, which only partially responds to our spiritual quest. The gospel offers true life starting now, unlike materialist

---

13. https://en.wikipedia.org/wiki/List_of_cities_by_murder_rate.

ideologies which promise fleeting successes and deceptive pleasures far from true happiness.

Those who love do not seek to force the truth in which they believe on others. They recognize the right of everyone to make mistakes. It is God who somehow, temporarily at least, gives this right to all human creatures. God suspends his judgment and gives people time to reflect on the love he has shown them in Jesus Christ. This period will end with the second coming of Christ. Until then, we live in "the time of the nations [or 'gentiles']" (Luke 21:24), marked by God's patience towards us. Far from being indifferent to evil, of which violence is one expression, God gives us the opportunity to examine ourselves and to consider how we should respond to his love for us. The apostle Paul invites his readers, with a certain sense of urgency, to make use, before it is too late, of what the apostle Peter calls "our Lord's patience" (2 Pet 3:15):

> Do you show contempt for the riches of his kindness, forbearance and patience, not realizing that God's kindness is intended to lead you to repentance? (Rom 2:4)

5

Islam: Current Issues

This chapter will discuss difficult and sensitive issues relating to Islam and the Muslim community in France and around the world. Some of these questions are general, others concern the lives of Muslims in non-Islamic countries, and the situation of Christians living in predominantly Islamic countries. Many issues are topical and the subject of heated debate and endless controversy.

Islam and Christian Communities

Christians and Muslims have lived side by side since the birth of Islam in Arabia. Islamic law grants Jews and Christians the status of protected minorities. In his famous commentary on the Qur'an, Razi openly declares, in connection with verse 9:29, that this special status is a privilege meant to make Jews and Christians realize sooner rather than later that Islam is superior to their religions and to encourage them to convert to Islam.

A good number of Jews and Christians kept their religion. The presence of these two monotheistic communities alongside the *umma* is perceived by many Muslims as a permanent challenge, even an affront. The (relative) prosperity of the Jewish and Christian communities on a global scale makes Judaism and Christianity appear as competing religions and heightens the resentment felt by some Muslims.

Why do jihadists attack Christians in particular?

Terrorist attacks seem to target Christians specifically. Most of these attacks are not reported in the non-specialist media of secular countries. Exceptions include the following incidents:

- On Sunday 31 October 2010, an Islamic State commando targeted the Syriac-Catholic Cathedral in Baghdad killing forty-eight worshippers.
- On 15 February 2015, the same organization executed twenty-two Egyptian Coptic (Christian) men working in Libya.
- On 26 July 2016, two terrorists killed Father Jacques Hamel in Saint-Étienne church in St-Étienne-du-Rouvray, France.
- On 21 April 2019, Easter Sunday in Sri Lanka, eight Islamist attacks targeted, among others, three churches.
- On 29 October 2020, an Islamist young man killed three people inside the Basilica of Nice.

We could multiply such examples. What prompts jihadists to attack Christians?

There are several reasons for this. Basically, for Islamists, Christians are not only non-believers as they do not believe in the Prophet of Islam, they are disbelievers (*kuffar* – a very derogatory qur'anic term deeply rooted in history) who have a corrupt faith. They are enemies who have regularly opposed Muslims throughout history.

One of the facts regularly reported by the Arabic-speaking media is the growing number of Muslims who convert to Christianity, in the West as well as in Islamic countries. Christianity is thus seen as a serious competitor of Islam.

Christians are also blamed for their alleged complicity with Western governments which are considered Christian governments by many Muslims.[1] These governments are accused of interfering in the affairs of Islamic countries, of supporting corrupt regimes, and of shamelessly exploiting their people. Western interventions in Syria and Iraq over the past two decades have been catastrophic from this point of view.

Christian communities are an easy target – most of them are small communities, unable to defend themselves and little tempted to resort to violence. Church buildings are an ideal theater of operations, as it is highly unlikely that attackers will face armed opposition.

Arab Christians in particular represent a challenge for Islamists in that they have remained, despite all the pressures they have endured, faithful to their religion and have been able to resist Islam's attraction. Their presence alongside the Muslim community poses a fundamental question that hegemonic Islam

---

1. It cannot be completely ruled out that, in very rare cases, foreign secret services may have used Christians, nationals or expatriates, often without them being aware of being manipulated.

has always found problematic: otherness. Islamists seek to scare Christian minorities and encourage them to leave their country.

Finally, targeting Christians guarantees maximum global media coverage, which is precisely what jihadists look for.

Terrorist attacks partly explain why Christians from Islamic countries are leaving in greater numbers, proportionally, than their fellow Muslims. Economic and political problems are also behind this migration which considerably reduces the number of Christians in Middle Eastern countries such as Iraq, Syria, Palestine and Egypt.

The unenviable plight of Christians in many Islamic countries raises the question of the Christian attitude in the face of discrimination and persecution. Jesus warns his disciples that following him is costly: "Whoever wants to be my disciple must deny themselves and take up their cross and follow me" (Matt 16:24). Following Christ involves suffering in one form or another, and requires resilience and perseverance (Matt 5:11-12; cf. 1 Pet 3:8-18).

The international Christian community must show greater solidarity with Christians and other persecuted communities, but that does not necessarily mean helping them get out of their country. All Christian leaders in Islamic countries want their church members to stay in their homeland for as long as is reasonably possible. They consider that Christians have a witness to bear in Islamic lands. Christian leaders all over the world need to plead the cause of those who are persecuted (Christians, Muslims, etc.). As far as possible, it is their responsibility to contact political and religious representatives in their own country to speak on behalf of those who are generally ignored in the media and political institutions.

In Islamic countries, Christians do not fully enjoy freedom of worship; shouldn't we in return restrict religious freedom of Muslims in our country?

Except for a few countries (e.g. Algeria, Saudi Arabia, Iran), Christian communities are not openly persecuted in Islamic countries, at least not on a large scale. It is true that, in many countries, they are subject to severe restrictions and various troubles which are often caused by the local population rather than by the government. In rare cases (e.g. Abu Dhabi), Christian communities have received free land from local political authorities on which to build churches where they can freely worship.

Restricting religious freedom of Muslims in France would amount to holding them responsible for the politics of Islamic countries. This would be deeply unfair, because Muslims in France do not have much influence on the policies of Islamic countries that discriminate against their religious minorities.

Christians have received a clear instruction from their Lord, namely to treat others as they would like to be treated: "So in everything, do to others what you would have them do to you, for this sums up the Law and the Prophets" (Matt 7:12). The principle of reciprocity, in the sense of conditioning our actions by what others are prepared or not prepared to do, is therefore not a Christian principle, nor is the law of retaliation. If we recognize the rights of Muslims in our country, we will be all the more credible in asking Islamic countries to respect the rights of their religious or ethnic minorities.

In July 2020, the Hagia Sophia Church in Istanbul (first converted into a mosque, then into a museum), was converted again into a mosque. What do you think?

Hagia Sophia, built on the ruins of an ancient pagan temple, had a very eventful history since it was built in the fourth century and rebuilt by the Byzantine emperor Justinian in the sixth century. For centuries it was the seat of the Orthodox Patriarchate of Constantinople. During the fourth crusade, which saw the sack of Constantinople, the Church was plundered by the crusaders and became the Seat of the Latin Patriarch of Constantinople (1204–1261).

After the Ottoman conquest of the city in 1453, Constantinople was renamed Istanbul and became the capital of the empire. Sultan Mehmet II then decided to transform Hagia Sophia into a mosque, *Ayasofya*. Kemal Atatürk, the secular founder of the Turkish Republic, turned the mosque into a museum in 1934.

The present Turkish president, Recep Tayyip Erdogan, an Islamist-nationalist leader, seeks to revive his declining popularity in his own country as well as in surrounding Islamic countries. He also faces an international community increasingly unfavorable to him because of his authoritarian, nationalist, Islamist and aggressive policies. He had a card to play, namely giving *Ayasofia* back to Islamic worship, which he did in July 2020.

The decision of the Turkish president is therefore primarily a political one aimed at improving his image though a religious motivation cannot be ruled out for a political leader who is a self-confessed Muslim. Nevertheless, this decision is unlikely to ease tensions in the relations between Turkey and its European neighbors, notably Greece, or between Muslims and Christians in general. Turkey's ambition was to join the European Union until it realized several European countries were fiercely opposed to this idea.

Regrettable as it is, the conversion of Hagia Sophia into a mosque is not without precedent. Over the course of history, many churches have been converted into mosques and (in fewer numbers) mosques into churches. Hagia Sophia, however, is highly symbolic. The decision of the Turkish president, however unfortunate, is not hugely significant for the future of Christianity. Hagia Sophia is certainly a very beautiful building, very evocative from a historical and Christian point of view, but whether it remains a museum or becomes a mosque again is not of great importance for the parties involved. As for Christians, the vitality of the church is found elsewhere, especially in the dynamism of her mission and the fidelity of her members to the teaching of the Master.

What should we think of mixed marriages between Muslims and Christians?

Marriage is more than a legal contract between a man and a woman. According to Scripture, it is a spiritual union, sealed by bodily union. This union is like a parable (or a sign) of the love that binds Christ to the church (Eph 5:31–32). Marriage between two people, only one of whom is Christian, loses much of its meaning.

Marriage between a Muslim man and a Christian woman is permitted by Sharīʿa. In the New Testament there is no text that explicitly refers to the marriage of a Christian to a non-Christian. The Apostle Paul clearly advised against a Christian widow marrying a non-Christian (1 Cor 7:39). There is therefore no formal and general prohibition against a Christian choosing a Muslim spouse. But in this case, can the spouses fully live their faith within their marriage? There is good reason to doubt it. How could the two spouses be united in prayer and worship of God without their faith being reduced to the lowest common denominator? The Christian prayer par excellence is the Lord's Prayer. Since Muslims do not know God as their Father, they cannot say this prayer in sincerity. Jesus Christ is a great prophet to Muslims, but of lower rank than Muhammad, who is considered the last and greatest of all prophets. For Christians, Jesus is the incarnate Son of God, the Lord of the universe and the Savior of humankind. Muslim prayers are full of qurʾanic texts, many of which are difficult to reconcile with the gospel.

If one of the important tasks of parents is to pass their faith on to their children, sooner or later the question will arise: what faith will spiritually feed these children? A general faith in an abstract God, or a faith which will give concrete meaning to their life and enable them to find their place in the faith community?[2] Marriage is already under strain today, even for Christian couples. It would be very risky to commit to a lifelong human relationship, arguably the most intimate of all, when it is more than likely that this relationship will set them on a rocky road.

These same theological reasons make it nearly impossible for Christians and Muslims to sincerely unite in a common act of worship. It would be confusing as the differences between Christianity and Islam are not superficial. This does not prevent the two communities, Christian and Muslim, from praying *each according to their own tradition* in the same place to celebrate an event of general interest or to ask for divine blessing.

Apart from these two red lines (marriage and worship), Christians and Muslims have every reason to get involved in common actions for the common good. They share enough beliefs and values (as the last chapter will show) to tackle together the many challenges facing society.

Muslims in France

There are nearly six million Muslims in France (10 percent of the population). Most are second, third and fourth generation immigrants. Initially, many came from countries in North Africa at the invitation of the government or French companies. They helped rebuild the French economy, which was devastated by World War II. Family reunification policies have considerably increased their number. The economic crises in the former French colonies, including the Sahel countries, have kept migrants coming.

The Muslim population now represents a significant minority which is an integral part of the national fabric. Many Muslims, who have become full French citizens, claim their rights as citizens. The question of their integration into society is not as problematic as it is often said, although there are serious issues in certain suburban neighborhoods. It is imperative that Muslims feel at home in France, as part of the national community.

Radical Muslims and jihadists want to draw a wedge between Muslims in France and non-Muslim French people. It is the government's responsibility to fight against ghettos and community separatism through fair laws, but also and above all, through socio-economic and educational projects that tackle the root cause of ghettoization.

---

2. It is important to take into consideration the fact that according to Sharīʿa, children must always follow the religion of their (Muslim) father. This has legal implications in the event of divorce, especially if the marriage has been registered with an Islamic authority.

What can the French government reasonably expect from Muslim citizens?

The government is entitled to expect all citizens to be loyal to the country where they live. The government has the right to demand that everyone obey the laws of the land, especially those that are meant to preserve social cohesion and ensure national security. If citizens do not agree, they have the right to express their views by any means permitted by law. However, the government cannot ask Muslims (or Christians) to consider the laws of the republic superior to what they see as divine laws. For all monotheistic believers, the demand of placing human authority above God means nothing less than idolatry. In a democratic country (with a Christian tradition) like France, it is not clear which republican laws would directly oppose Islamic laws. If it does (e.g. abortion law), there is always the possibility of invoking the conscientious objection clause, or even civil disobedience.

Muslims in France can also appeal to the resources of Islamic jurisprudence which includes the principle of *'urf* (customary law). This allows Muslims living in non-Muslim countries to respect local laws while staying true to their beliefs. The Qur'an itself admits there are exceptional circumstances, when human life is at stake for instance, in which Muslims are allowed to break Sharī'a law. The code on dietary restrictions (e.g. pork, blood, dead animals) can be suspended if necessary, notably to save lives (2:173; 5:3; 6:145; 16:115).

Rather than enduring their minority status, Muslims can view their situation as an opportunity for them to take a fresh look at their religious heritage. It is also an opportunity that many use to share their faith and win new converts to Islam, which is part of their right as citizens. Muslims must recognize, however, that in the debate of ideas in France, people must be able to respectfully critique Islam without being immediately accused of Islamophobia. There are Islamophobic people who take their disagreement with Islam as a justification of their hostility to Muslims. Critiquing Islam does not necessarily mean being Islamophobic, even if the danger is not very far away.

The government would be ill advised to pass laws that target, even implicitly, only Muslims. The principle of equality must apply to all citizens, regardless of their religion. If this principle is accepted, it is difficult to see how halal meat could be banned when there are kosher meat slaughterhouses. Preaching in Arabic (or in other languages) cannot be made illegal since preaching in foreign languages is practiced and accepted in certain churches. Foreign imams cannot be barred when there are many foreign priests and pastors in France. The government is entitled to monitor, by appropriate means, the nature of messages delivered, in particular by foreign preachers. It is also responsible to monitor and regulate funding of organizations in general.

The government is also entitled to define its rules on migration and asylum. It will nevertheless have to honor its own values, particularly in terms of human rights, and to respect the international conventions to which it has subscribed. The French government, like many others, is entitled to require new immigrants and refugees to make an effort to learn French and to familiarize themselves with French history and culture. They are expected to show their agreement in principle with republican laws concerning marriage, divorce, secularity, religious freedom, women's equality with men, monogamy, female circumcision, etc.

It is legitimate that the government adopts a cautious attitude in its migration policy as terrorists have infiltrated migrants over the past decade. However, we should not have a distrustful policy towards migrants.

It is said sometimes that the principle of dissimulation or concealment (*taqiyya*) is accepted in Islam, which allows Muslims to lie in good conscience, especially in a non-Muslim society. Certain scholars first developed this principle to allow persecuted Muslims (especially Shi'ites under the reign of the first three caliphs) to save their lives by outwardly denying their religious affiliation. According to A. Amir-Moezzi, this principle (based on a very flimsy interpretation of a few qur'anic verses) has been implemented in two different contexts, one political and the other religious. Minority Muslim groups (Kharijites, Shi'ites, Druze, etc.) have used it to protect themselves in hostile environments. It has also been used to withhold esoteric teachings, "secrets" known only by the elite, which characterize Shi'a Islam and some Sufi groups.[3] Therefore, dissimulation is not an all-encompassing right to lie granted to Muslims by their religion. However, it is true that some ill-informed Muslims invoke the principle of dissimulation to cover up unethical behavior condemned by Islamic doctrine.[4] Islamic authorities should speak out publicly about what the principle of dissimulation really means.

The French government may not want to treat Muslims as a community but only as citizens of the national community, the only community recognized by the republic. However, it cannot prohibit Muslims from considering themselves to be a community, the *umma*, which is distinct from the national community. The *umma* brings together believers from all over the world. Like the church for

---

3. A. Amir-Moezzi, "Dissimulation," in *Encyclopaedia of the Qur'an*, ed. J. D. McAuliffe, vol. 1, 540–42.

4. According to a prophetic saying, lying is allowed only in three cases: when a husband wants to please his wife (perhaps by over flattering her), in a context of war, and to reconcile people who do not speak to each other; see Tirmidhi, *Birr* (Righteousness), 26.

Christians, it is a transnational community that knows no political, geographic or ethnic boundaries.

Responding to the government's request, on 16 January 2021 the CFCM (Conseil Français du Culte Musulman – French Council of Muslim Worship) approved a "Charter of the Principles of Islam in France."[5] The signatories of this charter, made up of ten articles, pledge "not to criminalize renouncing Islam, nor to qualify it as 'apostasy' (*ridda*), even less to stigmatize or call, directly or indirectly, to attack the physical or moral integrity of those who renounce a religion" (Article 3). Articles 3, 4 and 5 are entitled (presumably deliberately) "Liberty," "Equality," and "Fraternity," respectively. Article 6 openly rejects political Islam and the use of religion for political ends, and it also criticizes Salafism (Wahhabism) and the ideology of the Muslim Brotherhood. Article 8 endorses "attachment to secularity and public services." The charter affirms "the principle of equality between men and women," rejects the interference of foreign countries in the affairs of Islam in France, and ensures the compatibility of the Muslim faith with the French Republic laws. Although the CFCM does not represent all Muslims in France, this text marks a very significant step forward in the relations of Muslims with the French State.[6]

What can Muslims in France reasonably expect from the government?

Muslims in France are entitled to expect the government to respect the principle of secularity, hence not to interfere in the internal organization of their religion. The government may want to have an authorized spokesperson who is representative of the Muslim community, but it cannot impose its own preferences.

Muslims are also entitled to expect that secularity is not replaced with secularism which would be used surreptitiously to deprive Muslims of their rights as citizens. It is not for the government to decide whether the veil (i.e. head covering) is a religious obligation or a cultural sign. It can be one and/or the other, and the Muslim woman has the right to wear it in public spaces, although the government may deem it appropriate that the wearing of

---

5. The text of the charter is available on the website of the Grande Mosquée de Paris: https://www.mosqueedeparis.net/charte-des-principes-pour-lislam-de-france/.

6. On 5 February 2022 in Paris the Forif (Forum de l'islam de France) was launched in the presence of the Minister of the Interior. This new body, which took over from the CFCM, is expected to better represent Muslims in France and to serve as a national forum for dialogue with the government.

ostentatious signs of ethnicity or religious identity is not permitted in specific locations such as public schools and offices.

Wearing the veil is in no way a sign that Muslims reject secularity or that they refuse to integrate into French society. But the wearing of the full veil over the face (*niqab, burqa*) is different in that this veil raises the issue of public safety. Moreover, the face is the non-verbal means of communication par excellence, and in order to preserve a minimum of cultural identity, this kind of veil (i.e. face covering) could be banned. It is very unfortunate that some women are forced by their husbands, brothers or fathers to wear the veil, but new laws may not be the most effective way to combat this issue. The cure would, in this case, be worse than the disease.

Multicultural societies may also wish to preserve their cohesion by agreeing to make "reasonable accommodations." For example, if school canteens can offer vegetarian meals, why not offer meals without pork? Or why not offer female-only time slots in certain swimming pools? Thorny questions will always arise in multicultural societies and these issues need to be dealt with on a case-by-case basis, at the local level, while ensuring that no decisions are imposed from above without proper consultation with the relevant people.

Islam in the World

From the start, Islam wanted to be a missionary and universal religion. Islam is now a world religion, present on all continents; it is the second religion in Europe. The Muslim community is particularly active in European countries such as Germany, Spain, France, Italy and the United Kingdom. The spread of Islam worldwide raises questions in the minds of Europeans who are not familiar with this religion.

We will address some of these questions in the following section. We will also deal with some questions Muslims ask concerning Western civilization, and we will explore the special treatment the State of Israel seems to enjoy from Western governments and some Christians.

What are the reasons for the success of Islam in the world?

There are several reasons for the numerical growth of Islam. In the early days of Islamic history, preaching was instrumental in the spread of Islam. In Mecca, Muhammad was a simple preacher. In Medina, the Prophet faced opposition from Jewish tribes and eventually resorted to force in combating them. Thus, preaching and armed force were key factors in the early expansion of Islam.

Trade has also contributed significantly to the spread of this religion beyond the empire's known borders, into Southeast Asia in particular.

The fact that Islam has retained its territorial conquests wherever it has established itself, except in Spain, demonstrates Islam's intrinsic strength. This strength was first based on law enforcement since, in the conquered countries, Islam quickly became a state religion. This political advantage explains the conversions of numerous citizens who had a vested interest in belonging to the same religion as the ruling power.

Islam's force of attraction is also intellectual as this religion represents a coherent system of thought. It offers a plausible answer to people's spiritual quests. This response consists of faith in one God whose revelation is within the reach of the human mind, unlike Christianity with its mysteries. Islamic faith appeals to people's efforts and promises paradise as a reward to deserving Muslims, unlike the gospel which promises salvation not as a reward but as an undeserved grace.

Islamic mysticism, represented by Sufi brotherhoods, offers another possible alternative to people whose hearts are dissatisfied with legalistic Islam or rational theology. Unlike Islamism, mysticism has a low profile but it plays an important part in mission. Nowadays, Muslim mystics attract a significant number of Westerners.

Islam has also been able to contextualize itself by embracing the cultures of the countries where it has spread. In many places the cult of ancestors was replaced by the cult of saints. Polygamy was reduced but not abolished, which also favored the multiplication of the community.

The Muslim community has been growing mainly thanks to the high birth rate of its members, just like the Christian community. The number of new converts is relatively small, except perhaps in Africa among people with traditional religions. Today the heartland of both the Muslim and Christian communities is in the Majority World. Both are confronted with global secularization which increasingly penetrates developing countries.

Muslim converts from a Christian background are put in the fore much more than Christian converts from a Muslim background. The number of believers from a Muslim background has grown steadily over the past three decades. The growth rate of the two communities is actually very similar. Some Muslim apologists argue that of all religions, Islam is the fastest growing religion.

Is Islam a danger to Western civilization? Do Muslims want to convert Western societies to Islam?

There is no doubt that a number of Muslims have a very strong missionary zeal, just as with Christians. These Muslims work to convert Westerners and have some success in societies disenchanted with the cult of money, performance and pleasure. The few Muslims who really believe that Rome will soon become the European capital of a new Islamic empire are victims of wishful thinking. There is good reason to doubt that large numbers of conversions to Islam will occur in democratic societies. Conversion to Islam in great numbers is unlikely because of the critical mind that characterizes influential people in Western societies, and because of terrorism which gives a very bad name to Islam. That said, civilizations of the past collapsed not always because of external attacks but because of evils that plagued them from within. As Christians, we must not let our guard down. We need to take seriously our role of sentinels, "salt of the earth" and "light of the world" (Matt 5:13–14).

What advice would you give non-Muslims who want to live in peace with Muslims?

Non-Muslims must adopt a fair attitude towards Islam and Muslims, holding neither hostility nor naivety. This twofold attitude echoes the command Christ gave to his disciples: "Be as shrewd as snakes and as innocent as doves" (Matt 10:16). You need to be able to criticize Islam without falling into Islamophobia. Muslims should not be stigmatized or marginalized. They are our partners, especially in the fight against Islamist ideology. This battle must be carried out with appropriate "weapons," because the police or military response is not enough. The most effective weapons in the long term are education, socio-economic promotion and the development of critical thinking.

Christians must take their part in this struggle. Muslims are neither our competitors nor our enemies. They are our brothers in humanity and our cousins in faith. We need to show our solidarity with them. We have been through where they are now in terms of religious and cultural crisis. Modernity has put the Western church to the test, and it has emerged freed from the yoke of political power.

Secularity can also be an opportunity for faith communities. God's love, unconditional and universal as demonstrated in Jesus Christ, is at the center of the gospel. This is what makes the gospel stand out when compared to the message of Islam which emphasizes only divine mercy. Deep down in their hearts, everyone seeks love – but Muslims don't find it in their religion. The gospel is a relevant message for them too. To convince them of this message, arguments are not enough; one must live it out with them. It means respecting them unconditionally and avoiding provoking them with inappropriate words or attitudes.

In a sense Muslims are strangers to Christians in the religious sense of the term. They are doubly so in countries where they are immigrants. The Torah specifies that love for neighbors (Lev 19:18) includes love for strangers (Lev 19:33–34). Jesus perfectly linked these two commands in his famous parable of the "Good Samaritan" (Luke 10:25–37). When the time comes, God willing, our testimony will bear fruit.

Is Islam a religion of peace?

Traditional Islamic teaching permits and even commands the use of force under certain conditions, therefore it cannot be said to be just a peaceful religion. However, unbridled violence is not allowed, and jihad must obey certain rules that jihadists tend to ignore.

In a sense, Islam does not exist, only Muslims do. They are, like everyone else, very different from each other. Many are kind and friendly, some are less so. Their attitude towards us depends in part on our attitude towards them. Rather than asking whether Islam is a religion of peace, it might be more helpful to ask how we can be peacemakers with them. In a polarized world potentially exposed to the clash of civilizations, which some consider inevitable, everyone must take responsibility as best they can so that alarmist predictions do not come true.

Does not the moral decay of Western civilization prove the failure of Christianity and its values?

Christian values are those of God's kingdom as the gospels describe them to us. Among these values are the following: justice, love, truth, humility, peace, non-violence, non-discrimination, respect for human life, solidarity, and attention to the vulnerable, especially children.

In many ways, Western societies have evolved over the past decades in a direction far removed from the teaching of Jesus Christ. This is evidenced by ever-growing symptoms such as disintegration of the family unit, atheism, individualism, materialism, hedonism, abortion, sexual relativism, drugs, suicide and violence. It thus appears that Western societies are no longer (as many Muslims still believe) Christian societies. These are post-Christian societies marked by a demographic decline partially offset by migrants. People who claim to be Christian have become a minority, and not all of them are committed Christians. What is even more serious is that the teaching or behavior of some Christian leaders is clearly out of step with the gospel of Jesus Christ.

The growing secularization of Western societies partly explains their moral decadence. This situation is not necessarily worse than when the church was powerful in Europe – there were religious wars, persecutions of people deemed to be heretics, and military expeditions carried out in the name of Christianity, such as the crusades against Muslims in the Middle East and North Africa. Secularization allows those whose religion represents just a cultural or social veneer to distance themselves from the faith more easily. It can also inspire believers to live out their faith and share it with those who are seeking meaning to their lives.

Jesus did not mandate his followers to forcibly establish a Christian society. Christians endeavor to transform individuals and communities by appealing to the conscience of each. Christian influence in Western societies in the past and today should not be underestimated. The contribution of Christians is quite significant in many areas: education, access to medical care, attention to the homeless, the elderly, people with disabilities, the poor, the struggle for the abolition of slavery (old and new), and welcoming migrants. Pope Francis often insists on the need to show solidarity with poor countries from which most migrants come. Christians are also present in the fight for fair trade, respect for the environment, the cancellation of third-world debts, the denunciation of injustice, and the fight against torture, corruption, exploitation and war.

We must try to be fair in our judgment of Western and Muslim societies. Western societies reflect Christian values to some extent: tolerance, human rights, freedom, solidarity, equality, and democracy, although some of these secularized values are now extreme because they have been disconnected from their biblical context. The result is well expressed in the adage that "corruption of the best breeds the worst." Western civilization is therefore ambivalent, and our appreciation of it depends on the angle from which we consider it. The same could be said of Islamic civilization.

What is behind the strained relationships between Jews and Muslims?

The conflict between Muslims and Jews dates to the origins of Islam. Most Arabic-speaking Jews, who held political power in Medina, did not accept Muhammad as a prophet. Bitter religious controversies ensued between the two communities (5:57–64), but it was mainly political issues that fueled the conflict and ended up giving Muslims a clear victory. This religious background does not explain everything, however, as many Jewish communities subsequently lived peacefully for many centuries in Islamic countries. Their lot was generally better than in European Christendom.

The First Zionist Congress held in Basel, Switzerland, in 1897 was decisive in the events of the twentieth century. This congress adopted a program whose objective was defined in these words: "Zionism seeks to establish a home for the Jewish people in Palestine secured under public law." It is not unreasonable to think that Zionism, an essentially nationalist and secular ideology, developed in part in response to the centuries-old persecution of Jews in Europe.

At the end of the nineteenth century, the British government included members who were very sympathetic to the Zionist cause. Among them were politicians strongly influenced by Zionist Christians, inspired by dispensationalist theology. On 2 November 1917, Lord Arthur Balfour, British Foreign Secretary, addressed a letter to Lord L. W. Rothschild, leader of British Jewry and financier of the Zionist movement, in which he declared that "His Majesty's Government views with favour the establishment in Palestine of a national home for the Jewish people and will use their best endeavours to facilitate the achievement of this object."

France and Great Britain divided the countries of the Middle East between themselves in the aftermath of the Great War which saw the collapse of the Ottoman empire. Palestine thus came under British mandate, which favored the colonization of Palestinian lands by Jewish immigrants. World War II saw the persecution of Jews reach a climax under the Nazi regime, which undoubtedly accelerated the creation of the State of Israel in 1948 in Palestine. The UN swiftly sanctioned the creation of the Jewish State without the inhabitants of Palestine being able to exercise "the right to self-determination," even though this right is enshrined in the UN Charter. The Palestinians were enraged by the turn of these events which deprived them of an independent State over the whole territory of Palestine. Most of them took refuge in neighboring countries (Jordan, Lebanon, Syria, Egypt) and some migrated to other parts of the world.

Arab and Muslim peoples continue to have a strong sense of solidarity with the Palestinian people. For them, the Palestinians were unjustly compelled to pay a heavy price for the age-long persecution suffered by Jews in Europe, a persecution in which they had no part. Negotiations between the Israeli government and the Palestine Liberation Organization (whose ideology is nationalist and secular) have failed to give the Palestinian people a proper homeland. This has resulted in the consolidation of jihadist ideologies, especially among hardline Palestinian groups. These groups reactivate qur'anic texts hostile to Jews and point out that Jerusalem (entirely occupied by Israel following the Six-Day War in 1967) is the third holiest site of Islam, after Mecca and Medina. Arabs and Muslims continue to call Jerusalem *al-Quds*, "the holy place," because, according to Islamic tradition, one night the Prophet had a (spiritual) experience of ascending to heaven via Jerusalem.[7]

As long as the Palestinian-Israeli conflict persists, the Middle East will remain an unstable region, fueling extremist ideologies. However, in some Arab countries these days, political and economic interests seem to take precedence over other considerations. In 2020 several countries decided to normalize their relations with Israel – Bahrain, UAE, Sudan and Morocco (nearly 800,000 Jews of Moroccan background live in Israel today). Egypt and Jordan had already signed peace treaties with the Jewish State in 1979 and 1994, respectively. However, Arab peoples do not necessarily approve of the policies of their leaders, and Muslims continue to feel strongly for the Palestinian people, victims of the Zionist ideology and the biased policies of the great powers.

Why do Christians support the oppression of the Palestinian people by the State of Israel?

Most Christians do not unconditionally support the policies of the State of Israel. They do not identify this contemporary State with Israel of the Bible. Those who endorse these policies are mainly evangelical Christians in Western countries (today most Christians live in the Majority World).

Christians who support Israel do so for three main reasons. First, they have a lot of sympathy, and perhaps guilt too, towards the Jewish people because of the Holocaust of World War II in which the Nazi regime wiped out nearly six million Jews (as well as other minorities). Second, they believe that God promised to give the land of Canaan to Abraham and his offspring forever when he made a covenant with him (Gen 15:18–21). Third, they are misinformed about the historical events that led to the creation of the State of Israel, and they are largely ignorant of the suffering endured by the Palestinian people since then.

The theology of Zionist Christians, which relies mainly on Old Testament texts to justify their support for Israel, is far removed from the teaching of the four Gospels. Jesus foretold the destruction of Jerusalem and the exile of its

---

7. The qur'anic text alludes to this nocturnal journey (17:1) which is recounted in detail in several accounts of the Hadith; see Bukhari, *Manaqib al-Ansar* (Virtues of the *Ansar*), 43.

inhabitants because of their rejection of the Messiah, and he made no promise of their return to the land, much less of the political restoration of their nation (Luke 21:20–24). In the Old Testament, the themes of the Promised Land, the Chosen People, and the Temple belong to the particular historical context of the Old Covenant. They announce, beyond themselves, the coming of the Messiah, Jesus Christ, and the establishment of a new covenant which fulfills all the promises God had made to Israel (Matt 8:10–12; Matt 21:42–44; Luke 22:20; John 2:18–19; Acts 1:6–7).

When a country's constitution is closely associated with a specific religion, ideology or ethnic group, religious and ethnic minorities are bound to suffer. At best, these minorities are discriminated against, and at worst, they are oppressed and even persecuted. This was true of the so-called Christian nations during the middle-ages. Currently, the regime of European nations is in reality secular even in countries where there is an established church which has formal connections with the state (e.g. UK, Denmark). Today, religious and ethnic minorities continue to be discriminated against in many countries (e.g. Islamic Republics, Israel, China). A genuinely secular regime, free of any ethnic or religious affiliation, offers more favorable conditions for true democracy and the protection of human rights.

Many Westerners perceive Israel as a secular democracy, yet the reality is very different, at least for non-Jews. Any Jew in the world has the right to migrate to Israel while Palestinians living abroad whose parents or grandparents were born in Palestine have no right to live in this land. On 19 July 2018, the Knesset (Israeli parliament) passed a fundamental law which makes Israel "the Nation-State of the Jewish people." This law reinforces, for Muslim and Christian Palestinians with Israeli nationality (who make up about 20 percent of the population), the feeling that they are treated as second-class citizens, as if they are foreigners in the land where they were born.

Whatever their feelings or beliefs about Israel, Christians are called to seek justice and peace where there is conflict. It means showing solidarity with the Palestinian people, to whom the Israeli leadership continues to deny the right to a genuine homeland. Israeli policy is paradoxical when we consider how much the Jewish people struggled to have a homeland of their own. Palestinians are the largest refugee and stateless people in the world. Christians need also to be sensitive to the suffering of Israeli civilians targeted by terrorist attacks. Jesus is unambiguous in his condemnation of violence: "For all who draw the sword will die by the sword" (Matt 26:52).

Jewish prophets were the first to criticize their people when they strayed away from the teaching of the Torah, especially by oppressing the non-Israelites living among them (Jer 22:3; Mal 3:5). Today many courageous Jews speak out against the occupation of Palestinian land and the oppression of Palestinians who demand that their rights be respected.

Among Israeli organizations very critical of Israel's politics is B'Tselem, "The Israeli Information Center for Human Rights in the Occupied Territories."[8] On 12 January 2021, B'Tselem released a well-documented report titled "A Regime of Jewish Supremacy from the Jordan River to the Mediterranean Sea: This Is Apartheid." The report explains the meaning, according to international conventions, of the word apartheid: "'Apartheid' has long been an independent term, entrenched in international conventions, referring to a regime's organizing principle: systematically promoting the dominance of one group over another and working to cement it." Closely examining the very different realities faced by Israelis on one side and Palestinians on the other, the report underscores the institutional discrimination between the two peoples. It concludes that "the bar for labeling the Israeli regime as apartheid has been met."[9] Organizations like B'Tselem honor the outstanding heritage that Israel received in the Bible which should challenge all who claim this heritage.

Those who unconditionally support Israel do not contribute to a just and peaceful settlement of the conflict between the two peoples. Sometimes we hear that anti-Semitism and anti-Zionism are in fact the same thing. This argument is obviously intended to protect Israel from any criticism, even legitimate, of its policies towards the Palestinians. Anti-Semitism is hatred of Jews, just as Islamophobia is hatred of Muslims. In contrast, anti-Zionism is the political opposition to the Zionist hegemonic and expansionist ideology of the Jewish State. The two terms are different and it is wrong to claim that they are interchangeable. We recognize, however, that there is a real danger of moving from a debate of ideas to hostility towards those whose ideology is being challenged.

---

8. The Center, founded in 1989, explains on its website that its name, which means "in the image of," was chosen by its Jewish founder, then a member of the Knesset, in connection with the text of Genesis 1:27 ("God created mankind in his own image, in the image of God he created them"), in order to express the Jewish and universal moral imperative to respect and support human rights for everyone. https://www.btselem.org/about_btselem.

9. Both quotes are found here: https://www.btselem.org/publications/fulltext/202101_this_is_apartheid/, under the section "No to Apartheid: That Is Our Struggle." In its most recent World Report (published on 2 February 2022) Amnesty International considers that "Israel imposes a system of oppression and domination against Palestinians across all areas under its control: in Israel and the OPT [Occupied Palestinian Territories], and against Palestinian refugees, in order to benefit Jewish Israelis. This ammounts to apartheid as prohibited in international law". Human Rights Watch reaches similar conclusions in its own annual report (see amnesty.org and hrw.org).

Violence always feeds violence and increases suffering for all. Sadly, this is particularly the case in the Arab-Israeli conflict, which continues to claim many victims on both sides. Thankfully, more and more Israelis and Palestinians are engaging in non-violent actions for a just and peaceful resolution of the conflict. They really need our support so that one day Jews and Palestinians may enjoy the same rights on the same land.

Why are most Islamic countries poor, underdeveloped and ruled by authoritarian regimes?

Not all Muslim-majority countries are poor, underdeveloped and ruled by authoritarian regimes. Some are very wealthy and developed (e.g. Malaysia, Gulf States). Islamic solidarity would require these countries to invest their petrodollars in developing Islamic countries rather than in Western banks and large international corporations. If they did, they would significantly contribute to improving the lives of many Muslim populations.

It is not always pertinent to associate poverty and underdevelopment with religions or religious practices specific to a particular context. Many poor and developing countries are not Islamic. In fact, a number of overwhelmingly Christian-majority countries face similar socio-economic issues (e.g. Haiti, Philippines, Central African Republic).

Material poverty is not in itself evil. Many poor people are actually happier than rich people. Wealth is neither good nor bad. The question is: "How did you get rich and what do you do with your wealth?" Poverty and wealth expose us to different temptations: corruption, exploitation, a sense of self-sufficiency, power and invulnerability, theft, pride, contempt for others, etc. In the book of Proverbs we find this beautiful prayer:

> Two things I ask of you, LORD;
> do not refuse me before I die:
> Keep falsehood and lies far from me;
> give me neither poverty nor riches,
> but give me only my daily bread.
> Otherwise, I may have too much and disown you
> and say, "Who is the Lord?"
> Or I may become poor and steal,
> and so dishonor the name of my God. (Prov 30:7–9)

A number of Islamic countries are poor because they have few natural resources (Mali, Mauritania, Niger). Their hot and dry climate, and the increasing desertification of their land, make agriculture difficult and do not stimulate the development of tourism. Therefore, it is not surprising that these countries have a harder time than others lifting their populations from the poverty line. Challenges, in particular economic ones, faced by Islamic countries have various internal causes (e.g. bad governance, corruption) as well as external ones. Among the latter is the fact that Western countries and large multinationals often impose their rules on the global economy. For instance, the price of coffee is decided not by countries where coffee is grown (such as Ivory Coast, Ethiopia, Brazil, Yemen) but by multinational corporations.

There may be some correlation between economic hardship and religious beliefs when Muslims, or Christians, misinterpret their Scriptures. Muslims strongly believe in God's sovereignty, which leads some to have a fatalistic mindset at the expense of personal responsibility. Like any religion, Islam has gone through periods of reform and stagnation.

Islamic thought has gradually become fossilized for several reasons. Islamic civilization was prosperous and flourishing at a time when Europe was much less so (between the eighth and fourteenth centuries). Islam has given rise to great scholars in several fields, such as mathematics, medicine, astronomy, historiography, sociology and philosophy. Among Muslim scholars who exercised a great influence on the development of science in Europe, we find the mathematician al-Khwarizmi (AH 235/AD 850), the physician Ibn Sina known in the West as Avicenna (AH 428/AD 1037), the physicist Ibn al-Haytham, a.k.a. Alhazen (AH 430/AD 1039), the philosopher Ibn Rushd known as Averroes (AH 595/AD 1198), and the sociologist Ibn Khaldun (AH 808/AD 1406). Many of their works were translated into Latin and studied in European universities. Much of philosophical and scientific work was first translated from Greek into Arabic, then into Latin, before reaching medieval Europe. Muslim Spain has played a decisive role in the transmission of this rich heritage, thanks to the harmonious and fruitful collaboration of Jewish, Christian and Muslim scholars.

Human development is not only measured by technological and scientific progress. Civilization is not just about freedom, human rights and democracy. Spiritual growth and personal development are integral to the fullness of human life. Moral values are inseparable from human activity. Western civilization can certainly boast of tremendous success in many areas, impressive efficiency, and great economic prosperity. But it is also marked by the breakdown of its moral and spiritual values. Taken as a whole, as we have already indicated, its record is a mixed one.

Part Two

Islam and Christianity

6

The Corruption of the Bible: Myth or Reality?

The second part of this book will examine key theological issues that have been debated between Christians and Muslims from the beginning of Islam to the present day. The two religions are based on two holy books held to be divinely revealed, the Bible and the Qur'an, and regarded as God's word respectively by Christians and Muslims.

Islamic theology challenges the reliability of the biblical text. We must therefore begin by looking into Islamic criticisms of the Bible. Indeed, the credibility of Scripture is a prerequisite for any meaningful discussion on the person of Jesus Christ and his mission (ch. 7) as well as on God with the two versions of monotheism offered by the biblical and the qur'anic traditions – trinitarian monotheism on one side, unitarian monotheism on the other (ch. 8). Salvation of humankind through forgiveness of sins is at the center of the gospel (Luke 24:47). What concepts of salvation do the two Scriptures teach and what divine attributes are they based on? Chapter 9 will attempt to answer these questions in Islam and Christianity.

The final chapter of the book will stress that, despite the crucial theological differences between Christianity and Islam, there are many convergences between Christians and Muslims in terms of their religious beliefs and ethical principles. This common ground forms a solid base for Islamic-Christian cooperation aimed at making a significant contribution to the well-being of the society in which we live.

"The People of the Book"

Judaism and Christianity are two revealed religions, according to Islam, both based on Holy Scriptures – respectively the Torah, given to Moses, and the Gospel, preached by Jesus. The Qur'an also mentions the *Zabour* of David, a word that probably refers to the book of Psalms. The expressions "Old Testament" and "New Testament" are therefore alien to the Qur'an as well as to the vast majority of Muslims. Muslims are familiar with the biblical stories that are told in the Qur'an, which mentions about thirty biblical characters and prophets, although the narratives concerning them do not reproduce the biblical text exactly. In fact, there is no direct quotation from the Bible in the Qur'an, with perhaps just one exception.[1]

Bible stories are repeated in the Qur'an in a shortened form and with a typically Islamic perspective. Anything in these stories that does not seem to agree with Islamic faith, especially monotheism, is ignored. The mission of the Prophet is integrated into the biblical history of revelation. Thus, the two qur'anic accounts of the Annunciation made to Mary (3:45–48; 19:16–21) speak of the virgin conception of Jesus but without describing him as "the Son of the Most High" as the Gospel of Luke does (Luke 1:26–38). Likewise, Abraham, as a monotheistic believer, is the father of all Muslims according to the Qur'an (22:78). He was neither a Jew nor a Christian because he lived before Moses, the founder of Judaism, and of course long before Christ. In fact, Abraham was a Muslim before his time and his most worthy heirs are Prophet Muhammad and his community (2:65–68).

For Islam, Abraham's two sons, Ishmael and Isaac, were both prophets. From the elder brother came the Arab people and from the younger came the Jewish people. Jesus was the last Jewish prophet sent to Jews just as Muhammad was the last Arab prophet sent to Arabs. Abraham, with the help of his son Ishmael, built the Ka'ba temple in Mecca. Both asked God to send a messenger to their offspring to instruct them in the truth. For Muslims, the coming of Muhammad represents the fulfillment of this prayer:

> Our Lord! Send among our people after us an Apostle of their own kin, who will recite to them Your revelations, teach them the Book and the Wisdom and purge them from evil. For You are Almighty and Wise. (2:129)

---

1. Sūra 21:105 says: "Before this, We (God) wrote in the Psalms after the Reminder: 'My righteous servants shall inherit the earth.'" This verse probably quotes Psalm 37:11 and 29, which is almost certainly behind one of Jesus's beatitudes: "Blessed are the meek, for they will inherit the earth" (Matt 5:5). As for the "Reminder" (*Dhikr*), it refers probably to the Torah of Moses.

The divine origin of the Bible (Old and New Testaments) is therefore recognized by Islam, at least in theory. However, Muslim writers challenge the reliability of biblical texts for a reason easy to understand: the teachings of Judaism and Christianity contradict the doctrine of Islam on very important points. How can we explain the discrepancies between various Scriptures, all given by God? This is precisely the role assigned by Muslim theologians to the theory of the falsification of the Bible. Christians have no difficulty in explaining the discrepancies since for them the Qur'an does not represent a divine revelation, God having crowned his revelation with the incarnation of his Son (Heb 1:1–3).[2]

Was Muhammad Foretold in the Bible?

Historically the first divisive issue between the Muslim community and the other two monotheistic communities was Muhammad's prophethood: Was he really sent by God? According to the Qur'an, Muhammad was announced in the two parts of the Bible:

> I shall ordain mercy for . . . those who follow the Apostle, the unlettered, *ummi*, Prophet, whom they find mentioned in their own [Scriptures], in the Torah and the Gospel. (7:157)[3]

Jesus himself is said to have predicted the coming of Muhammad:

> O Son of Israel! I am the Apostle of God sent to you, to confirm the Torah and to announce to you an Apostle who will come after me and whose name will be Ahmad. (61:6)[4]

---

2. Readers who want to delve into the issue of falsification of the Bible according to Islamic teaching are invited to read chapters 2 to 5 and 20 of my book, *Faith to Faith: Christianity and Islam in Dialogue*.

3. The word *ummi* is understood by most Muslim authors to mean illiterate, a person who cannot read or write. The same word is found in other qur'anic texts which clearly refer to religious illiteracy, namely, ignorance of the Holy Scriptures. This ignorance characterized the Arab people who, unlike the people of Israel, did not receive any Scripture prior to the Qur'an (3:20, 75; 62:2). This ignorance is also ascribed to certain Jews who misunderstand the meaning of their own Scriptures (2:78). Muhammad Hamidullah is among a few Muslim exegetes who understand Muhammad's illiteracy in a religious sense. In his French translation of the Qur'an, "the *ummi* prophet" in verses 7:157–158 is understood as "the gentile prophet," the one from the Gentiles, that is the "Nations" or the "pagans" (see Rom 1:16; 15:8–9). In this sense Paul considered himself, as M. Hamidullah points out, "the apostle to the Gentiles" (Rom 15:15–18; Gal 2:8).

4. The name "Ahmad" is a variation of "Muhammad." Both names mean "the one worthy of praise."

The Muslim community expected the People of the Book to recognize in Muhammad a prophet sent by God, but they did not. Jews and Christians found no predictions about the coming of an Arab prophet in their respective Scriptures. It is worth noting that the two texts just quoted do not refer to any biblical text in support of their claim. Muslim theologians responded to Jews and to Christians as follows: "You do not find in your Scriptures any mention of our prophet? Then they must have been falsified!"

Muslim theologians subsequently looked in the Qur'an for texts that could support their charge against the authenticity of the Bible. They found about twenty verses that criticize the way the People of the Book deal with their Scriptures.[5] These verses refer to Jews rather than Christians. Indeed, after Muhammad's migration to Medina, the Muslim community found itself in open conflict with the Jews of that city.

The most significant of these texts are the four verses which use the verb "falsify" (*harrafa*) (2:75; 4:46; 5:13, 44). None of these four verses explicitly mentions the biblical text. One text speaks of "the Word of God" (2:75), which could refer to the Torah, the Gospel and even the Qur'an, as Tabari points out. If it is the Qur'an, a plausible hypothesis, this would mean that the Jews distorted the word of God preached by the Prophet in order to discredit him.

Assuming it is indeed the biblical text that has been altered, several unanswered questions remain. These texts say nothing about the time when the falsification would have occurred or how the falsification was done. They are also obscure as to who carried it out, and what the objective and motive were. Muslim authors have tried to answer these questions which are related to each other.

Two Theories about the Corruption of the Bible

Very few Muslims know that there are two schools among Muslim scholars about the corruption of the Bible. The first group of theologians believe the corruption involved the biblical text itself. This is what has come to be called "textual (or literal) corruption." According to the second group, the falsification means giving wrong interpretation to the text, which has not changed. Thus, "the falsification of meaning" is the result of bad interpretations given by the Jewish and Christian scholars to their sacred texts. Theologians who subscribe to the theory of textual falsification include Ibn Hazm, Juwayni and, to some extent, Ibn Taymiyya. Maurice Bucaille, a French doctor converted to Islam,

---

5. See Qur'an 2:12, 59, 79, 135, 144–146, 174; 3:65–67, 71, 78, 187; 5:15; 6:91.

has made their views very popular in a best-selling book first published in 1979 (see bibliography). Among scholars who adopt the theory of falsification through misinterpretation we find Razi, Baqillani, Avicenna, Ghazali, and closer to us Muhammad 'Abduh.

Corruption of the Text

Many Muslim authors trace the falsification of the Torah back to the invasion and destruction of Jerusalem (587 BC) by Nebuchadnezzar, king of Babylon (cf. 2 Kgs 24–25). For them, this tragic event resulted in the destruction of the temple and the Torah manuscripts. Upon their return from exile, the Jews attempted to recover their Scripture from memory. Ezra, who was the chief agent of this enterprise, was not a prophet, hence his work was faulty. This would explain the unreliability of the Torah, its many internal inconsistencies, and its contradictions with history, geography, and especially with the teaching of the Qur'an.[6]

The major flaw of the reconstituted Torah is that the texts announcing the coming of Muhammad are no longer there. According to most Muslim theologians, the biblical text was changed not deliberately but due to historical circumstances; however, some argue that the texts were intentionally altered to remove the passages about the coming of Muhammad. This deletion therefore took place during the Prophet's time to justify his rejection by the Jews.

According to proponents of textual falsification, the evidence that the Gospel has been tampered with is obvious. The Qur'an attests that God revealed to Jesus only one Gospel, yet according to Christians there are four Gospels, none of which is ascribed to Jesus. These books were written decades after Jesus ascended to heaven. In addition, they were written in Greek whereas Jesus's language was Aramaic. This would explain the unreliability of the Gospels and the many contradictions they contain.[7]

---

6. Contradictions include the length of the stay of the Israelites in Egypt (Gen 15:13; Exod 12:40), the unlikely existence of the first two rivers of Eden (Gen 2:10–14), the age of the patriarchs (not the same in the Hebrew text and the Greek text of the Septuagint), and even the creation of Adam in God's image (Gen 1:26–27). In the Qur'an nothing in creation is like God, not even human beings (42:11).

7. Texts in support of literal falsification include the two genealogies of Jesus (Matt 1:1–17; Luke 3:23–38), the time when Jesus expelled the merchants from the temple (Mark 11:15–17; John 2:13–17), the attitude of the two robbers crucified next to Jesus (Matt 27:38–44; Luke 23:39–43), Jesus's declaration that he did not come to abolish the law of Moses (Matt 5:17) which goes against what he said about divorce and the law of retaliation (Matt 5:31–32, 38–48).

Some Muslims today claim that the true Gospel is "the Gospel of Barnabas" which despite its title has nothing to do with one of the apostle Paul's companions (cf. Acts 13–14). The alleged author of this document is called Barnabas and replaces Thomas in the list of the twelve apostles. This so-called Gospel confirms Islamic doctrine on many points, in particular, Jesus's repeated prediction concerning the coming of a prophet whose name will be "Muhammad."

Muhammad is described in the Gospel of Barnabas as the "Messiah," whereas the Qur'an reserves this title for Jesus. Scholars who have closely studied this writing all agree that it is a fake, probably written in the sixteenth century by an Italian convert to Islam. The only manuscript we have of this pseudo-gospel is in Italian and is kept in a library in Vienna. Moreover, the fact that none of the ancient Muslim theologians mentions this document confirms that it was written relatively recently.

The other books of the New Testament (Acts, the Epistles, and Revelation) simply have no place in God's word according to Muslim scholars. As the authors were not prophets, their writings are not divinely inspired and therefore cannot be trusted.

Many Muslims consider that the true founder of Christianity was not Jesus but Paul, the author of much of the New Testament, yet Paul was not one of Jesus's twelve Apostles. For them Paul has turned Christianity from a Semitic monotheistic religion into a tri-theistic religion strongly influenced by Greek thought. He also invented the doctrine of salvation by faith in the atoning death of Jesus.

Proponents of textual falsification highlight that there are too many Bible manuscripts with key differences between them. They also point out that a lot of contradictions can be found in various translations of the Bible. Some highlight the fact that some Bibles have sixty-six books while others have eight more. This is clear evidence for them that the Scriptures have been corrupted.

Textual falsification advocates disregard qur'anic texts which seem to give credit to the biblical text. The Qur'an says it confirms the Torah and the Gospel (2:89, 91, 97, 101; 3:3, 81; 5:48; 6:92; 35:31). Does it make sense for the Qur'an to confirm falsified Scriptures? The Torah and the Gospel are described in the Qur'an as "light and guidance" (5:46). Can corrupt Scriptures be described in this way? Muslims are called to believe in the Torah and the Gospel (3:84, 119; 4:136). Jews and Christians too have an obligation to comply with the rulings of their Scriptures (5:43, 45, 47) and to follow their teachings (5:66, 68). These are strange ways to talk about "falsified" Scriptures!

Corruption of the Meaning

Some renowned Muslim theologians dispute the theory of textual falsification and adopt that of the falsification of the meaning. Proponents of this second theory make theological and rational arguments. God's word, they say, must reflect the character of its divine author. As God is truthful, his word must also be truthful and therefore trustworthy. They hold that the theory of textual falsification undermines divine truthfulness. According to the Qur'an, God has pledged to protect the veracity of his word: "There is nothing that can alter the Words of God" (6:34; cf. 10:64; 15:9; 18:27).

If God did not watch over his word to preserve it from all corruption, asks Razi, what can guarantee us that the Qur'an itself has not been altered due to the vicissitudes of history? 'Abduh uses a rational argument: it is highly unlikely that a religious community manipulates its own sacred texts. Jews and Christians were hostile to each other, and if some had tampered with their Scriptures, they would have immediately been denounced by others.

Finally, the texts of the Torah and the Gospel were widely disseminated throughout the Mediterranean region. Had the two communities wanted to modify their Scriptures to remove the texts concerning the coming of Muhammad, says 'Abduh, on a practical level they would not have been able to accomplish it. Another major argument of proponents of alteration by misinterpretation is this: without God's commitment to preserve his word from corruption, his decision to reveal that word makes no sense, is absurd and thwarts his truthfulness.

Proponents of textual falsification do not claim that the entire biblical text has been altered. They consider that large portions of this text have remained unchanged, which include prophetic passages about the coming of Muhammad. Conversely, proponents of falsification by misinterpretation do not entirely rule out that a very limited number of passages could have been modified, for instance, the ones about the coming of Muhammad.

All Muslim theologians seek to interpret biblical texts in a way that makes them agree with the qur'anic message. They resort to metaphorical and rational interpretations to deny the divinity of Christ and the divine Trinity. As for the announced mission of Muhammad, the prophecy of Deuteronomy concerning the "new Moses" is often quoted (Deut 18:15–18). In this prophecy God tells Moses that he will send to the Israelites "from among their brothers" a prophet "like you." It is argued that Arabs and Jews are brothers since their respective ancestors (Ishmael and Isaac) were brothers. Muhammad, it is claimed, is much more like Moses than Jesus is: both were born in an ordinary way and died naturally, both were legislators, prophets and political leaders at the same time.

Christians agree that certain traits are common to Moses and Muhammad; however, Moses's mission foreshadowed that of Jesus on several points. The first freed his people from the slavery of Egypt, the second freed his from greater slavery, that of sin and death. The first was God's spokesperson, the second was himself God's word. In the context of Deuteronomy, the brothers of the Israelites are other Israelites as opposed to foreigners (cf. Deut 17:14–15). Jesus knew he was the prophet announced by Moses (John 5:46). His disciples also knew he was the new Moses, notably Peter who quoted the text of Deuteronomy 18 in one of his speeches (John 1:45; Acts 3:20–22).

The texts of the New Testament most often quoted in favor of the coming of Muhammad are the ones about "the Paraclete," the Comforter, the Helper, the Counsel for the defense, the One who will come to the aid of Jesus's disciples after his departure (John 14:16, 26; 15:26; 16:7). Muslim authors, including Maurice Bucaille, argue that the Greek word *parakleetos* may very well have replaced (inadvertently or intentionally) a very similar Greek word, namely *periklytos*, which, translated into Arabic, could mean "one who is praiseworthy," that is Muhammad. However, no manuscript of the Gospel of John has *periklytos*. Furthermore, Jesus clearly identifies "the Paraclete" in the Gospel as "the Spirit of truth" and "the Holy Spirit." He also asked his disciples not to leave Jerusalem because the promise he made to them would be fulfilled "within a few days" (Acts 1:5; cf. Luke 24:49). It was indeed fulfilled ten days after Jesus ascended to heaven (Acts 2:1–4).

The following section will look at a specific issue that illustrates the difference between Christian and Muslim theologies in the ways they define the reliability of divine revelation in scripture.

Are Prophets Sinless?

For all Muslim theologians, biblical texts that report sins attributed to certain prophets pose a serious problem. According to Islamic doctrine, because prophets are God's messengers, they must be blameless and even infallible. They enjoy what is known as "prophetic impeccability" or sinlessness. Prophets would discredit themselves if they committed sins and would seriously damage the glory of the One who sent them. Prophets are also spiritual leaders of their communities; as such, they are role models for their people and must set an example through their conduct as well as through their words. Therefore, they do not commit serious sins, at least not after they were called to the prophetic ministry.

We do find in the Bible many accounts that expose the immoral behavior of great men of God in certain circumstances: Noah's drunkenness (Gen 9:20–21), Abraham's lie about his wife Sarah (Gen 12:11–13), Lot's offer to his fellow citizens to sleep with his daughters in order to protect his guests (Gen 19:8), the dishonorable treatment of this same Lot by his daughters (Gen 19:31–35), the outrageously wicked attitude of Judah towards Tamar, his daughter-in-law (Gen 38:11–26), the murder of an Egyptian man by Moses (Exod 2:11–12), and David's adultery and act of murder (2 Sam 11).[8] Jesus's miracle at the wedding feast at Cana (John 2:1–11) is inconceivable for Muslims (since Islam forbids consumption of alcohol) as is his apparently uncharitable attitude towards the Syro-Canaanite woman (Matt 15:26). Indeed, according to the Qur'an, unlike any prophet, Jesus was without sin from his birth to the end (19:19).

Some of these stories are echoed in the Qur'an. Qur'anic texts that reference sin committed by prophets are interpreted by the Muslim authors in such a way as to protect the honor of God's messengers. Thus, Moses had not yet received the prophetic call when he killed the Egyptian (28:15–16), nor Adam when he disobeyed divine command (7:23). Abraham did not lie when he told Pharaoh that Sarah was his sister, for she was his sister in faith. Lot invited his fellow citizens to marry single women belonging to their people. He called them "my daughters" metaphorically because as a prophet he was like a father to them (11:78). Noah's sin (different from that mentioned in Genesis) was unimportant (11:41–47), like the sin committed by Muhammad, which nevertheless earned him a rebuke from God (80:1–10). As for David, the Qur'an casts a modest veil over his sin and presents it as a simple test (38:21–24).

The Qur'an (and Muslim exegetes) therefore exonerates the prophets unlike the biblical text, which, in the eyes of Muslim theologians, shows that the Bible is unreliable, or at least misunderstood. The Qur'an was revealed to restore the truthfulness of the Bible and correct its misinterpretations.

Islamic reinterpretations miss the way in which the biblical text shows its reliability. After all why would the Jewish author of the first book of Samuel report facts that dishonor Israel's greatest king? Would it not have been more advantageous for him and his people to protect David's honor by covering up these facts? Shouldn't national chauvinism have led the author to gloss over the misdeeds of the great king? The fact that the author relates this dark page of David's life indicates paradoxically that his story is true. This shows that

---

8. Surprisingly, the conduct of King Solomon, whose wives and concubines numbered in hundreds (1 Kgs 11:2–4), and who had departed from the Lord at the end of his life, does not seem to have caught the attention of the Muslim authors.

the author does not care about the reputation of a man, however famous he is; the author's only concern is to speak the truth even when it is very hard to hear. The intention of this story is to warn us against all temptation and to encourage us to repent when we commit sin, following the example of David, who wrote one of the most beautiful psalms on repentance in the Bible (Ps 51).

It might be rationally desirable for prophets to be sinless so as not to undermine their message in any way. However, the very fact that they were not sinless bears witness to the reality of human condition and is consistent with the biblical revelation that humans are not just sin*ners* but sin*ful*. Our spiritual misery should prompt us to place all our hope in divine mercy. Jesus is the only prophet who was without sin. His encounter with the Syro-Canaanite woman, when studied carefully, shows his compassion and even his admiration for this foreign woman. Moreover, consumption of wine is not condemned in the Bible, unlike drunkenness (Ps 104:15; Eph 5:18).

Two Very Different Concepts of Revelation

Careful examination of the two Islamic theories about the alteration of the Bible clearly shows that these theories are based on a deep misunderstanding of the biblical notion of revelation. Muslim authors apply to the Bible the Islamic concept of revelation, which is very different from the Christian concept. For Muslims the Qur'an in Arabic is the word of God, word for word, hence the extreme reverence they have for the book. Their reverence is so strong that the Qur'an, which is only God's word when it is in Arabic, is not divided into paragraphs, has no subtitles or punctuation marks or footnotes, etc., so as not to add anything human to the divine word.

In contrast, for Christians, the Bible is God's word transmitted through its human writers. God is the ultimate author of the biblical text (2 Tim 3:16), which guarantees its authenticity. This text was not dictated by an angel (as is the case with the Qur'an); the Spirit of God inspired it. This means that God, far from bypassing the human writers, has fully used their personalities, their intelligence, their sensitivity, and their emotions, as well as the cultural background and historical context of the recipients.

The use of various languages in the Bible helps clarify what revelation means for Christians. The Old Testament is in Hebrew because it was written by Jews for the people of Israel.[9] It was translated into Greek a few centuries

---

9. Parts of the Old Testament are in Aramaic because they were written after the Jews came back from their exile in Babylon where they started to speak Aramaic.

later by Jews residing in Egypt when Greek began to spread around the Mediterranean Sea. This translation, known as the Septuagint (LXX) because of the (approximate) number of its translators, includes eight books the Hebrew Bible does not have.[10] The New Testament is in Greek because the gospel is a universal message, and Greek was the most common language when it was written in the first century AD.

It thus appears that the biblical languages are not sacred languages. They do not play at all the same role as the Qur'an's Arabic language. For the Qur'an, Arabic is an integral part of the revelation and its supernatural standard is one of the main proofs for Muslims of the divine origin of the Book. This "qur'anic miracle" is especially convincing for Muslims because they believe the Prophet was illiterate. Biblical languages are only the vehicle of revelation. What matters most is the conveyed message, which has as its ultimate object God's revelation in Christ: "The Spirit of prophecy [who] bears testimony to Jesus" (Rev 19:10). The Old Testament foretells the coming of Christ and the New Testament declares the fulfillment of this announcement.[11]

While Muhammad is seldom mentioned in the Qur'an (his name appears only four times) we meet Christ on every page of the Gospels. Christ is at the heart of the gospel. The unity and diversity of biblical revelation are illustrated by the duality of the *gospel*, as the one message preached by Christ, and as the four *Gospels*, namely the four writings that bear witness to Christ, his identity and his mission. The Christian concept of inspiration explains why we can speak of the Gospel *according* to Matthew, Mark, Luke and John as well as of the Gospel *of* Matthew, Mark, Luke and John. The Gospels give us four different and complementary portraits of Jesus that can be described in broad terms as follows: Jesus is the Messiah of Israel promised by the prophets (Matthew), the tireless Servant who came to help the needy (Mark), the compassionate man who identifies with all people and with the poorest in particular (Luke), and the Son of God who gives himself out of love for the salvation of humanity (John).

These four portraits are inspired by the life, teaching and deeds of Christ. The reality of the reported facts and words is as important as how each evangelist reports and interprets them. The Gospels are therefore not historical accounts in the modern sense of the term, they are faith testimonies whose

---

10. Catholic translations of the Bible include these eight books. All of them belong to the Old Testament and are described as "deuterocanonical." The Protestant Bibles retain only the sixty-six "canonical" books of the Hebrew Bible, the eight others are considered "apocryphal" (not authentic).

11. See Mic 5:2 with Matt 2:1–6; Isa 61:1–2 with Luke 4:16–21; Isa 52:13–53:12 with Acts 8:29–35; Ps 16:8–11 and 110:1 with Acts 2:22–36.

theological purpose matters more than historical accuracy (in the modern sense of the term). Readers of the Gospels will therefore seek above all to discover who Christ is and his message.

According to Christian tradition, of the four evangelists, two were among Jesus's twelve Apostles (Matthew and John), a third was one of his disciples (Mark) – very close to an apostle (Peter) – and the fourth one (Luke) opens his Gospel by emphasizing that his account is based on trustworthy eyewitnesses (Luke 1:1–4). The central importance of Christ in the Scriptures is such that Christians are not so much "the People of Scripture" (as the Qur'an calls them) but the People of the Word, namely God's eternal word, made man in the person of Jesus Christ (John 1:1–2, 14). This is why the disciples of Christ are pleased to be called "Christians" (Acts 11:26) while Muslims do not like being called (as they used to be) "Mohammedans."[12]

The Muslims who were close to Muhammad are known as his "companions" and those who wrote down his message are not considered prophets like him. It is quite different with Christ's disciples who were commissioned by him to proclaim the gospel (Matt 28:18–20; Luke 24:44–48). The disciples proclaimed this message verbally and some put it in writing in the four Gospels.

After his ascension to heaven and his enthronement with God, Christ chose a persecutor of his disciples to make him an apostle, Saul of Tarsus, who became the apostle Paul. Christ appeared to Saul as he was on his way to Damascus to arrest the church leaders in that city and bring them to Jerusalem to be judged by the Jewish authorities. Saul was charged with proclaiming Christ especially to non-Jews (Acts 9:1–16). God has the right to call through his Son whomever he wants to make his messenger. Is God not sovereign in his decisions? The apostle Paul was therefore one of Christ's apostles; he did see the risen Christ on the road to Damascus (Acts 22:6–16; 26:12–18) and later in his visions (2 Cor 12:2–4). With his colleagues, he founded several churches around the Mediterranean. His thirteen letters to some of these churches and his associates are part of the New Testament. The teaching developed in these letters is in perfect accord with the foundational teaching of Jesus in the Gospels. It is to one of his companions, the evangelist Luke, that we owe the book of Acts and its account about the birth of the church and its expansion

---

12. The Qur'an and most Arabic-speaking Muslims refer to Christians as *nasaara*, a term of obscure origin which may be linked to the city of Nazareth, *Naasira*, where Jesus grew up, or to the Nazarenes, a now defunct Christian sect, or even to those who supported (*nasara*) Jesus when he was confronted with the hostility of his enemies (cf. 3:52).

in the first century of our era. The New Testament (consisting of twenty-seven books in all) contains other books written by Christ's apostles and followers.

Why the Bible Has Not Been Corrupted

Muslims may rightly ask us the question: How do we know that it was God who inspired all the authors of the New Testament (and of the Bible in general)? The answer to this legitimate question is simple and it makes sense. God decided to reveal himself through his eternal word (Christ), therefore it is to be expected that he also reveals his word in the form of a document (the New Testament) so that we can recognize and understand his revelation, otherwise, his initial decision to disclose himself would be absurd and ineffective. It was God who revealed his word to the people of his choice, and who made sure that it was recognized as such by the leaders of the early church. It is a similar reasoning that leads Muslims to believe in the preservation of the qur'anic text.

The theory of textual falsification raises a very serious theological question expressed by theologians who argue for the falsification of the meaning, not the text. We can endorse their argument: if God is true, his word, which reflects his character, must also be true and remain so. The qur'anic promise that God protects his word from corruption has its equivalent in the Bible. Jesus is not afraid to equate his own word with God's word when he declares: "Heaven and earth will pass away, but *my* words will never pass away" (Matt 24:35; emphasis added; cf. Ps 119:89–90; 1 Pet 1:24–25). To God's truthfulness one must add his faithfulness to his word and to his people (Deut 7:9). If he allowed his word to be corrupted, he would be true neither to his word nor to his people, who would have inevitably been misled . . . unless one thinks that God is unable to protect his word, which is utter nonsense for both Christians and Muslims.

It has already been noted that according to some Muslim authors it would have been impossible, if only for practical reasons, to deliberately falsify the biblical texts. The manuscripts were widely spread – getting them all together and agreeing on what to change and how to do it would have been an impossible task. Add to this the fact that the Gospels (and other parts of the New Testament) were, as early as the first centuries AD, already translated into many languages (e.g. Syriac, Coptic, Ethiopian, Armenian, Latin). Therefore any attempt at falsification would have been doomed to total failure.

We no longer have the original manuscripts of the Bible, nor of the Qur'an. The earliest manuscripts of Old Testament texts, discovered in 1947 in Qumran Caves near the Dead Sea, date from the first century AD. The only whole manuscript, the first of Isaiah (1 QIs[a]), is dated 125 BC. The oldest manuscripts of Gospel texts date back to the second century. We do, however, have at our disposal hundreds, even thousands, of ancient biblical manuscripts, unlike Qur'anic manuscripts. According to Islamic sources, manuscripts deemed to be inauthentic were destroyed very early on by the authorities of the time.

Paradoxically, the multiplicity of biblical manuscripts increases the chances of identifying the original text. Some Greek manuscripts of the Bible (Old and New Testaments) predate Islam. The Codex Sinaiticus (kept in the British Museum in London) and the Codex Vaticanus (kept in the Vatican Library) are from the fourth century. The Codex Alexandrinus (also in the British Museum) dates from the fifth century. Compared to later manuscripts, these manuscripts show that the text of the Bible has not undergone any modification. In other words, the fact that Jews and Christians did not accept Muhammad as a prophet had no bearing on their Scriptures. Regardless of their religious beliefs, experts who have examined the Bible manuscripts have concluded that the Bible has been handed down with exceptional accuracy.

The textual variants, which are many but not significant, are not such as to cast doubt on the reliability of the biblical manuscripts or their message. The absence of some passages in certain manuscripts (e.g. Mark 16:9–20; John 7:53–8:11; John 21) in no way undermines the reliability of the Gospels or the clarity of their message.

The fact that the Bible is God's word transmitted in human languages makes its translation possible and even highly desirable, since its message is addressed to all people. Today, the Bible (in whole or in part) is available in 3,495 languages.[13] Christians consider good translations of the Bible to be God's word, unlike the Qur'an, which is only God's word in Arabic. This raises the question about its accessibility to non-Arabic speakers as well as the universality of its message. Contemporary translations of the Bible are based on the same manuscripts, Hebrew (and Aramaic) for the Old Testament, Greek for the New. The differences in translations are due not so much to the manuscripts as to the particularities of each translation depending on whether it is more literary or more literal, done in simple or sophisticated language, etc. As human languages develop over time, it is normal for translations to evolve too.

Another major feature differentiates biblical revelation and qur'anic revelation – the writing of the Bible took place over a very long period, approximately a thousand years, and the people who wrote it were many, about

---

13. According to Wycliffe statistics from October 2021, the entire Bible is available in 717 languages. In addition, the New Testament is available in 1,582 languages, and portions of the Bible in 1,196. See https://www.wycliffe.net/resources/statistics/.

forty. The writing of the Qur'an took place over a twenty-three-year period (AD 610–632) and was received by only one man, Muhammad. Therefore, it is not surprising that the Bible has very diverse literary genres (e.g. narrative, parabolic, legislative, poetic, philosophic, historical, apocalyptic, and even romantic). We find these genres in the qur'anic sūras too, but to a much lesser degree. This difference may explain why the unity of the Qur'an seems greater than that of the Bible. The internal consistency of the Bible, despite its literary diversity and the multiplicity of its authors, enhances its veracity.

How to Interpret the Bible

So far, we have seen that the Bible as God's revealed word is significantly different from the Qur'an in terms of how it was revealed, through inspiration not dictation, its timescale, its many human authors, its numerous literary genres, the role of its languages as sheer vehicle of divine revelation, and (last but not least) its main purpose which consists in pointing to God's ultimate revelation, namely Jesus Christ. When all this is taken on board, it is fair to say that the biblical text has not been corrupted in any way. However, the reliability of the Bible does not guarantee sound interpretation of its text. There are some basic principles that can help us understand correctly its message.

Jesus himself once pointed out to his Jewish opponents that their reading of the Torah was inadequate: "You study the Scriptures diligently because you think that in them you have eternal life. These are the very Scriptures that testify about me, yet you refuse to come to me to have life" (John 5:39–40). Jesus does not accuse his interlocutors of falsifying the text of the Torah. He never did. He blames them for their servile attachment to the text which prevents them from seeing the person to whom this text points, namely himself. When reading the Bible, we need to keep in mind the fact that at the heart of Scripture is God in person who wants to disclose himself through the life and mission of Jesus Christ.

The only truly qualified interpreter of God's word is the Holy Spirit who led people to write it down (2 Pet 1:20–21). It is very important to always seek his help in our efforts to understand the biblical text. We need to be divinely guided in this activity even more than in our other human activities.

To the extent that the Torah and the New Testament constitute a revelation from God about God, this revelation is not confined to human rationality. Therefore, our approach should not be a rationalist one ruling out all that is supernatural. We need to acknowledge that our intellectual resources are limited and cannot explain everything. Moreover, as the Bible is also a human word, it is necessary that we respect certain rules of interpretation each time we want to understand a given text. We know that the Bible is a very old text written in a specific social and cultural environment very different from ours.

Each text must be placed in its historical context without reducing its significance to this context. The length of the hair and the wearing of the veil had a special meaning in Corinth that they no longer have in our society (cf. 1 Cor 11:4–16). They are therefore irrelevant for us; however, it is important for Christian men and women to dress modestly out of respect for others. Another example concerns slavery which was accepted in antiquity. Neither the Bible nor the Qur'an denounce this practice. This does not mean that the Bible approved or justified slavery. Like polygamy, slavery was tolerated and specific instructions were given to both masters and slaves who were reminded that they all have one master, Jesus Christ (Eph 6:5–9). Slave trading is unambiguously condemned in at least one text in the New Testament (1 Tim 1:10). Let us not forget new forms of slavery, more subtle but no less real, that affect many of our contemporaries.

We must also take into account the literary genre of the biblical text under consideration. An apocalyptic text should not be interpreted literally. The book of Revelation is full with symbols and numbers that need decoding. Likewise, we will not take literally a poetic story; for example, this book speaks of 'the four corners of the earth [and] the four winds of the earth' (Rev 7:1; cf. Rev 20:8). Obviously, this language is not to be interpreted literally.

A narrative text does not necessarily establish a model for us to follow. The texts relating the sin of some prophets do not excuse them. Quite the contrary. These texts teach us that sin is rooted in our heart, so we must be careful not to let it dominate us. The so-called imprecatory psalms, which call on God to severely punish enemies, faithfully express the feelings of their author without necessarily enjoying divine sanction (e.g. Ps 109:6–15; Ps 137:8–9).

In general, the natural meaning of a text must be retained without seeking, when it disturbs us, to deflect this meaning with a metaphorical interpretation. This would amount to falsifying it! Unfortunately, some Muslim authors fall into this trap when confronted with New Testament texts that clearly teach, for instance, the divine sonship of Jesus Christ.

Reading the Bible should also take onboard that Jesus Christ brought about a radical change in taking divine revelation to its ultimate fulfilment. Therefore, we must read the Old Testament in light of the New Testament, just as Jesus and his apostles did. For example, the notion of the "Promised Land" (of Israel) is no longer relevant, and the only implicit reference to this land in the New Testament is found in the Beatitudes: "Blessed are the meek, for they will share the earth [land]" (Matt 5:5; cf. Acts 15:15-17). The same is true of the temple in Jerusalem, which has been replaced by the risen Christ: "Destroy this temple, and I will raise it again in three days" (John 2:19). Obsolete too are the concept of "Chosen People" (Israel) to the exclusion of all others (Gal 3:28-29), the dietary code (Mark 7:19), polygamy (Matt 19:4-6), circumcision (Gal 6:12), and, of course, the Mosaic penal code, in particular about adultery (Lev 20:10; John 8:1-11) and apostasy (Deut 13:6-10).

The Bible enjoys internal consistency because it was revealed by the one and same God. The biblical texts are diverse but consistent. Therefore, the Bible should be interpreted by the Bible as much as possible. This way, one will avoid interpreting the biblical text in light of modern science, because the Bible is not primarily a scientific book. This obviously should not stop us from looking for connections between the biblical text and data belonging to other religious texts, to extra-biblical history, to human sciences, to archeology, etc.

Christians try to understand the most difficult biblical texts in light of easier ones dealing with the same subject. Foundational texts must also serve as reference points on all thorny subjects. Among these texts is the first chapter of Genesis about the creation of man and woman in God's image (Gen 1:27). This text provides a solid ground for major truths such as equality between men and women, and between all human beings regardless of their creed, culture or color, and sex.

To fully understand a text, it must be approached with an open mind. The intention of the author must be discerned from possible colorful or even clumsy expressions. Rather than finding contradictions at all costs (as proponents of textual falsification do), the texts should be harmonized with each other as much as possible. Flexibility in interpretation would resolve many difficulties. The stay of the Israelites in Egypt for 400 years (Gen 15:13) or 430 years (Exod 12:40) does not represent a real contradiction, any more than certain chronological discrepancies in gospel narratives, for those who keep a sympathetic and humble attitude towards the biblical text. Let us not forget that the authors of the Gospels, and of the Bible in general, do not claim that their writings follow a strict chronological order. Likewise, the figures they quote are approximate as it can be seen from the "thousands" often quoted in the New Testament (Matt 14:13; 15:29; 18:24; Luke 12:1; Acts 21:20; Heb 12:22; Jude 1:14; Rev 5:11).

Our efforts at interpreting Bible texts will not eliminate all difficulties. These are due in part to our limited knowledge and in part to the manuscripts themselves. The manuscripts include texts in which the meaning is unclear. Divine inspiration enjoyed by Bible writers does not extend to copyists, although the latter have copied the manuscripts with remarkable seriousness and care. Studies of biblical manuscripts by scholars (believers and non-believers) have shown that the integrity of the biblical text is not undermined by its textual variations.

For believers the clarity of the Bible message is not in doubt as, once again, it does not make sense for God to give us a revelation whose core message is beyond our reach. Despite the doctrines that characterize different churches (Catholic, Orthodox, Protestant), they all subscribe to the first professions of faith, such as the one known as "the Apostles Creed." Someone helpfully made the following comment: "What for me is a real problem is not the relatively few texts that I do not understand, but all those texts that I do understand and have great difficulty to implement." We should not let textual difficulties obscure the clarity of the gospel to us, nor discourage us in our reading of the Scripture. These difficulties should not lead us into a situation where we cannot see the forest for the trees!

> As the rain and the snow
> come down from heaven,
> and do not return to it
> without watering the earth
> and making it bud and flourish,
> so that it yields seed for the sower and bread for the eater,
> so is my word that goes out from my mouth:
> It will not return to me empty,
> but will accomplish what I desire
> and achieve the purpose for which I sent it. (Isa 55:10–11)

7

Jesus Christ

Jesus is mentioned in about a hundred qur'anic verses scattered in several sūras. The main ones are the following:

- Sūra 3 "The Family of 'Imran" (Mary's father's name in the Qur'an), verses 35-55. The story begins with Mary's birth, whose parents were childless. As soon as she is born, Mary is given by her mother to God. She grows up in the temple of Jerusalem under the care of Zechariah (vv. 35-37). Then comes the account about the miraculous birth of John the Baptist, *Yahya* (vv. 38-41), followed by the birth of Jesus, not only miraculous but unique since he was born of a virgin woman (vv. 42-47). Jesus's mission and miracles are told from verses 48-55.
- Sūra 5 "The Table," verses 110-117. The sūra takes its title from the miracle Jesus performs in response to the request of his disciples who wanted God to send down from heaven a table with food to confirm the divine origin of his mission (112-115).
- Sūra 19 "Maryam" (Mary), named after Jesus's mother, the only woman named in the whole Qur'an. It begins, like Sūra 3, with the account of John's birth (vv. 2-15), and then that of Jesus (vv. 16-34). Jesus speaks in the cradle to defend the honor of his mother who was accused of committing adultery since she was not married. The Qur'an makes no mention of Joseph, Mary's legal husband and Jesus's foster father.[1]

We begin this chapter by reviewing Jesus's names and titles, then we consider his sinless life, miracles, and claims before focusing on his mission. We will close the chapter by looking at the Islamic story concerning the end of

---

1. For an in-depth study of who Jesus is in Islam, see my book *Faith to Faith*, chapters 10-17.

Jesus's life on earth and the objections Muslim writers level against the historic and redemptive death of Christ.

Jesus's Names

In the Qur'an Jesus is called *'Isa*. The derivation of this name is uncertain and its meaning is unknown. Muslim scholars simply tell us it is the Arabic equivalent of his name in Hebrew. As there is no mention of Joseph in the Qur'an, Jesus is often called "Jesus, son of Mary" while in Arab society, children are referred to in connection with their father.[2] There are two narratives in the Qur'an relating to the virgin conception of Jesus (3:42–48; 19:16–21). They are both similar and different from the Gospel accounts (Luke 1:26–38; Matt 1:18–25). In both accounts, Mary is overwhelmed by what she has just heard from the angel: "How can I have a boy when no man has touched me and I am not a prostitute?" (19:20; cf. 3:47). Therefore, all Muslims accept Jesus's miraculous birth as they take seriously what their holy Book says.

In the Arabic Bibles, Jesus is called *Yasu'*, a word that comes directly from the Hebrew *Yeshua* via the Greek *Yesous*. God gave the name and the specific mission of Jesus. When the angel appeared to Joseph, he announced the birth of Jesus in these terms: "She [Mary] will give birth to a son, and you are to give him the name Jesus, because he will save his people from their sins" (Matt 1:21; cf. Luke 1:31).

Al-Masih is another name given to Jesus in the Qur'an; in fact, it is a title which has become a name. It comes from the Hebrew *Mashiah*, meaning "Messiah." This word has been translated into Greek as *Christos*, Christ. The Qur'an does not explain the meaning of this name. No prophet receives this name either in the Bible or in the Qur'an. Muslim writers have recognized the basic meaning of the word, namely "anointed one," and have offered a dozen explanations (e.g. the pure, the truthful, the king). In the Bible, this word means "the one chosen by God" and refers to the King appointed by God to carry out a specific mission, namely to establish God's universal and everlasting kingdom on earth. The angel Gabriel describes the mission of Jesus when he announces his birth to Mary:

> He will be great and will be called the Son of the Most High. The Lord God will give him the throne of his father David, and he will

---

2. Jesus is called "Mary's son" only once in the Gospels (Mark 6:3).

reign over Jacob's descendants forever; his kingdom will never end. (Luke 1:32–33)

Paradoxically, the prophet Isaiah depicts this King in the fourth "Servant of the Lord" poem, "a man of suffering, and familiar with pain" (Isa 53:3). Jesus explained to his disciples that he would accomplish his messianic mission through his suffering and victory over death: "From that time on Jesus began to explain to his disciples that he *must* go to Jerusalem and suffer many things at the hands of the elders, the chief priests and the teachers of the law, and that he *must* be killed and on the third day be raised to life" (Matt 16:21; added emphasis).

Jesus's Titles

The Qur'an ascribes several prestigious titles to Jesus. Among the most significant ones are the following four:

- *Prophet and Apostle* (5:75, 110). Jesus is the last messenger sent to the children of Israel. According to Muslim theologians, a prophet delivers an oral message to his people while an apostle leaves a holy written scripture after him. Among all prophets, there are only four apostles: Moses, David, Jesus and Muhammad.

- *Word of God.* Jesus is God's word (3:39, 45) and a word from God (4:171). The Qur'an does not provide any explanation for this title, which is not given to any other prophet. Muslim writers have offered several interpretations, all of them downplay its significance. Jesus is God's word because, like Adam, he was created directly by the divine word which made him come into being (cf. 3:59); because his birth was a fulfilment of the word spoken by the angel to Mary; because as a prophet he was God's spokesperson; or because his mission was a fulfilment of the ancient prophecies about his coming. Why, in these last two cases, is Muhammad not called God's word, since for Muslims he was the last and the greatest prophet? Why, in the first case, is Adam not called God's word?

    Jesus is described in the Gospel of John as God's eternal word revealed in a man (John 1:1–2, 14). To a certain degree, one can compare Jesus, as the eternal word revealed in human form, to the Qur'an. For Sunni Muslims, God's eternal and uncreated word is revealed in the form of a Book, namely the Torah, the Gospel and ultimately the Qur'an. For Christians, Jesus is the manifestation of

God, full and perfect, while for Muslims, the Qur'an discloses only the will of God and his names.

- *Spirit of God*. Jesus is a spirit from God (4:171). For lack of qur'anic explanations, Muslim exegetes have made several suggestions which all amount to taking this title in the metaphorical sense and referring to the purity of Jesus, his divinely inspired and kind message, and the miraculous way in which he was created. These explanations have one thing in common: they honor Jesus who is the only prophet to receive this title. In the biblical context, the risen Christ is referred to as a life-giving spirit at work in a new humanity with whom he shares his victory over death: "So it is written: 'The first man Adam became a living being'; the last Adam, a life-giving spirit" (1 Cor 15:45; cf. Gen 2:7).

- *Servant of God*. In spite of all the qur'anic titles exclusive to Jesus, he remains a mere human being: "He [Jesus] is only a servant whom We [God] have showered with blessings and whom We have designated as an example to the children of Israel" (43:59). His one-of-a-kind birth does not mean that he is of divine origin. He is essentially a human being, like all prophets, although his coming into existence was miraculous like that of Adam: "The likeness of Jesus before God is as that of Adam; He created him from dust, then said to him: 'Be.' And he was" (3:59; cf. 15:29; 32:9; 38:72).

    In the Bible too, Jesus presents himself as the servant of God. Far from disdaining this status of servant (cf. Qur'an 4:172), Jesus owns it with no reservation: "For even the Son of Man did not come to be served, but to serve, and to give his life as a ransom for many" (Mark 10:45). He is the Servant par excellence, who perfectly served God by giving his life for humankind. He is servant not only in the sense he is fully a human being, but also in that he fulfilled God's will to save humanity through giving "his life [as] an offering for sin" (Isa 53:10).

Jesus's Sinless Life

The Qur'an does not hide the fact that all prophets did not lead exemplary lives. Regarding the prophet of Islam, God once rebuked him for his uncharitable and discriminatory attitude towards a blind Muslim man who approached him and asked him to instruct him in the faith. The prophet was busy preaching to non-believing Meccan leaders and so he dismissed the poor man (80:1–10).

In several qur'anic texts the Prophet is encouraged to invoke God's mercy: "Implore forgiveness for your sin" (40:55), "for your sin and the sins of believing men and women" (47:19). God is willing to forgive the Prophet "his past and future sins" (48:2). Muhammad must "ask for forgiveness" from his Lord (110:3). According to Islamic tradition, the Prophet was fully aware of his shortcomings to the point that when his companions asked him a question regarding his merits, he did not hesitate to recognize his deep need for divine mercy:

- I heard God's messenger say: "A man's actions will not earn him paradise."
- They asked him: "Not even you, O God's messenger?"
- He responded: "No, not even me, unless God covers me with His favor and forgiveness."[3]

Muslim exegetes minimize Muhammad's sin by explaining that his irritation at the blind Muslim man was understandable, though he could have had a better course of action. The sins referred to in the other texts are either his own minor sins (e.g. inadvertence, sin of omission), or the sins of the Muslim community which are transferred onto him because he is their leader and therefore their representative.

The Hadith accounts contain many prayers in which the Prophet earnestly pleads with God to forgive him:

> O God! Wash away my sins with snow and hail water.
> Purify my heart from sin as the white garment is cleaned from
> dirt, and keep sin away from me as East is kept away from West.[4]

It appears that the doctrine about Muhammad's sinlessness is a later theological construct aimed primarily at honoring the Prophet of Islam. It would be more judicious to recognize that Muhammad and all prophets were sinful men, like all of us, hence they too needed divine mercy, just like us.

In the Qur'an, Jesus is blameless. The angel describes the child who will be born to Mary as "a pure boy" (19:19). The Prophetic Tradition confirms

---

3. Bukhari, *Marda* (Sick People), 19.

4. Muslim, *Dhikr* (Invocation Prayers), 14. Prayers of the Prophet which include praise as well as repentance, and calls for help and imploring divine forgiveness are found in most collections of the Prophetic Tradition, for example: Bukhari, *Tawhid* (Monotheism), 8; *Da'awat* (Non-ritual Prayers), 9; Muslim, *Musafirin* (Travelers), 16, 26; Tirmidhi, *Da'awat* (Non-ritual Prayers), 29, 39, 78; Nasa'i, *Isti'adha* (Seeking Refuge with God), 62; *Tahara* (Ritual Purity), 4; Ibn Majah, *Du'a'* (Non-ritual Prayer), 2; Abu Dawud, *Witr* (Praying with an Odd Number of Prostrations), 25–26.

the qur'anic teaching. A saying attributed to the Prophet puts Jesus and his mother in a unique place among all humans: "There is none born among the offspring of Adam but Satan touches it. A child, therefore, cries loudly at the time of birth because of the touch of Satan except Mary and her child."[5] There is in this statement a hint at what Christians call "original sin" from which Jesus was preserved (as well as his mother).

When he was twelve years old, Jesus knew he had a very special relationship with God, "his Father" (Luke 2:49). Later, he challenged his detractors: "Can any of you prove me guilty of sin?" (John 8:46; cf. 2 Cor 5:21; 1 John 2:1-2; Heb 2:17-18; 7:26; 9:14). Jesus came to save sinners, which is why, from the beginning of his mission, he wanted to identify with them by receiving from John the baptism of repentance (or conversion). John at first refused to baptize Jesus, because he knew that since Jesus was sinless, he did not need to be baptized. Jesus insisted and John finally gave in (Matt 3:13-15).

Some Muslim writers, apparently ignorant of the teaching of their own Scriptures, claim that Jesus was not without sin. They sometimes quote the Lord's Prayer which Jesus taught to his disciples: "Forgive us our sins, as we have forgiven those who sin against us" (Matt 6:12 NLT). But this prayer is in response to the disciples request for Jesus to teach them to pray, and he answered: "When *you* pray, say . . ." (Luke 11:1-2; emphasis added). Even if Jesus included himself in this prayer, he would have done it out of solidarity with us. Indeed, there is no text, neither biblical nor qur'anic, which suggests that Jesus committed the slightest sin. It is precisely his sinless life that qualified him to offer his life for sinners, "for the forgiveness of [our] sins" (Matt 26:28).

Jesus's Miracles

Islam teaches that God grants his messengers the power to work miracles in order to confirm in the eyes of their people the divine origin of their mission. Qur'anic texts mention many miracles performed by Jesus. Some are found in the four Gospels (healing of lepers and blind people, raising the dead) and others in the "apocryphal" gospels written much later than the four canonical Gospels and whose veracity is not certain at all.

Among the miracles that have most captured the attention of Muslim writers – mystics in particular – are the creation of birds from clay and the resurrection of the dead (3:49; 5:110). Regarding the creation of birds, the qur'anic text uses the verb *khalaqa*, which is the same verb used for God when

---

5. Bukhari, *Anbiya'* (Prophets), 44.

he created the world. In other words, Jesus stands out among all prophets thanks to this divine attribute which enabled him to perform miracles that had to be from God. The resurrection of the dead is also a very special miracle since it is God who "gives life and takes it back" (57:2). It is also true that the Bible reports to us several resurrection miracles performed by prophets and apostles.

Muslim writers point out that it was with God's permission that Jesus was able to work these miracles. The question remains: why did God want to honor Jesus by granting this permission to him and to no other prophet? Doesn't this mean that Jesus is an exceptional prophet?

In Christianity as well, miracles are a sign which authenticates the divine mission of a prophet. In the case of Jesus this sign is much more significant because some miracles carry a meaning that Jesus himself disclosed in connection with these miracles. After feeding a hungry crowd, he declared: "I am the bread of life. Whoever comes to me will never go hungry, and whoever believes in me will never be thirsty" (John 6:35). Likewise, before raising his friend Lazarus from the dead, he declared: "I am the resurrection and the life. The one who believes in me will live, even though they die; and whoever lives by believing in me will never die" (John 11:25–26). Before restoring sight to a blind person, he declared: "While I am in the world, I am the light of the world" (John 9:5).

Jesus's Claims

These three statements, which all include the words "I am," have an unsuspected significance. Indeed, they echo the very name of God revealed to Moses: "I AM who I AM" (Exod 3:14; cf. John 8:28). In John's Gospel, Jesus makes other statements that begin with the same words:

> Very truly I tell you . . . before Abraham was born, I am! (John 8:58)

> I am the light of the world. Whoever follows me will never walk in darkness, but will have the light of life. (John 8:12)

> I am the good shepherd; I know my sheep and my sheep know me. (John 10:14)

> I am the way and the truth and the life. No one comes to the Father except through me. (John 14:6)

There are many other texts in the Gospels which reveal the divine identity of Jesus. His word is eternal and imperishable (Matt 24:35); his personal authority is supreme and superior to the law of Moses (Mark 2:27–28); he is the new temple where people can meet and worship God (Matt 26:61; John 2:21); nature is under his authority (Matt 8:23–27) and demons too (Luke 11:26–39). Very significant also are the incidents where Jesus forgives people their sins (Mark 2:1–12; Luke 7:36–50; John 8:1–11). He does this in his own name and not by asking God to forgive them. A paralyzed man was once brought to Jesus to be healed. Contrary to what was expected of him, Jesus said to the paralytic: "My son, your sins are forgiven." The law teachers were outraged: "Why does this fellow talk like that? He's blaspheming! Who can forgive sins but God alone?"

Apart from God no one has the right to forgive people their sins. This is what Jews and Christians believe as well as Muslims. According to the Qur'an, granting forgiveness of sin is typically a divine prerogative: "Who forgives sins except God?" (3:235). To convince his opponents that he has the authority to forgive sins, Jesus turns to the disabled man and orders him to stand up: "Get up, take your mat and go home." The man obeys. To everyone's surprise, the man gets up, takes his stretcher and leaves (Mark 2:1–12). Would God have given Jesus the power to perform this miracle if he had no right to forgive the paralyzed man his sins?

Jesus takes on the role of judge on the last day. The prophet Daniel had announced the coming of a king whose kingship would be universal and eternal. This king receives the title "Son of Man" (Dan 7:9–10, 13–14). Jesus takes for himself this seemingly very ordinary title which can be applied to all human beings; however, for those familiar with the Scriptures, this title also refers to the Supreme Judge who, on Resurrection Day, will judge everyone:

> When the Son of Man comes in his glory, and all the angels with him, he will sit on his glorious throne. All the nations will be gathered before him, and he will separate the people one from another as a shepherd separates the sheep from the goats. He will put the sheep on his right and the goats on his left. . . . Then they will go away to eternal punishment, but the righteous to eternal life. (Matt 25:31–33, 45; cf. Matt 7:21–23; John 5:24–27)

Jesus's claims are extraordinary in that they are first and foremost about his person which is at the center of his message. The Jewish authorities perfectly understood the meaning of these claims. Since they did not accept him as the promised Messiah, they accused him of blasphemy and condemned him to death on this very charge (Mark 14:61–64).

Jesus's Mission

According to the Qur'an, Jesus's mission was to preach monotheism like all prophets (3:50-51). God entrusted him with a holy scripture, the Gospel (*injil*), to be preached to the people of Israel.

Muslims do not know the meaning of the word *injil* (gospel), as it derives from Greek. Its Arabic equivalent would be *bushra* or *bishara* (good news). Indeed, the central message of Jesus is about not condemnation but forgiveness of sins thanks to God's unconditional love. Taking over from John the Baptist, Jesus placed his preaching under the theme of the kingdom of God now accessible to everyone through conversion and faith: "After John was put in prison, Jesus went into Galilee, proclaiming the good news of God. 'The time has come,' he said. 'The kingdom of God has come near. Repent and believe the good news!'" (Mark 1:14-15).

Jesus's mission was not simply to proclaim God's kingdom – its purpose was to provide access to that kingdom through his death and resurrection. As soon as the disciples recognized their master as the promised Messiah (Matt 16:16), Jesus began to reveal to them the crowning of his mission:

> From that time on Jesus began to explain to his disciples that he *must* go to Jerusalem and suffer many things at the hands of the elders, the chief priests and the teachers of the law, and that he *must* be killed and on the third day be raised to life. (Matt 16:21; emphasis added)

It took time for the disciples to accept the Messiah's mission in these terms. For them, the purpose of this mission was to liberate Israel from the Roman occupation (cf. Luke 24:20-21; Acts 1:6). They retained – from the Messianic prophecies – the victorious image of the "Lion of the tribe of Judah" (Rev 5:5; cf. Gen 49:9) who triumphs over his enemies. The figure of "the lamb [led] to the slaughter" (Isa 53:7) had completely escaped their attention, despite the fact that John the Baptist had designated Jesus in these terms: "Look, the Lamb of God, who takes away the sin of the world!" (John 1:29). One day when Jesus announced to his disciples his imminent death, Peter did not want to know anything about the sufferings that awaited his Lord. His reaction was immediate and robust:

> Peter took him aside and began to rebuke him. "Never, Lord!" he said. "This shall never happen to you!" (Matt 16:22)

Jesus recognized in the apparently kind words of his disciple nothing less than a devilish temptation to divert him from the way of the cross:

Jesus turned and said to Peter, "Get behind me, Satan! You are a stumbling block to me; you do not have in mind the concerns of God, but merely human concerns." (Matt 16:23)

For Jesus the salvation of the world meant dying on the cross, hence the imperative in the announcement of his death to his disciples: he *must* suffer and be killed. This death was all the more dreadful as it was not the result of a mere death sentence. It was a demonstration of extreme love (John 13:1) manifested in the atoning sacrifice of his life for the forgiveness of our sins (Matt 26:28). Jesus knew that he had to drink the cup of judgment (John 18:11) and did not hide how upset he was when he approached this decisive hour. At the very beginning of his agony, he confessed: "Now my soul is troubled, and what shall I say? 'Father, save me from this hour?' No, it was *for this very reason* I came to this hour. Father, glorify your name!" (John 12:27–28; emphasis added).

While two of the Gospels completely ignore the miraculous birth of Jesus (Mark and John), all four devote a disproportionate amount of space and detail to the last week of his life, from his triumphant entry into Jerusalem until his ascension into heaven, through his crucifixion and resurrection. Among all the apostles, only John was at the foot of the cross, "the disciple whom Jesus loved." The others had fled. Several women were also present including Mary, the mother of Jesus, her sister, and Mary Magdalene. Before dying, Jesus took care to entrust his mother to John (John 19:25–27).

On the third day Jesus rose from the dead to the surprise of all his disciples. He appeared to them many times, individually and in groups (John 20). He also appeared to a crowd of five hundred people (1 Cor 15:5–8). For forty days Jesus continued his teaching about the kingdom until the day he was lifted up into heaven with God (Acts 1:1–3). The resurrection of Jesus from the dead has several meanings: first, through it, God gave the factual demonstration that Jesus faithfully fulfilled the mission entrusted to him; second, the unprecedented statements he had made about himself were all true; and third, everything he had done was in perfect accordance with God's will.

Islamic Objections to Jesus's Death

Unlike the Gospels, qur'anic texts focus on the miraculous birth of Jesus (3:42–48; 19:16–34). There are only four short texts about the death of Jesus: two speak of his death as an ordinary one (5:120; 19:33), another is variously interpreted (3:55), whereas the fourth one seems to categorically deny the reality of Jesus's death and crucifixion (4:157–158).

This last relatively short text is the one on which Islamic theology has based its argument against Jesus's death. It is in the light of this text alone that the other qur'anic texts are understood. It is by no means a historical account of events as they happened. It is part of an anti-Jewish controversy whose primary purpose is not to deny the crucifixion but to defend Jesus against the Jews. Their arrogance reaches a climax when they make the following statement:

> They claim, "We killed the Messiah Jesus, son of Mary, the [one who claimed to be the] Apostle of God."
>
> But they killed him not, nor did they crucify him. They were under the illusion that they had. Those who differ about this matter are full of doubts. They have no real knowledge but follow only conjecture. Assuredly, they did not kill him. On the contrary, God raised him to himself, and God is Almighty and Wise.
>
> And there are none of the People of the Book who will not believe in him (Jesus) before his death. On the Day of Resurrection he (Jesus) will be a witness against them. (4:157–159)

This text is the peak of a series of charges against the Jews: they broke God's covenant, uttered an infamous lie against the chastity of Mary, and put to death many prophets (4:155–156). According to the Qur'an, in their arrogance, the Jews go as far as to claim they put to death the one who said he was the Messiah, the messenger of God. The Jews think they have thus proved that Jesus was not really the Messiah, because, in their eyes, God would not have let the Messiah be put to death. The Qur'anic text vindicates Jesus by claiming that he was indeed the Messiah, which is why God did not let the Jews carry out their murderous plan. The Jews plotted against Jesus and God plotted against them: "They (the Jews) plotted and planned [against Jesus] and God too plotted and planned [against them], and the best of planners is God" (3:54). Thus, it was through a "trick" that God thwarted the ignominious plan of the Jews.

According to the traditional Islamic interpretation of this text, God immediately stepped in to snatch Jesus from the hands of his enemies. God made a man look like Jesus (some accounts identify this man with Judas, the disciple who betrayed Jesus), and this lookalike was crucified in place of Jesus, who was raised to heaven where he is now. The Jews did not realize what really happened due to divine intervention. They thought they had crucified Jesus because they did not realize that a lookalike was crucified in his place. They were not the only victims of this enormous delusion. It seems that everyone got it wrong, including Jesus's own disciples, starting with his mother and his beloved disciple, despite the fact they were at the foot of the cross! Why would

God let the Jews kill several prophets whereas he stepped in to foil their plot against Jesus? The Qur'an does not answer this question but one can make a suggestion: the prophets killed by the Jews were anonymous men while Jesus was an exceptional prophet.

Here we remember Peter's belief which led him to rule out the possibility that the Messiah could be humiliated and suffer an infamous death (Matt 16:22). This is typical human reasoning: who would readily admit that his "hero" could be defeated, let alone if this hero is an illustrious messenger of God? Jesus said to Peter: "You do not have in mind the concerns of God, but merely human concerns" (Matt 16:23). The Qur'an (like the Bible) maintains that God remains faithful to his people (cf. 22:40; 40:51; 47:7), therefore God's loyalty to his servants and his power would have been challenged had he allowed his faithful servant to suffer the abject fate to which his enemies had condemned him.

Christians agree with Muslims that God is always faithful to his servants and his power has no limits. God was faithful to Jesus by raising him from the dead, not by sparing him death, for this was part of his eternal plan announced by the prophets (Acts 2:23; Matt 26:53–54). This purpose reflects God's limitless love for humanity which he created and which he decided to save powerfully through Christ.

According to Islamic thought, Jesus will return at the end time to complete his mission (started two thousand years ago). He will then fight the Antichrist (*al-masih al-dajjal*) and defeat him. He will establish Shari'a law through which he will rule the entire earth. Justice and peace will characterize his reign, the duration of which varies depending on various stories. Everyone will then believe in him as Muslims do today. Christians will realize he is not the Son of God, and the Jews will accept him as the Messiah God promised them.

Jesus will die a natural death and will be honored by all Muslims, who will bury him next to Muhammad in Medina. The death of Jesus will give the signal for the last day and the general resurrection (cf. 43:61).[6] Then all human beings will appear before their Creator to be judged according to his perfect justice.

The Islamic version of how Jesus's life ended on earth is significantly different from the Christian version. Renowned exegetes such as Razi admit that the Islamic rendition raises serious difficulties. It amounts to questioning God's moral integrity as he would have led everyone to believe that Jesus was crucified when he was not; yet, comments Razi, we cannot think that God (who is true) can deceive people, believers in particular. Despite this

---

6. Bukhari, *Anbiya'* (Prophets), 49; *Fitan* (Trials), 26.

intractable difficulty, Razi still believes that the qur'anic text is divinely inspired and therefore should be trusted no matter what. Some Muslims, however, think that this text (4:157–158) is obscure and the traditional interpretation (based mainly on various accounts in the Prophetic Tradition) is not necessarily the right one. For them, Jesus was crucified and it was his spirit that was taken up to heaven.

Compared to the biblical text, which reports in detail the facts transmitted by eyewitnesses, the qur'anic text, written six centuries after the event, doesn't seem very convincing. The Bible narrative points out that after his resurrection Jesus appeared to his disciples for forty days before ascending to heaven. To the disciples who doubted his resurrection, he showed the marks of his crucifixion on his body (John 20:19–29).

Later Muslim thinkers sought to legitimize the qur'anic texts and to refute the gospel message by appealing to three theological arguments:

1. The first is that Jesus's atoning death was not necessary, because God does not need a sacrifice to forgive our sins. He forgives us out of sheer generosity and because he is merciful. The Bible emphasizes that God's love is boundless; at the same time it affirms that his absolute righteousness requires that sin be judged. The second sūra of the Qur'an, entitled "the Cow" (or "the Heifer"), mentions a special sacrifice prescribed in the law of Moses (2:67–71; cf. Num 19:1–10). The biblical text specifies that the cow to be sacrificed should be "without defect or blemish," and that it is "a purification from sin" (Num 19:2, 9). The sacrifices of the old covenant foreshadowed the sacrifice of Christ whereby God can forgive our sins without undermining his righteousness (cf. Heb 9:22; 10:1–4, 10–12).

   God's forgiveness is what Jews celebrate on Atonement Day, *Yom Kippur*, and Christians at Easter. Muslims associate divine forgiveness with the "feast of sacrifice," called the Great Feast, during which they commemorate the sacrifice of Abraham (37:100–111). In fact, God redeemed the patriarch's child with "a great sacrifice" (37:107).[7] Can an animal be described as a great sacrifice? Can this

---

7. The qur'anic text does not name the child. Early Muslim commentators, familiar with the Genesis account (Gen 22:1–18), thought the child was Isaac. Later on, Muslim exegetes affirmed it was Ishmael for two reasons: first, the qur'anic account mentions Isaac immediately after the sacrifice story (37:112); second, in the biblical narrative God asks Abraham to sacrifice his "only son," which means that Isaac was not yet born. However, Ishmael was no longer living in his father's house at time of sacrifice (Gen 21:18–21), and Isaac was, according to Genesis, the only "son of the promise" (Gen 17:15–21). Today, Muslims are almost unanimous in saying that

sacrifice be a veiled announcement of another sacrifice, far greater than that of a lamb, namely Christ on the cross?

2. A second argument against the atoning death of Jesus consists in emphasizing individual responsibility of all of us in connection with our own actions. We will be judged according to our works because, as the Qur'an says, "no one bears someone else's burden" (6:164). To say that our salvation depends on a sacrifice offered by another person, in this case that of Christ, contradicts this principle. The Bible also affirms the principle of personal responsibility: "The one who sins is the one who will die. The child will not share the guilt of the parent, nor will the parent share the guilt of the child. The righteousness of the righteous will be credited to them, and the wickedness of the wicked will be charged against them" (Ezek 18:20).

   The Bible maintains that we should have no illusions about our ability to save ourselves with our own deeds (cf. Isa 64:5; Rom 3:11–18). Our responsibility is fully dependent on how we respond to God's revelation in Jesus Christ in general and to the salvation he achieved for us in particular. Furthermore, Sunni doctrine teaches that the Prophet will intercede on judgment day on behalf of Muslims and many will come out of hell thanks to his intercession, which is based on Muhammad's merits. Christ, thanks to his life offered for us, promises salvation to whoever confesses him as his Savior. "Savior of the world" is one of Christ's most prestigious titles ascribed to him in John's gospel (John 4:42; cf. 1 John 4:14).

3. A third argument used by Muslim theologians against Christ's crucifixion is that it would be unjust, even immoral, for God to accept the sacrifice of an innocent man, namely Jesus Christ, on behalf of sinners. For Christians, God did not force Christ to lay down his life for us – Christ willingly gave his life as an atoning sacrifice for us. In fact, it is God himself through his Son who has done us this extraordinary service, essential to our salvation. Through his extreme humbling, which led him to the cross, Christ became the perfect Servant-Savior. In response God exalted him and "gave him the name that is above every name," so that "every

---

the story is all about Ishmael. The biblical and qur'anic texts have in common that God tested the faith of Abraham by this sacrifice and the patriarch showed exemplary and obedient faith.

tongue acknowledge that Jesus Christ is Lord, to the glory of God the Father" (Phil 2:9, 11).

A careful examination of the qur'anic texts concerning Jesus shows that he is a truly unique prophet by virtue of his miraculous birth, his exceptional names, his prestigious titles, his blameless life, his meaningful miracles and his unparalleled claims. His mission was also matchless since God did not allow him to be defeated by his enemies. God raised Christ to himself and he is in heaven with God. His expected return by Muslims confirms that he is a very special prophet.

But it is the Gospels that reveal the mystery of Jesus in all its fullness. This prophet, unique among all prophets, is in reality much more than a prophet. He is not just God's messenger; he is God's eternal word. He is the Son of God who discloses to us the mystery of God: Father, Son and Holy Spirit.

The next chapter will examine the objections raised by the Qur'an and Islamic tradition against the cornerstone of the Christian faith, namely the divine Trinity and its corollary – the deity of Christ.

8

One God in Three Persons

The last chapter showed that Jesus is a unique prophet in the Qur'an and even more so in the Gospels. His uniqueness is a clue that he is actually much more than a human being. Jesus did not leave his disciples in any doubt about who he was. He disclosed to them that he was God's only Son. He also revealed to them that God is his Father and that the Holy Spirit is the eternal link that unites him to the Father.

On the threshold of his mission, when Jesus was baptized by John, the Father and the Spirit publicly bore witness to him:

> As soon as Jesus was baptized, he went up out of the water. At that moment heaven was opened, and he saw the Spirit of God descending like a dove and alighting on him. And a voice from heaven said, "This is my Son, whom I love; with him I am well pleased." (Matt 3:16–17)

The Father and the Spirit were fully involved in Jesus's mission as the three have been intimately united from all eternity. The Father sent the Son on a mission to save humanity and Jesus was filled with the Spirit in the fulfilment of that mission. At the end of his mission, Jesus commissioned his apostles to preach the gospel to all nations. He promised them that he would stay with them even after he ascended to heaven, thanks to the Holy Spirit whom he would send to them in a very few days:

> Then Jesus came to them and said, "All authority in heaven and on earth has been given to me. Therefore go and make disciples of all nations, baptizing them in the name of the Father and of the Son and of the Holy Spirit." (Matt 28:18–19; cf. Acts 1:4)

Qur'anic Monotheism versus Biblical Monotheism

Muslim writers rightly point out that the word "Trinity" is not found in the Gospels (nor in the Bible). It is a technical word coined by theologians of the early centuries to denote a truth Jesus taught. Strictly speaking, we should say "Tri-Unity" to make it clear that it is both about the oneness of God and the trinity of his persons. One may also observe that the Arabic word *tawhid*, namely monotheism, is not found in the Qur'an. It was made up by Muslim theologians to refer to that central doctrine of Islam.

There are three qur'anic texts that denounce the Christian Trinity but only one explains what kind of trinity is rejected. It is not the Christian doctrine of the Trinity but a misconception of this doctrine. The text in question, from Sūra 5, anticipates the day of judgment on which Jesus will be questioned by God about the teaching he gave to his followers.

> God said:
> - Jesus, son of Mary, did you ever say to people, "Adopt me and my mother as two gods in disregard of God Himself?"
>
> Jesus replied:
> - Glory be to You. It is not in me to say what I have no warrant for. If I had ever said such a thing, You would have known it. For You know my innermost being and I do not know Yours. I said to them only what you commanded me to say, namely, "Worship and serve God, my Lord and your Lord." As long as I was among them I bore witness to them and when You took me to Yourself it was You who were watcher over them. For You are a witness to all things. (5:116–117)
>
> Believe, then, in God and His apostles and do not talk of three [gods]. You are well advised to abandon such ideas. Truly God is one God. Glory be to Him, He is above having a son, to Him belong all things in the heavens and the earth, and He is the one and only guardian. (4:171)
>
> Surely they are disbelievers who say that God is the third of three [gods]! There is no god but One. (5:73)

These texts exempt Jesus from any false teaching that he would have given to his disciples. The Gospels show that Jesus never taught his disciples that *he and his mother* were to be worshipped alongside God. Quoting the Torah, Jesus recalled this central commandment of Scripture: "Worship the Lord your God, and serve him only" (Matt 4:10). Jesus had great respect for his mother, but he never elevated her to the rank of a deity (cf. Luke 1:27–28). Therefore these qur'anic texts rightly reject the trinity made of God-Mary-Jesus in which Jesus is "the third of three" (5:73). The church has never taught this tri-theism though we cannot completely rule out that some Christians, through certain practices, may have misled some into believing that the Virgin Mary had a divine status. This is therefore a serious misunderstanding of Christian doctrine. However, we should not, because of this confusion, blame the Qur'an too quickly for attributing to Christians a doctrine that has never been part of Christian teaching. The Council of Ephesus (431) ruled that it was legitimate to call Mary "the Mother of God." This decision was taken, not to glorify Jesus's mother ("the Lord's servant," in her own words) (Luke 1:38), but to highlight the divinity of Jesus and the non-separation of the two natures, divine and human, in the one person of Christ.[1]

Today, the Virgin Mary is acclaimed, particularly in the Catholic and Orthodox churches, as "our Mother," and "the Mother of the Church." As Christians, we confess that God is our Father and Jesus Christ is the Son of God. Therefore we should not be too surprised when Muslims perceive the Christian Trinity as being the Father, Mary and Jesus. Excessive devotion of some Christians to the Virgin Mary does nothing to help remove misunderstandings about Christian teaching. Many Muslims remain ill-informed about this teaching and it is common for them to think that Christians worship three deities, Mary included. When the opportunity presents itself, it is important to dispel this misunderstanding. Muslims who are well informed about the Christian faith continue to think that the qur'anic criticism is not totally unjustified because it targets, if not a belief, at least a reality that can still be found with many Christians who seem to worship Mary.

Well-informed Muslim thinkers know that Christianity teaches God's oneness in three persons: Father, Son, and Holy Spirit. They nevertheless reject the Christian doctrine about the Trinity in the name of qur'anic monotheism. Is this doctrine really incompatible with monotheism? We do not think so. We are here in the presence of two monotheisms, unitarian on the one hand, and trinitarian on the other. Muslim theologians take a rationalist approach in their rejection of the Trinity: either God is one or he is three, he cannot be one *and* three at the same time. However, Sunni theology is not characterized

---

1. Even if the title *theotokos* ("mother of God") is theologically sound, from a missiological point of view it was ill suited to the largely polytheistic environment like the Arab society on the eve of the birth of Islam. Christians of the Assyrian tradition (known as "Nestorians"), present in northern Arabia, did not accept this title for Mary.

by rationalism – it defines faith above all as an act not of intelligence but of trust in God (*tasdiq*). The same is true of the Christian faith. A rational, but not rationalistic, approach to faith is all the more appropriate in Christianity because the object of revelation is God himself and not simply his will for his servants.

God is described four times in the Qur'an as "the one who knows in full the hidden mysteries" (5:109, 116; 9:78; 34:48). For Christians, God decided to unveil these mysteries through Jesus Christ, including the mystery of the divine Trinity. By definition, mysteries are inaccessible to us because they concern our Creator. He is an infinite God and we are limited creatures; how could we know him other than through self-disclosure? We are sinners and sin affects our whole being, including our minds. The only way to have a sound knowledge of our Creator is to trust what he tells us about himself. Muslims like to say *allahu akbar*, literally "God is greater." He is greater than anything, and of course, greater than our understanding. If we could capture him with our intellect, we would have made him an idol. Voltaire's aphorism would prove to be quite accurate in this case: "God created people in his image, and they did the same to him!"

Christian theologians have emphasized that the Christian faith, far from being irrational, is in search of intelligence. It makes sense that we are not able to penetrate the mystery of our Creator. We must humbly seek to understand the mystery that Christ has revealed to us. Some theologians, like St. Augustine, understood the Trinity in light of the statement that "God is love" (1 John 4:8). Love is inherently relational. From before the creation of the world, the Father loves the Son, the Son loves the Father, and the Holy Spirit is the One who expresses this love. According to another analogy used by Arab Christian theologians in the Islamic context, the Father is the Intellect, the Son the Intelligent, the Holy Spirit the Intelligible.[2]

Although creation is only a pale reflection of the Creator, we can still see that unity and diversity coexist within the same reality. The human being is one, and he is body and soul. The sun is one, and at the same time it is a disc, light and heat. These examples, although they fall short, may help us start understanding the Trinitarian monotheism of the Bible. God is absolutely one in his essence (or nature), which is fully possessed by the three persons – the Father, the Son and the Holy Spirit.

---

2. See Kuhn, *God Is One*, Appendix 2, Ibn al-Tayyib, "A Treatise on the Divine Attributes," 233–61.

God the Father: Above Us

Unlike Muhammad, Jesus lived in a Jewish environment that had been monotheistic for many centuries. For the Jews, there was only one God. So Jesus did not need to insist on this truth. He came to lift the veil on the mystery of who God is by giving full revelation of his being. The great new truth that Jesus brought from the beginning of his mission is that God is Father – Father in the absolute sense of the word.[3]

In the Old Testament, God is rarely described as Father though he is likened to a father. He is the father of the people of Israel (Deut 32:6; Jer 3:19; 31:9). He promised to have a father-son relationship with the Messiah, foreshadowed imperfectly in the relationship God had with Solomon, King David's son (2 Sam 7:14; Ps 89:26). He presents himself as "a father to the fatherless, a defender of widows" (Ps 68:5). He has a fatherly compassion for his human creatures: "As a father has compassion on his children, so the LORD has compassion on those who fear him" (Ps 103:13). In Jesus's day, some Jewish believers called God *abinu*, "our Father."[4] Before explaining this title, we should point out that the Qur'an never uses the word "father" for God, not even metaphorically, and it is of course not among "his most beautiful names" (59:22–24).[5]

To elucidate the meaning of the word "father," it is helpful to first explain what it does not mean when it is used for God. Indeed, this word can easily be misunderstood if we project on God our understanding of human fatherhood. In the Lord's Prayer, Jesus underscores that our Father is *in heaven*. What he meant is that human fatherhood and divine fatherhood are not the same. If we can say, by analogy, that God is Father, we must not equate our heavenly Father with a human father. In some ways God is like human fathers, but he is very different from them in other ways. God the Father is different from human fathers in many ways:

(1) Divine nature belongs exclusively to God. We have the same human nature as our earthly fathers, but we do not have the same nature as our heavenly Father. We are his adopted sons and daughters, not, as

---

[3]. This section is based on what I developed in my book, *Two Prayers for Today: The Lord's Prayer and the Fatiha*, ch. 3, "God in the Lord's Prayer," 37–45.

[4]. This designation is found in three of the famous "Eighteen Benedictions" of Jewish prayer.

[5]. According to Prophetic Tradition, God has ninety-nine names, some of which are found in the Qur'an. This number is to be taken symbolically since there are two lists of divine names which have in common only seventy-three names, so the total number is one hundred and twenty-five names. See *Two Prayers for Today*, Appendix 1, "God's 99 Names as Reported in the Hadith," 125–30.

it were, his "natural" children. The heavenly Father does not share his divine essence with any of his creatures.

(2) Divine fatherhood is spiritual while human fatherhood is both biological and spiritual. God has no female partner and he is not a gendered being. He is neither male nor female; he is beyond sexual differentiation that characterizes humans and many other creatures.

(3) God is perfect and self-sufficient while fathers (and mothers) are dependent beings (like all human beings). They are also fallible and sinners. At the same time, God's love for us is much greater than the love our human parents have for us or the one we have for our children: "If you, then, *though you are evil*, know how to give good gifts to your children, *how much more* will your Father in heaven give good gifts to those who ask him!"(Matt 7:11; emphasis added).

(4) Unlike human parents, God is eternal and immortal.

(5) God is spirit (John 4:24). He is not a material being. He cannot be in one place because he is present everywhere in the universe he created.

(6) God is worthy to be honored *and* worshipped, whereas we only need to honor our parents (Exod 20:12).

(7) There are a multitude of human fathers, but there is only one heavenly Father: "Do we not all have one father? Did not one God create us?" (Mal 2:10). These are obviously rhetorical questions.

(8) Human fathers have a limited number of children while our heavenly Father is the Father of all humans. He is the universal Father.

What does it mean for God to be "Father"? Here are some biblical texts that will help us grasp the meaning of divine fatherhood.

(1) God is our Creator
   We owe our existence and our life to God because we have been created by him (Isa 64:8).

(2) God takes care of us
   God provides for all our needs, material and spiritual (Matt 7:9–11).

(3) God is good to us
   Our Creator knows us best. He knows that we are weak and he is full of compassion for us (Ps 103:13–14).

(4) God educates us
> Our Creator is also the one who teaches us. He helps us to grow morally and spiritually. When necessary, he also corrects us (Prov 3:11–12; Heb 12:5–10).

(5) God is our divine Friend
> Because God is our Father, we can have an intimate relationship with him: "Have you not just called to me: 'My Father, my friend from my youth, will you always be angry? Will your wrath continue forever?'" (Jer 3:4–5). Jesus calls his disciples his friends and explains to them why: "I no longer call you servants, because a servant does not know his master's business. Instead, I have called you friends, for everything that I learned from my Father I have made known to you" (John 15:15).

(6) God loves us
> God loves all his creatures with no exception (John 3:16). Jesus explains to his disciples how far love can go: "Greater love has no one than this: to lay down one's life for one's friends" (John 15:13). Jesus offered his life on the cross to show his disciples the extent of his love for them.

(7) God is our Savior
> We have all disobeyed God and his law, and thus we have strayed far from the right path. We have not given him the honor due to him (Isa 63:16; Mal 1:6). We deserve divine punishment; however, since God loves us, he wants to forgive us our sins and save us from death. This is exactly what he has done through Jesus's mission.

Unlike any other creature, humans were all made in God's image (Gen 1:27; cf. Gen 5:1–2). This means that we are all equal before God regardless of our gender and our ethnic, social or religious backgrounds. It also implies that we are very close to each other despite all our differences. All human beings are brothers and sisters to the extent that they belong to the same human family.

Divine fatherhood is not the same as human fatherhood, but it is similar to it. Human fatherhood reflects divine fatherhood to some extent. The immanence of God, including the resemblance of character that humans have with him, must be maintained along with his transcendence, namely the essential difference between him and creation.

God the Son: With Us

Muhammad was born and lived in a polytheistic society. Arabs believed in a supreme god known as *Allah*. This word simply means "God" in Arabic. It was in use among Arabic-speaking Jews and Christians who lived in Arabia. Arab Christians continue to refer to God as "Allah" as evidenced in the Arabic translations of the Bible. It is likely that polytheistic Arabs believed in Allah as the Supreme God because they were influenced by Jewish and Christian communities. However, they ascribed partners to Allah, male and female, as well as sons and daughters. The Prophet's mission was to convince his people that God had no associates, as the following texts show:

> They ascribe as partners unto Him the *jinns*, although He did create them, and impute falsely sons and daughters unto Him not knowing [He has neither sons nor daughters]. Glory to Him for He is far above what they ascribe (unto Him). (6:100)

> They ascribe daughters unto Him [whereas] they prefer [to have sons]. (16:57; cf. 17:40; 43:16)

> Say: "He is God, One and Only . . . He begets not, nor is He begotten. And there is none like unto Him." (112:1–4)

> The very Creator of heavens and earth: How could He have a son when He has no female partner? He created all things, and He has full knowledge of all things. (6:101; cf. 72:3)

These texts give us an idea of Arab polytheism at the time of Muhammad, known in the Qur'an as *shirk*, literally "associationism." It is the only sin that God will never forgive (4:48). In such a context, it is not difficult to misunderstand the meaning of the title "Son of God" given by Christians to Jesus Christ. The divine sonship of Christ is conceived and rejected as a biological conception, which has nothing to do with the Christian understanding:

> The Jews call 'Uzayr a son of God, and the Christians call Christ the son of God. What they say is like what the disbelievers of old used to say. May God fight against them: how they are deluded [from the truth]. (9:30)[6]

---

6. The identity of 'Uzayr is uncertain. Some Muslim commentators believe this to be Ezra because of the prominent role he played after the return of the Jews from exile in Babylon. The word used for Christians is *nasaara*, lit. "Nazarenes"; see note 12 on this word in chapter 6 (about the corruption of the Bible).

They are disbelievers who say: "God is Christ, the son of Mary." Christ [himself] said, "O Son of Israel! Worship God, my Lord and your Lord." (5:72; cf. 5:17)[7]

They (Christians) say: "God gave Himself a son." Glory to Him. Everything in heavens and on earth belongs to Him. All are devoted to Him. (2:116)

Our Lord, may He be always exalted, gave Himself neither a companion nor a child. (72:3)

Taken together, these qur'anic verses make it clear that, as with the Trinity, it is a misconception of the divine sonship of Jesus that is rejected. Indeed, Jesus's sonship is construed as a biological sonship, hence Jesus is misunderstood as the son of God by virtue of a physical relationship between God and a female partner, possibly Mary. This is obviously not what Christians believe. Jesus is the only and eternal Son in the spiritual sense of the term. He became a man without giving up his divine nature. The fact that he was born of the Virgin Mary is a hint at his status as the Father's eternal Son, not the evidence for his divinity.

Muslim authors criticize the Torah for presenting God with human features. However, the Qur'an also uses an anthropomorphic language for God. For example, it speaks of the face of God (2:115), his eyes (11:37), his hand (3:26), and seems to locate him in the heavens (67:17) where there is a throne on which he is seated (7:54), to say nothing of the wrath of God (1:7) or his plotting character (8:30). One can easily interpret these anthropomorphic expressions, as do Muslim theologians, in a metaphorical sense. Christians do the same with similar expressions found in the Bible.

Conversely, Muslim theologians criticize Christians for equating a man, in this case Jesus, with God, in a way similar to what Arab polytheists used to do (10:68; 18:4; 19:88; 21:26; 23:91). The Bible never says "God gave himself a son" to quote the qur'anic verse (2:116); Jesus has always been his Son. What the Qur'an denounces is actually a Christian heresy, namely "adoptionism," the belief that Jesus was adopted as the son of God when he was baptized.[8]

Muslim theologians who are familiar with true Christian doctrine use several arguments to explain why they reject this doctrine. One of these arguments is that the Gospels present Jesus as a human being. He was hungry

---

7. Disbelievers are those who have an inauthentic faith; the word *kufr* denotes not the absence of faith but a corrupted faith.

8. This heresy is attributed to Theodotus of Byzantium who lived in the second century AD.

and thirsty (Matt 4:2; John 4:7), was tempted by the devil (Matt 4:1), was tired (John 4:6), needed to sleep (Matt 8:24), was deeply moved to the point of weeping (John 11:35; Luke 19:41), was troubled at his imminent death (John 12:27), confessed his ignorance of certain things (Mark 13:32), and confessed that "the Father is greater than [him]" (John 14:28). Muslim theologians also point out that Jesus identified with his disciples when he declared to one of them: "Do not hold on to me, for I have not yet ascended to the Father. Go instead to my brothers and tell them, 'I am ascending *to my Father and your Father, to my God and your God*'" (John 20:17; emphasis added).

Thus, since Jesus was fully human, Muslim theologians say that he cannot be the Son of God. One has to choose – either Jesus is a man or he is God. He cannot be both at the same time. This either-or argument ignores the teaching of the gospel that Jesus was at the same time human and divine. The four Gospels do display the full humanity of Jesus, which explains that Jesus experienced the same limitations and weaknesses as all human beings.

For Muslim authors, to say that Jesus is both human and divine doesn't make sense. As with the Trinity, they hold a rationalistic reasoning even though Islam is not, as has already been said, a rationalistic religion. As for the words of Christ, "my God and your God" (John 20:17), it echoes the words that Christ in the Qur'an pronounces before his people: "My Lord and your Lord" (5:72, 117).[9] Muslim commentators miss the point when they take these words to mean that Christ puts himself at the same level as his disciples. In fact, it is just the opposite: Jesus never identified with his disciples in saying "our Lord," "our God" or "our Father." He always calls God "the Father," "your Father" or "my Father." By referring to God in this way, he highlights precisely that his relationship to God is unique, for he is the eternal Son. His disciples are invited to enter into a relationship with God similar to the relationship he has with the Father from all eternity. It is therefore an obvious misinterpretation of John 20:17 when this verse is used to demonstrate that Jesus is not the Son of God.

Another argument used by Muslim authors such as Ghazali is to understand "Son of God" in a metaphorical sense. Muslim authors argue that the Torah ascribes this title to the people of Israel as a whole (Exod 4:22) and to the Messiah (Ps 2:7–9; 2 Sam 7:14) and even to angels (Job 1:6). And they argue that in the New Testament, Adam is called the son of God (Luke 3:38) as well as the disciples of Jesus (Matt 6:9). However, Jesus is the "only son": "No one has ever seen God, but the one and only Son, who is himself God and is in

---

9. In the Qur'an these words are also uttered by the Arab prophet Houd (11:56) and by Moses (40:27).

closest relationship with the Father, has made him known" (John 1:18; cf. John 1:14). We, who are created in the image of God (Gen 1:27), are called to enter into a filial relationship with God following the example of the only begotten Son and thanks to him. It is he who saves us from death and opens the door to eternal life for us: "For God so loved the world that he gave his one and only Son, that whoever believes in him shall not perish but have eternal life" (John 3:16; cf. John 3:18). And because he perfectly fulfilled the mission entrusted to him by the Father to save humanity, he has also been appointed as the one who will judge all humans on the last day:

> For just as the Father raises the dead and gives them life, even so the Son gives life to whom he is pleased to give it. Moreover, the Father judges no one, but has entrusted all judgment to the Son, that all may honor the Son just as they honor the Father. Whoever does not honor the Son does not honor the Father, who sent him. (John 5:21–23)

It emerges from these texts that the Son is equal to the Father and has the same prerogatives as him. Nothing differentiates him from the Father except precisely the fact that he is the Son. In other words, Jesus is divine because, as the Son of God, he has the same nature as the Father.

Muslims point out that Jesus never says in the Gospels, "I am God," and they think that this casts a serious doubt on his divinity. There are, it seems, two main reasons why Jesus never uttered these words. First, by his incarnation – his lowering himself to become a human being – Jesus wanted to signal that God is great, but he is not arrogant. On the contrary, he is humble, as the conditions of Jesus's birth demonstrate as well as his triumphal entry into Jerusalem on the back of a donkey (Mark 11:1–7). Jesus's self-humbling came to a head in his passion: his arrest, his unjust trial, his atrocious flogging and his dreadful crucifixion. On the eve of his crucifixion, he dressed as a servant and began to wash the feet of his disciples to enact the meaning of his imminent death (John 13:1–5). He will wash away the sins of those who believe in him. Thus, Jesus's humility would have been undermined if he said openly that he was God.

Second, Jesus refrained from saying bluntly, "I am God," because he carried out his mission among the Jewish people who were fiercely monotheistic. If he had directly declared that he was God, he would have run the risk of being misunderstood, appearing as if he was reducing God to his person (whereas he is only the second person of the Trinity), or as if he was challenging God's oneness and transcendence as taught in the Torah. However, and while being very careful with the language he used, Jesus deliberately performed acts and uttered words which left no doubt that he was of divine status, at least for those who had "ears to hear" (Mark 4:9). His listeners, and his learned opponents in particular, were not mistaken. They perfectly understood the significance of his statements and it was because of his claim to divinity that he was condemned to death (Mark 14:60–64). Some Muslims say that the judges who condemned Jesus to death misunderstood his words. If that was really the case, Jesus would undoubtedly have taken the trouble to explain himself at his trial. Far from correcting their understanding, he confirmed it and agreed to pay the price.

Muslim authors also argue that divine majesty is irreconcilable with the humbling of God manifested in the incarnation, and even more so with the humiliation of the cross. It would be demeaning and degrading for the King of kings to become a servant just as all human creatures. It is inconceivable that the author of life, the immortal, should suffer death. This argument is of course understandable. It helps us appreciate the extraordinary character of the gospel (cf. 1 Cor 2:9). It helps us measure the depth of God's mystery and the extent of his love. Have we, as humans, the right to challenge the sovereign and almighty God about the way he decided to demonstrate his love, namely by becoming like one of us and even dying for us?

For Christians and Muslims, death does not mean the end of one's existence; it is the passage from life on earth to the next life. Jesus promised the repentant thief that he would be with him in paradise on the very day they were crucified (Luke 23:42–43). True love puts itself at the service of others. Perfect love gives itself to the loved one. This is what we, human beings, experience in our family, social and even national relationships. Faced with God's immeasurable love, the only fitting attitude for us is to respond to his love with love and to worship the One who never ceases to teach us, in word and in deed, what genuine love really means.

The rationalist approach of Muslim theologians, when they consider the issue of Christ's divinity, is because they want to preserve God's oneness – Islam's central doctrine – at all costs. While sharing their concern to protect monotheism from any alteration, their approach seems to be based on a reading of the Qur'an that does not sufficiently take into consideration the religious context of Arabia at the beginning of the seventh century. They argue as if the Qur'an rejects the biblical teaching on the Trinity and the divinity of Christ. We have seen that it is actually a misrepresentation of this teaching that is refuted in the Qur'an. Christians also condemn this misrepresentation. Let's close this discussion with a qur'anic text in which God calls for the Prophet to accept divine revelation even if it appears to him to be irrational: "Say: 'If the All-Merciful had a son, I would be the first to worship [this son]'" (43:81).

God the Holy Spirit: Within Us

The words "Holy Spirit" are found three times in the Old Testament (Ps 51:11; Isa 63:10–11) and over ninety times in the New Testament. The Spirit of God is God's agent at work in the cosmos. The word *ruah* in Hebrew can mean spirit, wind or breath. Associated with God, the preeminent Holy One, *ruah* refers to the Spirit by which God acts in creation (Gen 1:2; 2:7), and in the midst of his people. The Spirit inspires the prophets (Zech 7:12), guides the leaders of the people such as Moses (Num 11:17), gives wisdom to the judges of Israel (Num 11:25–29), and empowers certain people (Judg 14:6).

The prophets predicted the time when the Spirit would no longer rest only on the elite but on the whole people (Joel 2:28–29). This time will be marked by the revelation of God to his people through his Spirit (Ezek 39:29), making each one capable of following the law of God (Ezek 36:27). A new covenant will then be made between God and his people. This covenant will be marked by a universal knowledge of the Lord, who will forgive his people their sins and will inscribe his laws within their hearts (Jer 31:31–34). The Messiah will play a key role in these events because, moved by the Spirit of God who will rest on him, he will bring good news to the poor, to the captives and brokenhearted (Isa 61:1–2).

The New Testament describes the Holy Spirit in terms that indicate that he is a person and not just a divine attribute. Jesus is conceived by the Spirit in the womb of the Virgin Mary (Luke 1:35). The Spirit descends on him when he was baptized in the form of a dove (Matt 3:16). He is given without measure to Jesus for the accomplishment of his mission (John 3:34). In the synagogue of Nazareth, Jesus claims to be the foretold messenger who, under the anointing of the Holy Spirit, comes to proclaim the Good News to the poor (Luke 4:16–21). Jesus works miracles by the power of the Spirit (Matt 12:18, 28), but his opponents reject his message and accuse him of being the devil's agent (Matt 12:24). Jesus warns his disciples that they too will be persecuted, but they need not worry, because the Spirit of God will come to their aid (Matt 10:20). The only sin that will never be forgiven is the sin against the Holy Spirit, which consists in deliberately refusing the truth about Christ when one has witnessed a powerful manifestation of that truth (Matt 12:24–32).

Before leaving them, Jesus promises his disciples that he will not abandon them. He will send them "the Holy Spirit," also called "the Spirit of truth," who comes from the Father. The Holy Spirit will always be with them and in them (John 14:16–17). He will manifest the presence of the Father and of the Son in the life of the disciples (John 14:23). His mission will be to remind them of the teaching of Christ (John 14:26), to bear witness to him (John 15:26), and "to guide them into all the truth" (John 16:13).

The action of the Spirit will extend to everyone, since "he will prove the world to be in the wrong about sin and righteousness and judgment" (John 16:8). Just before ascending into heaven, forty days after his resurrection, Jesus reminds his disciples of the promise he made to them concerning the Holy Spirit: he will clothe them with power and equip them to carry his message to all peoples (Acts 1:8). Ten days later, the promise came true. In the speech the apostle Peter gave on the day of Pentecost, he declared that the ancient prophecies were fulfilled by the outpouring of the Spirit on Israel (Acts 2:16–21), and, sometime later, on the nations represented by Cornelius, the Roman officer (Acts 10:44–45).

The expression "Holy Spirit" (*ruh al-qudus*) occurs four times in the Qur'an: once in connection with the revelation of the Qur'an (16:102) and three times with the mission of Jesus: "We gave Moses the Book and followed him up with a succession of messengers; We gave Jesus the son of Mary clear proofs and strengthened him with the holy spirit" (2:87; cf. 2:253; 5:110). The word "spirit" is found twenty-four times in the Qur'an with a wide range of meanings, including "breath":

- God created man and "breathed His spirit into him" (32:9; cf. 15:29; 38:72).
- He sent his spirit to Mary, who appeared before her in the form of a perfect man (19:17).
- Mary "preserved her private part and We breathed into her with Our spirit" (21:91; 66:12).
- Jesus is God's spirit (4:171).
- The agent of qur'anic revelation was "the faithful spirit" (26:193).
- God sends his spirit to whomever he wants (40:15).
- He upholds believers with his spirit (58:22).
- We must not despair of the spirit of God (12:87).

These texts give us an idea of the action that God performs with his Spirit, in creation as well as in revelation. The identity of the spirit is not as clear in the qur'anic text as in the New Testament. When the first Muslims asked the Prophet about the spirit, the meaning of his response was not obvious:

"They ask you (Muhammad) about the spirit. Say: 'The spirit is part of my Lord's business, and you have been given only little knowledge'" (17:85). This verse shows that the status of the spirit of God is rather obscure. Muslim scholars have offered several explanations. The most common one is to identify him with an angel, possibly Gabriel. This interpretation aims at ruling out the possibility of considering something divine which is distinct from God himself. This minimalist interpretation strangely resembles the minimalist interpretations given to the title "Word of God" ascribed to Jesus in the Qur'an. The concern of Muslim commentators is clearly to protect qur'anic teaching from anything that could undermine God's oneness. However, the Qur'an makes a clear distinction between the spirit and angels (*mala'ika*) as shown in several verses (16:2; 70:4; 78:38; 97:4).

The coming of Jesus Christ represents for Christians the ultimate revelation made by God to humankind. Through his teaching, we know that God is not only one, he is also unique in the sense that he exists in three persons, each of whom manifests divine love in a distinct and personal way. God the Father is *above* us. He has loving *authority* over us and shows us his love by exhorting us to follow the right path revealed in his written word, the Bible. God the Son is *with* us: his name is "Emmanuel . . . God with us" (Matt 1:23). Through his incarnation and redemptive mission, he demonstrated close *solidarity* with us to the extent of making us God's adopted sons and daughters. God the Holy Spirit is *within* us. He dwells in us deep within our being. The felt *intimacy* of his presence is none other than that of the Father and the Son. The life he communicates to us is the very life of God, the foretaste of which we experience in this life while as we wait for the full realization of Christian hope when God will be all in all.

Is God the Same in the Bible and the Qur'an?

This chapter has enabled us to identify the main difference between Christian and Islamic monotheisms. The question we still need to consider is this: Is God the same in the two religions?[10]

This question is not simple, as each religion has many "faces" significantly different from each other. For Christianity, there are of course the different churches (Catholic, Orthodox, Anglican, Protestant, Evangelical, etc.). There

---

10. An attempt to answer this question can be found in *Two Prayers for Today*, ch. 8, "Is God the Same in Christianity and Islam?", 85–93.

are also various trends that cross all churches: mystical, social, conservative, liberal... The same applies to Islam with its different groups (Sunni, Shiʿa, ʿIbadi, Khariji, etc.) and streams (mystical, social, reformist, conservative, political, radical, and violent). Individuals live out their faith in a very personal way and believers cannot be reduced to their community. Our response will rely on mainstream Islamic and Christian teachings.

One point is clear: in the Qurʾan God is not a Triune God, as he is in the New Testament. Among his most beautiful names, listed in the Prophetic Tradition, we do not find the three names which are at the center of the Christian faith: "Father," "Savior," and "love." In Islam humans are not really lost and therefore, strictly speaking, they do not need salvation as the Muslim scholar Ismail al-Faruqi has pointed out. They have simply gone astray but they can find their way back to the straight path thanks to Sharīʿa guidance and divine help. Likewise, God is merciful (*rahim*), but he is not loving (*muhibb*), for he is too much above humans for an intimate and personal loving relationship to exist between the Creator and his humble creatures. Moreover, love is associated by Muslim theologians with a state of weakness and dependency because the lover needs the beloved whereas God is powerful, self-sufficient and needs nothing. The mere fact of naming God "Father" arouses in Muslim thinkers (mystics excepted) a whole series of misunderstandings and suspicions. If we stick to this information, the answer to the above question must be "no."

A fair and informed answer to this question must also consider the qurʾanic "portrait" of God, in particular, his most beautiful names. None of these names, when closely examined, is alien to biblical revelation. Even the name "avenging" (*muntaqim*) could be understood in the sense of someone who punishes, judges and implements justice (cf. Rom 13:4; 1 Thess 4:6; Rev 6:10). In Islam, God is personal, creator of all things, perfect, just, sovereign, trustworthy, generous, lenient, close to his servants, etc. Islamic theology speaks of five attributes exclusive to God: unity, eternity, otherness, self-existence and self-sufficiency. His main attributes, which are shared with human creatures to a certain degree, are seven: power, knowledge, will, life, speech, hearing and vision. This convergence between God's biblical and Islamic "portraits" suggests that Christians and Muslims do worship the same God though they do not know him in the same way. This by no means lessens the theological differences between the two religious traditions.

The question about God applies in almost the same terms to the one about Jesus. Is Jesus the same for Christians and Muslims? In the Qurʾan, Jesus is a monotheistic prophet, born of the Virgin Mary, sent to the people of Israel, entrusted with a Holy Scripture (the Gospel). Despite the many miracles he performed (e.g. healing of the sick, raising the dead), he encountered fierce opposition from the religious authorities of his people, who wanted to put him to death. Is there any other historic character to whom this description could apply? Obviously not. But what about Jesus's death, resurrection and divinity, which are all alien to qur'anic teaching? Do Christians and Muslims believe in the same Jesus? We cannot answer with a simple "yes" or "no." Rather, to take into consideration everything said in the holy books about Jesus, we should answer with a "yes" and a "no."

In Jesus's time there was a community of mixed origin in Palestine: the Samaritans.[11] They lived in Samaria, a province sandwiched between Galilee in the north and Judea in the south. The Samaritans were a monotheistic community and they believed only in Moses as a prophet. Hence, their Holy Scripture was limited to the Pentateuch (the first five books of the Bible). They worshiped God on Mount Gerizim and awaited the coming of the Messiah. Very strong tensions characterized the relations between Jews and Samaritans because of their religious disagreements and the wars which set in opposition the two communities (cf. Ecclesiasticus 50:25-26; John 4:9; 8:48).[12]

Unlike his fellow Jews, Jesus shows much sympathy towards Samaritans. To a teacher of the law who wanted to know how people can love their neighbor, Jesus gives the example of the "Good Samaritan" (Luke 10:25-37). He also praises the Samaritan man who came back to thank him for having healed him, and Jesus contrasts the grateful attitude of this foreigner with that of the nine Jews who had also been healed but showed no gratitude to him (Luke 17:11-18). One day a whole Samaritan village did not welcome Jesus and his disciples. The disciples were very angry and wanted God to destroy all the villagers, but Jesus rebuked them (Luke 9:51-56). Jesus surprises a Samaritan woman, who had a bad reputation, when he humbly takes the initiative to establish a relationship with her (John 4:4-42). After a long conversation, he tells her who he was: the expected Messiah. The woman is overjoyed and becomes a successful evangelist among her own people.

---

11. Samaritans were the product of intermarriage between Assyrians and Jews in the northern kingdom of Israel (cf. 2 Kgs 17:24-33). Today, a small Samaritan community still lives in Nablus, a town in the West Bank.

12. Here is how Jesus, son of Sirach, a devout Jew, described the Samaritan community: "There are two nations that my soul detests, and the third is not a nation at all: the inhabitants of Mount Seir (Edomites), and the Philistines, and the stupid people living in Shechem (Samaritans)" (Ecclesiasticus 50:25-26; Jerusalem Bible). Ecclesiasticus is a deuterocanonical book written in the second century BC.

During this personal and highly theological interfaith dialogue, Jesus says to the woman: "You Samaritans worship what you do not know; we (Jews) worship what we do know, for salvation is from the Jews" (John 4:22). Jesus does not say that the Samaritans worshipped an idol. They did worship God but they had inadequate knowledge of him since they did not accept all the Jewish prophets that came after Moses. This did not make them a pagan people without any knowledge of God; however, Jesus does not hesitate to declare to the woman, at the risk of offending her, that "salvation comes from the Jews."

Several lessons can be drawn from Jesus's very meaningful encounters with Samaritan people. First, God is at work everywhere, including in religious communities, and we must humbly and joyfully acknowledge his action. Thanks to this action, people of other faiths (and of no faith) sometimes act in a wonderful way to the point of shaming us as Christians. Second, Christians are neither worse nor better than non-Christians. When we become aware of our shortcomings, we need to admit them and ask forgiveness from God and others. Third, humility and kindness towards others, which should characterize our behavior, are not incompatible with boldness in our faith. If we truly believe that God is our Savior in Jesus Christ, and that we cannot have adequate knowledge of our Creator if we do not know him as such, then we must confidently share our convictions in contextually appropriate ways. Can we consider that the Muslim community is in a similar position to that of the Samaritans? It appears that mainstream Muslims and mainstream Christians do worship the same God, but because of their faith in Jesus Christ, Christians, unlike Muslims, know God as the heavenly Father and their loving Redeemer.

9

Forgiveness in Islam and Christianity

Many people still remember 11 September 2001, a day that changed the world in terms of how non-Muslims perceive Islam and Muslims.[1] Since then, violent acts committed in the name of Islam have dramatically increased in France, in Islamic countries and in many other countries. These attacks have a very negative and lasting impact on the image of Islam in public opinion. More often than not, Islam is seen as an aggressive, violent and revengeful religion. So much so that when I happened to say that my PhD research in Islamics was on forgiveness in Islam, many were surprised and asked if forgiveness really exists in this religion.[2]

This chapter will sketch Islamic thought on forgiveness, first in its vertical dimension (forgiveness received from God), then horizontal (forgiveness given to others). In the last part, a Christian perspective on forgiveness will be offered.

In Islam God is one, personal and creator. Among his most beautiful names (or attributes) we find "the One who forgives sins." Süra 40 is entitled "He who absolves." Divine forgiveness is determined mainly by three attributes which are all highlighted in the qur'anic text. God is *sovereign* (he has the freedom to decide what he wants and the power to implement his decisions), *just* (he rewards human creatures according to their merits) and *merciful* (he grants

---

[1]. Young readers may not know that this was the day when several coordinated terrorist attacks were carried out against the United States, including in New York where around three thousand people were killed when the World Trade Center Twin Towers collapsed.

[2]. The viva (defense) took place in 1994 at the EPHE (École Pratique des Hautes Études), department of religious sciences (part of the Sorbonne University). A book based on the thesis is available in English, *The Search for Forgiveness: Pardon and Punishment in Islam and Christianity*. This chapter is an outline of the book which provides all the relevant references to the treatises on Islamic theology and mysticism used in the following pages.

his blessings to all by virtue of his great generosity). There are different ways to articulate these three attributes, which explains why in Islamic thought on forgiveness, there are three main schools whose teaching differs significantly according to the primacy given to one or the other of these attributes.

1. God Will Forgive All Muslims according to His Sovereign and Merciful Will

For the Sunni school, the most influential in Islamic theology, God's *sovereignty* is paramount and comes before his mercy and justice. Many qur'anic texts speak of God's absolute right to forgive or to punish his creatures: "He will forgive whom He will and He will punish whom He will. For God has supreme power over all things" (2:284; cf. 3:129; 5:20, 43; 48:14). As a sovereign God, he decided not to forgive polytheists (who believe in more than one god) and atheists. By definition, Muslims are monotheists since the Islamic creed is all about God's oneness and Muhammad's apostleship.

Muslims are sinners like everyone else, because either they commit acts forbidden by Sharī'a or they do not fulfill all their obligations. If they sincerely repent of their transgressions, they will be forgiven. But what if they persist in their sins and do not repent? This is where divine sovereignty and mercy come in – it will be up to God on judgment day to freely decide who to forgive and what sins to forgive: "God does not forgive those who ascribe partners to Him,[3] but He forgives any other sin to whom He pleases" (4:48; cf. 4:116). Thus, not all Muslims will be forgiven; those who will (by virtue of divine mercy) will go to paradise, others will be condemned (because of divine justice) and will go to hell.

Unforgiven Muslims, however, will not stay in hell forever, for two reasons. First, because they did not commit the only unforgivable sin, namely polytheism. Second, because, on judgment day, the Prophet will intercede on behalf of his community. His intercession will especially benefit Muslims who are most in need of divine mercy, namely those who have committed particularly serious sins and have not repented of them. The God-given privilege of interceding for sinful Muslims is ascribed to Muhammad in several hadiths including this one: "On the Day of Resurrection my intercession will be in favor of members of my community who have committed major sins."[4] God having promised to answer the prayer of his Prophet, groups of Muslims

---

3. Or paraphrased: those who worship other gods alongside, or instead of, him.
4. Ibn Majah, *Zuhd* (Asceticism), 37.

will come out of hell one after another (after they have been forgiven) and enter heaven. In short, according to Sunni theologians, all Muslims will eventually find themselves in paradise, because they have not committed the only sin that God has sovereignly decided not to absolve.

2. God Will Forgive Only Muslims Who Have Not Committed a Major Sin

The Mu'tazili school is also important in Islamic theology, though it is less representative of the Muslim community. Theologians of this school place divine *justice* above all other attributes. According to them, God must punish sinners as it would be unfair to forgive those who deserve to be punished for their sins. This school divides sins into two main categories – major and minor – based on several qur'anic verses including the following: "If you keep away from major [sins], We will pardon your [minor] sins and introduce you [to Paradise] through a gate of great honour" (4:31; cf. 42:37; 53:32).

What is a major sin? It is any act which will lead the person to hell (if they don't repent). According to this school, it is not possible for us to know all major sins. We are aware only of some of them, in particular the sins for which the penal code prescribes a sanction.[5] It is on purpose and for our own benefit that God did not want to reveal to us all major sins. Our ignorance is both an incentive and a deterrent: it encourages us to obey God's law and warns us against any sin for fear of committing a major one.

Another characteristic of this school is that, unlike Sunni doctrine, it does not teach temporary punishment in hell. People in hell will remain there forever, including Muslims. For Mu'tazilis, God will forgive sinners because he is merciful, but he can only forgive minor sins as forgiving major sins would seriously compromise his justice. As a result, only Muslims who committed minor sins will go to paradise. Divine justice is so perfect that they will enjoy happiness in proportion to their merits. Likewise, the damned will receive a punishment in hell commensurate with their guilt. The Prophet will only intercede on judgment day on behalf of righteous Muslims, who are already in paradise, so that God may show his generosity and increase their reward and their happiness.

---

5. For example, apostasy, murder, adultery, theft, consumption of alcohol, and false accusation of immorality brought against a married Muslim woman. Among other great sins are polytheism, witchcraft, false witness, rebellion against parents, missing daily prayer, running away from battle, excessive trust in God's mercy, or the opposite, excessive fear of God's judgment.

Sunni and Mu'tazili theologians agree that good works are essential for salvation. Good works have a redeeming role as the following text attests: "The good deeds remove the evil deeds" (11:114). However, for Mu'tazilis, this compensatory role is restricted to minor sins; major ones can only be forgiven through sincere repentance.

Sunni theologians do not accept the distinction between major and minor sins. For them, God's sovereign mercy is such that he has the freedom to forgive all sins with or without the sinner's repentance. For all theologians, repentance is required from everyone who violates divine law.

What about Jews and Christians? Will divine forgiveness be available to them? The Qur'an recognizes Judaism and Christianity as two divine religions based on holy books (although their reliability is now uncertain). Therefore Jews and Christians are favorably referred to as "the People of the Book." Two verses from the Qur'an state that Jews and Christians have nothing to fear on the day of judgment because of their monotheistic faith (2:62; 5:69), however, the Qur'an levels serious criticisms against these two communities. Christians in particular are blamed for having corrupted God's oneness with their doctrines on the divine Trinity and the divinity of Christ. They are equated with disbelievers, even polytheists (2:105; 3:70; 5:72–73; 9:30–31; 98:1, 6). The simple fact that Jews and Christians do not accept Muhammad as prophet is enough to classify them as non-believers. As a result, traditional Islamic theology leaves very little hope for Jews and Christians with regard to their eternal destiny.

3. God Will Forgive Everyone because His Mercy Is Boundless

Mysticism is also an important trend within the Muslim community and mystics are often found in Sufi brotherhoods. However, the influence of their spirituality extends beyond the brotherhoods and reaches all Muslims who seek a personal and intimate relationship with God based on love, not just law.

Ibn 'Arabi is one of Islam's greatest mystics, and he attracts many of our contemporaries.[6] His thought is undoubtedly the most elaborate, rich and complex with regard to spirituality. He will serve as our guide as we outline the mystical perspective on forgiveness.

---

6. Ibn 'Arabi was born in Murcia (Andalusia) in AH 560/AD 1165 and died in Damascus (Syria) in AH 638/AD 1240. He is the author of numerous works, some of which are available in English, including his masterpiece *Al-Futuhat al-Makkiyya*, edited and published by M. Chodkiewicz (*The Meccan Revelations: Selected Texts of Al-Futuhat Al-Makiyya*). This volume comprises only short extracts from this monumental work of the Grand Sheikh.

For Ibn 'Arabi, *mercy* defines God's very essence and takes precedence over all other divine attributes. This mercy is limitless according to the Qur'an (7:156) whose sūras (except the ninth) opens with the invocation "In the name of God the All-Merciful, the Ever-Merciful." God manifests his mercy to all his creatures in this life and the next, for his mercy infinitely surpasses his anger.[7] Divine mercy finds its perfect expression in forgiveness which is also unlimited: "Say [O Muhammad], 'O my servants who have transgressed against their souls! Despair not of God's mercy. God forgives *all sins*, for He is All-forgiving, Ever-Merciful'" (39:53; emphasis added).[8]

Ibn 'Arabi comments that this verse is addressed to *all* God's servants, that is, to everyone. This text specifies that God forgives *all* sins with no exception; in other words, there is no sin that God does not forgive, not even polytheism. The author points out that forgiveness is completely free and depends on no condition, even repentance.

As a Sunni Muslim, Ibn 'Arabi admits that non-Muslims will go to hell (in accordance with divine justice) just like many Muslims. Punishment for Muslims will be less painful and shorter; in other words, all Muslims will eventually come out of hell and enter paradise. Muslims will be followed by Jews, Christians and all other monotheists. Only non-monotheists will remain in hell, but their punishment will also end once they have paid for their sins. They will however remain in hell which will then be turned into a place of bliss, different and of lesser degree than that of paradise. For Ibn 'Arabi, divine amnesty, sovereignly decreed, will be universal and will benefit all humanity with no exception. Everyone will ultimately be pardoned, for eternal punishment is not compatible with divine mercy.

Mystics have a much deeper understanding of sin and repentance than theologians. Sin is not simply disobeying divine commandments – it is estrangement from God and undue assertion of oneself. They understand repentance (*tawba*) in connection with the first meaning of the word, namely, "return" to God. Repentance is therefore the first and indispensable stage of a true pilgrimage leading ultimately not to Mecca but to God. This inner conversion, required from everyone (including practicing Muslims), radically transforms the existence of the repentant.

---

7. According to a divine hadith recorded in the Prophetic Tradition, the following inscription was placed before the divine throne when the universe was created: "My mercy will always prevail over My anger"; Bukhari, *Tawhid* (Monotheism), 15.

8. On the connection between divine mercy and forgiveness, see also Qur'an 2:286; 3:157; 7:23, 155; 23:109, 118.

Pushing this logic to its end, Ibn ʿArabi believes that sin is in reality a faux-pas (*zalla*), whose real author is God himself. This faux-pas provides the opportunity for repentance, a return to the divine Source. This return, from God through God to God, will be consummated when the entire universe becomes one with its divine Origin. Thus, the Andalusian thinker does not hesitate to celebrate sin as it grants repentant people, after they have completed their pilgrimage, the remarkable experience of merging with the only one Being who really exists and who Ibn ʿArabi defines as "the One who exists by Himself."

For Ibn ʿArabi, on judgment day, the Prophet will intercede for all people, not just for Muslims. Muhammad is seen as the universal Prophet who was sent to all nations through the prophets who were his deputies. He pre-existed Adam and received his prophetic call when Adam was created though he did not manifest himself to Arabs as prophet until the sixth century when he appeared as a human being. It is thanks to his intercession that humanity will be forgiven and saved.

The three understandings of divine forgiveness, just reviewed, reflect the theological diversity of Islamic thought. This diversity explains why Muslims have very different ideas on this subject, all based on the qurʾanic text. It is the way this text is interpreted and the precedence given to some passages over others that differentiate various schools of thought.

"Forgiving Is Closer to Righteousness [than Claiming One's Rights]" (Qurʾan 2:237)[9]

Islamic teaching urges Muslims to forgive their fellow Muslims as well as non-Muslims, taking God himself and the Prophet as a model.[10] Indeed, as we have just seen, God is merciful – he is "the best forgiver" (7:155). He forgives out of sheer generosity whereas we humans forgive either to show off or to free ourselves from pain.

The Prophet's mission was to disclose divine mercy to all peoples (21:107). He is called "the Prophet of mercy."[11] He is also called "the Prophet

---

9. Muslim writers often quote this verse (out of context) to highlight the importance of forgiving others. The text deals with divorce when it happens before the consummation of marriage. Forgiveness in this context refers to the giving up by the husband or the wife of the amount of dower which is due to them.

10. Muslims are encouraged to forgive in some fifteen qurʾanic verses as well as in many prophetic sayings.

11. Muslim, *Faḍaʾil* (Virtues), 34.

of repentance"[12] because his message calls everyone to repent and return to God. He himself used to repent daily.[13] In Mecca, he encountered a lot of opposition, and God commanded him to ignore the hostility of his enemies: "Show forgiveness, command what is right and turn away from the ignorant!" (7:199; cf. 45:14–15; 73:10). The Muslim community also had to be kind with their Jewish opponents: "Forgive them and bear with them *until* God brings about His Directive. God has power over all things" (2:109; emphasis added; cf. 5:13; 15:85; 43:88–89). This last text suggests that divine forbearance will end.

Muhammad was kind to the members of his community (9:128). He was to forgive them and ask God's forgiveness on their behalf (3:159). Muslims are also called upon to be lenient towards one another, especially towards their relatives (64:14). Believers are described as people "who forgive after they have been made angry" (42:37; cf. 42:43; 16:126). They need to fulfill their religious obligations and lead a life characterized by mercy: "[The results of] goodness and wrongdoing are not the same. Repel [evil] in the best possible way. Your enemy will then become like a close friend" (41:34; cf. 2:263; 4:149). A Muslim once asked the Prophet how many times he should forgive his servant who kept doing wrong to him. He replied: "Each day you will forgive him seventy times."[14] Forgiving others is therefore a good deed which will be rewarded, as will all good deeds. Muslims who "suppress their anger and forgive others" will be forgiven on the day of judgment (3:134; cf. 24:22).

In 622 (year one of the Islamic calendar), the Prophet left his hometown, Mecca, and migrated to Medina, accompanied by a few dozen Muslims. In Medina the Muslim community grew rapidly despite opposition from the large Jewish community. Jews were accused of plotting with Meccan polytheists against the Prophet and his community. Two years later, the conflict between the two communities reached a climax. It was then that two revelations came to the Prophet. First, Muslims should no longer pray towards Jerusalem as they had done before (2:127). Second, they were allowed, even commanded, to go to war against their enemies whereas previously they were to ignore them and even forgive them. Muslim commentators call this new revelation "the Verse about the Sword" (*ayat al-sayf*), without specifying what verse it is. It seems they have in mind the qur'anic texts concerning military jihad, in

---

12. Tirmidhi, *Birr* (Righteousness), 30.

13. The Prophet once declared: "By God, I implore God's forgiveness and return to Him more than seventy times every day"; Bukhari, *Da'awat* (Non-ritual Prayers), 3.

14. Tirmidhi, *birr* (righteousness), 31.

particular verses 5 and 29 of the ninth sūra (the only one which does not start with exalting divine mercy).

The question is whether the "Verse about the Sword" repeals previous qur'anic texts that encourage Muslims to forgive others, including non-Muslims. This question divides Muslims in two groups. For some the answer is not in doubt – Muslims are no longer required to forgive disbelievers. Others argue that Muslims must defend themselves when attacked or prevented from practicing their religion, as their community is the depositary of God's truth; however, on an individual level, Muslims should continue to be lenient towards Muslims and non-Muslims, because forgiving others reflects divine forgiveness, a virtue nothing can abolish.

While forgiveness is a virtue which must characterize believers, the qur'anic text does not go so far as to make forgiving others an obligation. Muslim authors, such as M. Allam, offer several explanations for this. First, forgiving someone is doing them a favor, and a favor is, by definition, not obligatory. Second, justice is also a virtue, hence we cannot blame people who demand justice. Third, if forgiveness were to replace justice in society, evil would very quickly take over because of the impunity that criminals would enjoy. Fourth, Muslim thinkers emphasize a principle repeated many times in the Qur'an, namely that "no soul shall have a burden laid on it greater than what it can bear" (2:233; cf. 6:164; 17:15; 38:18; 39:7; 53:38). This qur'anic teaching takes into account the fact that "humans were created weak" (4:28; cf. 8:66; 30:54). It would therefore be unfair to require the offended to forgive as the offense may prove to be too deep. For all these reasons, human forgiveness represents an ideal Muslims should aspire to and practice as far as they are able to.

"One God and One Mediator" (1 Tim 2:5)

We can understand forgiveness in Christianity similar to the way we understand it in Islam. The Bible also extols God's sovereignty, justice and mercy. To the extent that the Qur'an emphasizes God's mercy, the New Testament emphasizes God's *love*. Although in reality, love is not just a divine attribute, it is the very essence of God: "God is love" (1 John 4:8, 16).

Love is the motive that led God to come to the aid of sinful fallen humanity: "This is love: not that we loved God, but that he loved us and sent his Son as an atoning sacrifice for our sins" (1 John 4:10; cf. John 3:16). This text presents us with the death of Jesus Christ on the cross as the ultimate expression of divine love. Jesus offered his life as a sacrifice for us; he voluntarily chose to bear the judgment that we deserve because of our sins. He thus satisfied God's uncompromising *justice*: "[God] does not leave the guilty unpunished" (Exod 34:7; cf. Exod 23:7; Num 14:18; Nah 1:3). Since all people are sinners (Ps 14:3; Rom 3:10–12), it is impossible for humans to be saved by a human. But "what is impossible with man is possible with God" (Luke 18:27). God's *sovereignty* means that he took the unimaginable initiative of becoming a human to save us through his Son's death and resurrection. He thus placed his sovereignty at the service of his love so that his forgiveness would be granted to us without compromising his justice.

Christian monotheism is Trinitarian (one God in three persons) and it is inseparable from the historic mission of Jesus Christ, which culminated in his death and resurrection. Unlike all the prophets, Christ is above all the Savior whose earthly mission was to rescue humankind from the slavery of sin and death. He shares with God the title "Savior" because it is through him that God has achieved the salvation of the world.[15] Christian monotheism is therefore soteriological in the sense that it is centered on the redemption of humankind: "For there is one God and one mediator between God and mankind, the man Christ Jesus, who gave himself as a ransom for all people" (1 Tim 2:5–6).

The gospel enhances the three divine attributes that determine God's forgiveness in Islam. Love comes first, not just mercy as in Islamic mysticism. Divine justice is much more rigorous than in Muʿtazili theology since for Jesus, apart from the unforgivable sin against the Holy Spirit (Matt 12:31–32), there is no fundamental difference between minor and major sins (Matt 5:21–22, 27–28).[16] The root of sin is evil lurking deep within each one of us; therefore, it is not enough to confess this or that sin. We must (as Muslim mystics clearly understood) return with our whole being to God in response to the call made by Christ at the beginning of his mission: "Repent [or, convert], for the kingdom of heaven has come near" (Matt 4:17; cf. Matt 3:2). As for sovereignty, it manifests itself in the gospel, not in the way God freely decides to condemn certain sinners and to forgive others (as in Sunni theology), but in his will and capacity to save humanity through his Son.

The universal mediator of divine mercy according to the gospel is Christ, the Son of God, unique and eternal (John 1:14, 18; 3:16, 18), not Muhammad

---

15. In the New Testament God is described as "Savior" eight times (Luke 1:47; 1 Tim 1:1; 2:3; 4:10; Titus 1:3; 2:10; 3:4; Jude 25), and Jesus sixteen times (Luke 2:11; John 4:42; Acts 5:31; 13:23; Eph 5:23; Phil 3:20; 2 Tim 1:10; Titus 1:4; 2:13; 3:6; 2 Pet 1:1, 11; 2:20; 3:2, 18; 1 John 4:14).

16. Catholic theology makes a distinction, in addition to the seven capital sins, between mortal and venial sins. It also teaches the existence of purgatory, a place of purification where many believers will have to go to be entirely purified before reaching heaven. This doctrine is similar to the teaching about temporary punishment in Sunni theology.

as in Ibn 'Arabi's teaching. Whoever believes in him receives eternal life already in this life: "Very truly I tell you, whoever hears my word and believes him who sent me has eternal life and will not be judged but has crossed over from death to life" (John 5:24; cf. John 3:36; 6:40; 11:25; 17:3). Provided that our faith is a living faith, authenticated by a changed life committed to the service of God and of neighbor (Matt 5:14–16; Jas 2:17), we do not have to fear death or last day judgment. He who by his mission has become the "Savior of the world" (John 4:42) is the one who will judge the world in the Father's name (Matt 5:21–23; 25:31–46; John 5:22; Acts 17:31).

After his resurrection from the dead, Jesus appeared to his disciples for forty days (Acts 1:3). Before ascending to heaven, he entrusted his apostles with the mission of proclaiming the gospel which he summed up in these words: "*Repentance for the forgiveness of sins* will be preached in his name to all nations, beginning at Jerusalem" (Luke 24:47; emphasis added). The gospel promises unconditional forgiveness to everyone who converts (or repents), that is, who turns to God and believes in the salvation achieved by Christ.

Unlike Muslims, Christians do not need to wait for judgment day for Christ to intercede on their behalf. Ever since Jesus entered into the glory of the Father, he has been interceding on behalf of all his disciples (Rom 8:34). Through his intercession they benefit from divine mercy, and he strengthens them in their daily life. The Prophet's intercession on judgment day for his community is considered by Muslims as his privilege because, on one hand, he is the last prophet (33:40) and, on the other, God has already forgiven "his past and future sins" (48:2). Christ's intercession is based on a threefold privilege: (1) he is much more than a prophet – being God's Son he enjoys a unique relationship with God; (2) he is the only human being without sin (John 8:46; Heb 4:15); and (3) he gave his life "for the forgiveness of sins" according to his own words spoken on the eve of his crucifixion (Matt 26:28; cf. Mark 10:45). He is, therefore, the only intercessor truly qualified to intercede for us:

> My dear children, I write this to you so that you will not sin. But if anybody does sin, we have an advocate with the Father – Jesus Christ, the Righteous One. He is the atoning sacrifice for our sins, and not only for ours but also for the sins of the whole world. (1 John 2:1–2; cf. Heb 2:17; 7:26)

This text specifies that Christ gave his life not only for the Christian community but for "the whole world." What does this expression mean? It is very unlikely that these words imply a universal salvation since Jesus himself repeatedly warned that eternal punishment awaits those who have not accepted

God's love in their life (Matt 8:12; 23:33; 25:46). It is also possible to understand these words in the sense that salvation is offered to everyone but will only benefit those who accept Christ's death for them. A third interpretation focuses on God's loves for the whole world (John 3:16) and his grace to everyone with no discrimination whatsoever (Matt 5:45). He called Abraham and made him the father of the chosen people, Israel; however, he did not stop caring for other peoples, as demonstrated by Melchizedek, the Canaanite priest-king of Jerusalem. In fact, Abraham and Melchizedek lived at the same time and together they worshipped "God Most High, Creator of heaven and earth" (Gen 14:18–20). Thus, the church of Jesus Christ, "the Israel of God" (Gal 6:16), brings together all who believe in Christ.

According to Jesus, the Spirit of God, like the wind, "blows wherever it pleases" (John 3:8). He is at work inside and outside the church to reveal God to people of all ethnicities. Those who, thanks to the action of the Holy Spirit in their lives, realize their deep spiritual misery and trust only in divine mercy for their salvation, may also benefit from his saving sacrifice even if they have not heard the name Jesus Christ. This divine action is an expression of the universal and sovereign love of the "Father of compassion" (2 Cor 1:3). It remains mysterious for us and goes hand in hand with the mission entrusted by Christ to his church to make disciples of all nations (Matt 28:19).

"Forgive Us Our Sins as We Forgive Those Who Sin against Us" (Matt 6:12)

Jesus taught his disciples a prayer known as "the Lord's prayer" (Matt 6:9–13). The second part of this prayer deals first with our physical needs and then our spiritual needs: "Forgive us our sins as we forgive those who sin against us" (6:12).[17] Jesus establishes in this petition a very close link between forgiveness received from God and forgiveness given to others. In the only comment he makes on this prayer (6:14–15), he declares that divine forgiveness and human forgiveness are inextricably linked. But what exactly is the nature of this link?

The answer is given to us by Jesus himself in the parable of the "unmerciful servant" (Matt 18:23–35; cf. Luke 7:41–43). This parable clearly shows that God is the One who takes the initiative to forgive our sins unconditionally. He also expects us to show our gratitude to him by forgiving those who hurt us.

---

17. Most modern English translations have debts instead of sins, but this quote reflects the traditional usage which takes debts to be a way of referring to sin more broadly (as used by Jesus in the parable of the unmerciful servant in Matt 18:23–35).

We cannot sincerely ask God to forgive our sins if we are not ready to forgive others. Refusing to forgive others shows we have not adequately appreciated God's grace in forgiving our sins.

We should be prepared to forgive others with no time limit, just as God always forgives our sins. Peter once asked Jesus: "Lord, how many times shall I forgive my brother or sister who sins against me? Up to seven times?" Jesus's answer, very similar to the one given by the Prophet to the same question, was: "I tell you, not seven times, but seventy-seven times" (Matt 18:21–22). The apostle Paul sums up the attitude Christians should adopt towards one another as follows: "Bear with each other and forgive whatever grievances you may have against one another. Forgive as the Lord forgave you" (Col 3:13; cf. Eph 4:32).

The Christian perspective on forgiving others differs from the Islamic perspective in that forgiveness given is not a mere exhortation, it is an injunction. Love of neighbor, including one's enemy, is Jesus's command (Matt 5:43–45). Forgiving people is the supreme expression of our love for them. We cannot truly love someone and refuse to forgive them. In human relationships, forgiveness is one of the most eloquent demonstrations of love. It is true that there are circumstances in life when forgiving is extremely difficult. Is not living in a manner worthy of the gospel (Phil 1:27; Col 1:10) often beyond our reach without the permanent and decisive enabling of the Holy Spirit?

Another difference from qur'anic teaching is that forgiving is not a meritorious act, any more than our other good deeds. Our good deeds will never make up for our bad ones – only God's forgiveness can set us free from the guilt felt because of our evil actions. The gospel of forgiveness and non-violence (Matt 5:39; 26:52) can expose our lives to serious threats. In extreme cases, remaining faithful to the teaching of Christ can lead us to the ultimate sacrifice – martyrdom.[18] The example of Christ shows us that God is glorified, not when we want to take revenge or defend his honor, but when we are prepared to give our life for him (Luke 23:34; Acts 7:60). Using God's name to justify the violence that lies in our hearts is perhaps the worst witness to our Creator.

---

18. In the New Testament the Greek word for "martyr" means a witness.

10

Shared Beliefs and Values

The two chapters on Jesus Christ and God as well as the ones on the Bible and forgiveness have identified certain theological convergences between Christianity and Islam. They also highlighted real divergences, even irreducible contradictions, between the two faith traditions. The reader might be tempted to conclude that the differences between Christians and Muslims are such that it is almost impossible for them to work together in the service of society of which they are a part, unless they ignore their religious beliefs.

The purpose of this chapter is to show that such a conclusion is unwarranted. It is possible for Christians and Muslims to collaborate for the good of their society despite the doctrinal differences that separate them. We have a number of religious convictions in common which bring us together, including convictions on ethical issues. It is therefore important, before bringing this book to a close, to highlight what makes possible, even necessary, cooperation between Christians and Muslims.

The challenges facing our society are many: health, education, poverty, unemployment, violence in all its forms, xenophobia, drugs, pedophilia, global warming, terrorism, etc. These challenges can only be met if all people of good will join hands – believers of all persuasions as well as non-believers. Thankfully, this collaboration already exists but it needs to be increased, especially as Muslims are now an integral part of the national community in France, the UK and many other western nations. Our future depends in part on our ability to fight together the evils threatening our country. Terrorist acts committed in the name of Islam should not be allowed to discourage citizens in general, and Christians in particular, from engaging with Muslims to meet these challenges.

The beliefs and values discussed in this chapter are not abstract. I had the joy of implementing them on the field from 2006–2016, which I consider some of the happiest years of my life. I was then responsible for interfaith relations in a large Christian NGO, World Vision International. This development, relief and advocacy organization operates in many nations, including some twenty Muslim-majority countries. In all of these countries, the staff includes Christians and Muslims.[1] Here are the theological convictions and ethical values upon which cooperation between Christians and Muslims can be based.

1. One God, Creator of the Universe

Jews, Muslims and Christians form three monotheistic communities who believe that God created the entire cosmos. We have seen that the Qur'an considers Jews and Christians as "the People of the Book." Political conflicts in Medina, which set Muslims and Jews in opposition, explain the harshness of certain qur'anic texts towards Jews. Despite theological criticisms leveled against Christians, the Qur'an looks rather favorably on them:

> Certainly you will find the most violent of people in enmity for believers [Muslims] to be the Jews and the polytheists, and you will certainly find the nearest in friendship to believers to be those who say: "We are Christians," as there are priests and monks among them and as they do not behave proudly. (5:82)

The Bible does not mention Islam, which arose six centuries after Christianity. How can we look at Muslims? They are of course our neighbors, but what about the religious dimension of their identity? In general, Muslim people are shaped by their faith more than people claiming to be Christian; even non-practicing Muslims have a mindset strongly framed by religion. We could therefore consider them as "God-fearing people," because deep in their hearts they fear God and have a profound respect for the Creator.[2]

The three monotheistic communities who claim Abraham as their father (physical or spiritual) received a threefold call from God: to serve the Creator and obey his law; to worship the Lord and recognize his majesty; to witness to God, especially to those who do not know him. They respond to this call as best as they can in a world that faces very serious problems: economic, political, ecological, social, and above all spiritual. Followers of the three religious

---

1. In some countries Muslim staff outnumber Christian staff by far (Afghanistan, Mauritania, Somalia). However, in order to preserve the Christian identity of the organization, the leadership is always predominantly Christian.

2. The Qur'an celebrates the fear of God (35:28), as does the Bible, which considers this fear as the very principle of wisdom (Prov 1:7; 9:10; Ps 111:10).

traditions barely exceeds half of the world's population. Other religions exert more or less important influences. The number of those who do not adhere to any religion continues to increase, especially in Western countries. Add to this that religion is misused in many places, so instead of being a force for good, it only makes matters worse. People who believe that religion can be a force for good need to work together to convince those who think otherwise.

2. Humans Are God's Appointed Stewards on Earth

Christians and Muslims alike believe that God gave a mandate to all humanity just after they were created: to care for creation on his behalf. In other words, the Creator appointed humans as his representatives on earth in charge of managing his work. The Qur'an calls this role of representation *khilafa*.[3] Human creatures are therefore caliphs, God's lieutenants on earth responsible for running his creation:

> Behold, your Lord said to the angels:
> – I will place a vicegerent on earth.
>
> They said:
> – What! Will You place therein one who will make mischief therein and shed blood while we celebrate Your praise and glorify Your holy [name]?
>
> He said:
> – I know what you know not. (2:30)

> Then God said, "Let us make mankind in our image, in our likeness, so that they may rule over the fish in the sea and the birds in the sky, over the livestock and all the wild animals, and over all the creatures that move along the ground."
> So God created mankind in his own image,
> in the image of God he created them;
> male and female he created them.
> God blessed them and said to them, "Be fruitful and increase in number; fill the earth and subdue it. Rule over the fish in the sea and the birds in the sky and over every living creature that moves on the ground." (Gen 1:26–28)

---

3. This term can also have the meaning of succession, especially when used for mortal beings. The men who, after the death of the Prophet, succeeded him as head of the Muslim community are also called caliphs.

Thus, the mandate given to humans after they were created is expressed in equivalent terms in the second sūra and Genesis. The notable difference is that in the qur'anic text this mandate does not derive from the fact that humans were created in God's image as it does in the biblical account.

3. Human Beings Are Spiritual Creatures

God created the whole human being, body and soul. The two components of human nature, fruit of the one creative act, define the identity of each human being, created good as the whole of divine work. Humans are the only creatures made with a personal intervention from God who breathed life into them:

> Behold, your Lord said to the angels:
> – I will create a mortal being from clay. When I have formed him and breathed of My spirit into him, bow down to him. (38:71–72; cf. 32:7–9)

> Then the LORD God formed a man from the dust of the ground and breathed into his nostrils the breath of life, and the man became a living being. (Gen 2:7)

God values our physical and spiritual well-being, which is why he sent prophets to humanity to show us the way to follow. Our life on this earth has an inestimable price in God's eyes in both its material and spiritual dimensions. It is therefore important to have a healthy diet, take care of our bodies, and pay attention to our health. It is also necessary to take care of all aspects of our spiritual life (cultural, social, intellectual, religious, etc.).

Our relationship with God (or lack of it) plays a determining role in the choices and the decisions we make. Quoting the Torah, Jesus emphasizes that "man shall not live on bread alone, but on every word that comes from the mouth of God" (Matt 4:4; cf. Deut 8:3). Therefore, Christians and Muslims attach great importance to what nurtures our relationship with the Creator. Cultivating good relationships among believers of different faiths can help deepen our faith and preserve it from certain deviations (e.g. bigotry, spiritual pride, intolerance).

4. One Humanity

The Bible and the Qur'an tell us that God created one humanity. In other words, despite all differences that distinguish them, all people belong to a single species (or race). We have the same parents, Adam and Eve, and therefore we are members of the same human family. We are thus brothers and sisters whatever the color of our skin, our social background and our religious identity.

Our humanity is marked by the sexual difference between males and females. This is the only difference that belongs to creation. Gender is therefore an integral part of our identity. The first creation account emphasizes that man and woman were both created in the image of God: "God created mankind in his own image, in the image of God he created them; male and female he created them" (Gen 1:27). The second account emphasizes that man and woman are equal and complementary beings (Gen 2:18–23). It describes in symbolic terms that Eve was created from one of Adam's ribs. This means that the two are of the same nature, hence they are equal. The woman is the man's counterpart and vice versa; neither should dominate the other. The qur'anic text goes in the same direction: "O mankind! Fear your Lord who created you from a single person, and from that person created a partner. Then, from this couple, came many men and women" (4:1).[4]

The diversity of human beings goes hand in hand with the unity of the species to which they all belong. The Qur'an specifies that the diversity inscribed in humanity corresponds to a very specific divine intention:

> O mankind! We created you from a male and a female, and made you into peoples and tribes that you may know each other. The noblest of you, in the sight of God, is the one who fears him the most. God is the One who knows everything and is acquainted with everything. (49:13)

Thus, differences between humans, far from constituting barriers, are meant to motivate communication between them and enrich their dialogue.

5. Equal Dignity for All

The dignity of humankind is based on the fact that we are all created in God's image, according to the Bible (Gen 1:26).[5] According to the Qur'an, God created humans in "the finest form of creaturehood" (95:4; cf. 64:3). For the two holy books, we are all members of the same human family. Humans are such a

---

4. According to a prophetic saying, the woman was created from one of the man's ribs; Bukhari, *Nikah* (Marriage), 81.

5. According to a prophetic saying, "God created Adam in his own image"; Muslim, *Birr* (Righteousness), 115. This statement is variously interpreted by Muslim scholars; see my book *Faith to Faith*, ch. 6 "The Greatness of God," 84–88.

noble creature that the Creator summoned the angels to bow down to Adam, as soon as he was created, to acknowledge and praise God for his great work:

> And behold, We said to the angels:
> – Bow down before Adam!
> They bowed down except the Iblis (the devil) who was proud; he thus became a disbeliever. (2:34; cf. 38:74)

Therefore, all humans have the same dignity, regardless of their ethnic or religious background, their social status, their level of education, their criminal record, and their sexual conduct. They are of equal value in the sight of God and we should treat them without any discrimination. They have the same rights and obligations.

6. Human Solidarity

Since we are part of the same human family, we are expected to show solidarity with our brothers and sisters in the faith (cf. Gal 6:10) as well as with our brothers and sisters in humanity. We also need to care especially for the most disadvantaged people.

> Righteousness does not consist in the mere act of facing on the *qiblah* (direction) of the east or of the west. They are truly righteous those who believe in God and the last day, in the angels and in the Scripture and the prophets, who spend their money, for the love they have for Him, on their relatives, orphans, the needy ones, the travellers, beggars, and on the ransoming of slaves. (2:177; cf. 9:60)

> Religion that God our Father accepts as pure and faultless is this: to look after orphans and widows in their distress and to keep oneself from being polluted by the world. (Jas 1:27)

In the past, widows and orphans were among the weakest members of society. Who are the people most in need nowadays? Among the most vulnerable in our society are children, the elderly, the unemployed, the disabled, the sick, the prisoners, single parents, and foreigners. It is not mere compassion but justice that should motivate our commitment. These people have a dignity equal to the healthy, privileged and prominent people in our society, it is therefore important through concrete actions to demonstrate our respect for their dignity.

7. Love in Action

We saw in the last chapter that mercy is one of God's major attributes in Islam and in Christianity. A word attributed to the Prophet encourages Muslims to adopt the same moral attitude as God: "Have the same moral qualities as God."[6] Jesus also taught his disciples to model their lives on God: "Be perfect, therefore, as your heavenly Father is perfect" (Matt 5:48). God is good to all his creatures without any distinction. He showers us with many blessings through nature, through our loved ones and through people we do not even know. This is how righteous people are described in the Qur'an and the Bible:

> They (the believers) feed, for the love they have for Him, the needy ones, the orphan and the captive. [They say]: "We feed you for the sake of God. We do not expect any reward or gratitude from you." (76:8–9)

> If anyone has material possessions and sees a brother or sister in need but has no pity on them, how can the love of God be in that person? Dear children, let us not love with words or speech but with actions and in truth. (1 John 3:17–18)

Compassion and mercy are the hallmarks of the disciples of Jesus Christ according to the Qur'an, notwithstanding its criticisms of them (57:27). It should be the same for Muslims according to this saying of the Prophet: "God will not be merciful to those who are not merciful to others; He who is in heaven will treat with mercy those on earth who treat others with mercy."[7]

8. Faith in Action

The Bible and the Qur'an stress the importance of putting faith into practice, otherwise faith would be a simple intellectual agreement. True faith transforms the lives of believers in their relationship with God, with others and with themselves. There are sixty-two qur'anic verses that promise paradise to "those who believe and do good works."

> Proclaim the good news to those who believe and work righteousness. Their portion is gardens where streams flow. (2:25; cf. 2:82, 277)

---

6. This non-canonical prophetic saying is well known to Muslims and often quoted by Muslim writers (exegetes, theologians and mystics).

7. Bukhari, *Adab* (Good Manners), 18.

> What good is it, my brothers and sisters, if someone claims to have faith but has no deeds? Can such faith save them? Suppose a brother or a sister is without clothes and daily food. If one of you says to them, "Go in peace; keep warm and well fed," but does nothing about their physical needs, what good is it? In the same way, faith by itself, if it is not accompanied by action, is dead. . . . As the body without the spirit is dead, so faith without deeds is dead. (Jas 2:14–17, 26)

Good works are the hallmark of a living faith. They can be very varied, but they involve helping those who are vulnerable, regardless of what their vulnerability consists of. The Torah had prescribed tithing for the Israelites to support groups of people who lived in precarious conditions. The triennial tithe was to be assigned to "the Levite, the migrant, the orphan and the widow" (Deut 26:12; cf. Deut 24:19–21; Lev 19:10). The New Testament does not set a percentage but encourages generous giving (2 Cor 9:6–8). Jesus insists on the need to give alms almost secretly (Matt 6:1–4). He praises a widowed woman because she has given generously, not out of her abundance but out of her poverty (Luke 21:4). Islam prescribes *zakat* (legal alms) as one of the five pillars of religion. Muslims are also urged to make voluntary offerings.

We can give directly to those around us and to charities that care for people in need in our country and beyond. Material gifts is one good way to give, but donating your time is another important way to show your generosity to those in need. In relatively wealthy societies, like ours, many people suffer from loneliness because they cannot meet people who are willing to listen to them, spend time with them and help them with their difficulties.

9. Family First

Christian and Islamic monotheisms have important ethical values. God has given us precious teaching on how to behave as individuals, in our families and in our societies. Christians and Muslims share many values that stem from their religious beliefs, and many of these values revolve around the family:

– Respect for life from its conception to its end. This explains why Christians and Muslims often find themselves on the same side when it comes to issues such as abortion or euthanasia (so-called mercy killing).[8]

---

8. Christians have different views on the issues of abortion and marriage. The perspective of the Catholic and evangelical churches mentioned here is also ours.

- Honoring the elderly, and especially one's own parents.
 - Marriage as a lifelong commitment between a man and a woman. Divorce is admittedly authorized by Sharīʿa, but it is considered, according to a saying of the Prophet, "the most detestable thing among what is lawful."[9] Authorized in the Mosaic law, Jesus put an end to divorce without totally ruling it out in some cases (Deut 24:1–4; Matt 5:31–32; 19:3–9).
 - Faithfulness for married couples and chastity for single people. Of course, the Qur'an allows polygamy (limited to four wives), whereas it was tolerated without restriction in the Old Testament times. The qur'anic authorization must be understood in light of the historical context. There were a lot of widows at the time, partly due to tribal wars. In addition, the Qur'an sets as a condition for polygamy the fair treatment of the husband in his relationships with his wives (4:3). This condition is declared virtually impossible to fulfill: "You will never be able to be fair to each of your women even if you want to" (4:129). Jesus came to restore marriage to the way it was conceived by the Creator for the first human couple: "That is why a man leaves his father and mother and is united to his wife, and they become one flesh" (Gen 2:24). The union between a man and a woman makes polygamy obsolete (Matt 19:4–5).

10. The Child Is a Wonderful Gift from God

The Qur'an and the Gospels grant a special place for the child. Perhaps this is related to the fact that both Jesus and Muhammad had somewhat difficult childhoods. The Qur'an tells us (echoing accounts of apocryphal gospels), that the Virgin Mary was accused of having committed adultery because she was pregnant without being married (4:156). Several months after the birth of Jesus, his parents had to take him to Egypt to shelter him from king Herod who wanted to kill him (Matt 2:13–18). A few years later, Jesus was taken to Nazareth where he grew up.

Muhammad's father, Abdullah, died before he was born. His mother, Amina, died when he was six-years-old. Muhammad was then entrusted to his grandfather. When the latter died, it was his uncle Abu Talib who took charge of him. The Qur'an is relatively silent on Muhammad. However, he mentions his difficult childhood in Sūra 93:

> Did He (God) not find you an orphan and give you shelter?
> He found you lost and He guided you.

---

9. Ibn Majah, *Talaq* (Divorce), 1.

> He found you in need and He enriched you.
> Therefore, do not oppress the orphan,
> And do not reject the beggar.
> As for the favor of your Lord, proclaim [it]. (93:6–11)

God is the author of life. He gives children to parents as he pleases. Children are a blessing from God according to the Bible and the Qur'an:

> To God belongs the kingship of heaven and earth. He creates what He wills.
> He gives daughters to whom He wants, and sons to whom He wants;
> Or He gives both sons and daughters to whomever He wants.
> He makes sterile whoever He wills.
> He is the One who knows everything and can do anything. (43:49–50)

> Children are a heritage from the Lord,
>   offspring a reward from him.
> Like arrows in the hands of a warrior
>   are children born in one's youth.
> Blessed is the man
>   whose quiver is full of them. (Ps 127:3–5)

Newborns are all equally valuable, whether they are girls or boys. Before Islam, Arabs used to bury unwanted girls alive as soon as they were born. The Qur'an put an end to this practice (cf. 16:58–59). Mothers are encouraged to breastfeed their babies for two years (2:233). We need to take care of children, especially orphans:

> They ask you [Prophet] what they shall spend [in charity].
>   Say: "Whatever good you spend [has to go] to your parents, your relatives, the orphans, those in need and travelers. God knows perfectly very well whatever good you do." (2:215)

> Learn to do right; seek justice. Defend the oppressed.
>   Take up the cause of the fatherless; plead the case of the widow. (Isa 1:17)

Children should respect and honor their parents, acknowledge their authority, care for them in their old age, and pray for them:

> We entered into a covenant with the children of Israel in these terms: "You will worship only God, you will treat with kindness

> your parents, your relatives, the orphans and people in need. Use good words with people; be steadfast in prayer and give alms." (2:83)

> Your Lord has decreed: "You will worship only Him. He [prescribed that you treat] with kindness [your] parents." When one or both of them reach old age in your house, do not bully them or push them away, speak kind words to them. Out of mercy, lower to them the wing of humility, and say: "O my Lord! Be merciful to them, as they were to me when I was a child." (17:23–24)

> Honor your father and your mother, so that you may live long in the land the LORD your God is giving you. (Exod 20:12)

> Children, obey your parents in everything, for this pleases the Lord. (Col 3:20)

Parents should not abuse their authority over their children. They should love them and respect their rights: "Fathers, do not embitter your children, or they will become discouraged" (Col 3:21). Touching the goods belonging to orphans is a very serious sin according to the Qur'an (4:6).

Legal adoption of a child is not lawful in Islam (33:4–5), as adoption is seen as a potential source of confusion in family relationships and a possible cause of conflict between adopted children and biological ones. However, nothing prevents sponsorship or informal adoption, a very common practice in Muslim societies. There is no explicit teaching on adoption in the New Testament. The fact that followers of Christ are the adopted children of God means there is a rather favorable bias towards adoption in Christianity.

Male circumcision, unlike female, is a religious obligation although it is not prescribed in the Qur'an. The Torah requires the Israelites to circumcise their male firstborn as a sign of the covenant God made with them (Gen 17:10–11; Lev 12:2–3). This practice is no longer required in the New Covenant (1 Cor 7:19; Gal 6:15).

Excessive attachment to children and parents can go against the love one should have for God. Jesus warns his disciples against this danger. The same warning is found in the Qur'an where Muslims are warned against the temptation of wealth and undue affection for children. Our loyalty must go to God above all:

> Believers! Let not your riches and your children deter you from remembering God. Those who succumb to this do so at their expense. (63:9; cf. 8:28; 64:15)

> [Jesus says:] Anyone who loves their father or mother more than me is not worthy of me; anyone who loves their son or daughter more than me is not worthy of me. (Matt 10:37)

For Jesus, children can teach us important spiritual lessons. He even taught his disciples that they should model their attitude on that of the child: "Truly I tell you, unless you change and become like little children, you will never enter the kingdom of heaven. Therefore, whoever takes the lowly position of this child is the greatest in the kingdom of heaven" (Matt 18:3–4). Our faith would greatly benefit from having the same qualities found in children, at least those who are brought up in homes where they feel appreciated and loved. Among the inspiring qualities found in children are trust, humility, dependence, simplicity, candor, obedience, and a sense of wonder. Jesus encouraged his disciples to take care of children to the point of identifying himself with one of them: "Whoever welcomes one such child in my name welcomes me" (Matt 18:5). A child is a gift from heaven whom we need to welcome unconditionally and wholeheartedly.

11. Judgment Day

Among all of creation, humans are unique in many ways – we are blessed with many qualities: reason, freedom, language, spirituality, etc. We are appointed by the Creator as his representatives to manage the earth. The Lord did not leave us without equipping us. He sent us prophets and revealed his law to us so that we could successfully fulfill our mandate.

This privilege does not go without responsibility. The Scriptures adhered to by monotheistic believers teach that one day we will appear before God to give an account of how we have carried out our mission. The supreme Judge will judge fairly according to his unfailing justice:

> On that day people will proceed in groups to be shown their deeds. Whoever has done an atom's weight of good shall see it. Whoever has done an atom's weight of evil shall see it too. (99:6–8)

> Do not be amazed at this, for a time is coming when all who are in their graves will hear his voice and come out – those who have done what is good will rise to live, and those who have done what is evil will rise to be condemned. (John 5:28–29)

In the Gospels Jesus presents himself as the king who will judge all human beings on the last day. According to him, what makes the difference between genuine and nominal believers is the way they related to the most vulnerable people. He goes so far as to identify with those people he considers "the least of [his] brothers."

> Then the King will say to those on his right, "Come, you who are blessed by my Father; take your inheritance, the kingdom prepared for you since the creation of the world. For I was hungry and you gave me something to eat, I was thirsty and you gave me something to drink, I was a stranger and you invited me in, I needed clothes and you clothed me, I was sick and you looked after me, I was in prison and you came to visit me."
>
> Then the righteous will answer him, "Lord, when did we see you hungry and feed you, or thirsty and give you something to drink? When did we see you a stranger and invite you in, or needing clothes and clothe you? When did we see you sick or in prison and go to visit you?"
>
> The King will reply, "Truly I tell you, whatever you did for one of the least of these brothers and sisters of mine, you did for me." (Matt 25:34–40; cf. Matt 7:21–23; John 5:24–27)

For Christians and Muslims, helping those in need is not an option – it is an obligation that serves to authenticate their faith. This requirement is based on the fact that God takes care of all his human creatures, especially the weakest. God has shown his unreserved solidarity with us in Jesus Christ. What about Islam, which resolutely rules out the possibility that God can be embodied in a human being? According to a divine saying reported by the Prophet, the supreme Judge is not so distant from his needy human creatures. He can be found wherever a disadvantaged person calls for help. The following narrative undoubtedly echoes that of Jesus cited above:

> God will say on the Day of Resurrection: "O Son of Adam, I was sick and you did not visit Me."
>
> He (the Son of Adam) will reply: "O My Lord, how could I visit You and You are the Lord of the worlds?"[10]
>
> "Didn't you know that My servant so-and-so was sick and you did not visit him? Had you visited him, you would have found Me there. O Son of Adam, I asked you for food and you fed Me not."

---

10. In the Qur'an God is described forty-two times as "the Lord of the worlds," starting with the first sūra (1:2). In their everyday language, Arabic-speaking Muslims often use this expression when talking about God.

"My Lord, how could I feed You and You are the Lord of the worlds?"

"Didn't you know that My servant so-and-so was in need of food and you did not feed him. Had you fed him, you would have found him by My side."

"O Son of Adam, I asked you for water and you did not give Me to drink."

"My Lord, how could I give you water and you are the Lord of the worlds?"

"Didn't you know that My servant so-and-so asked you for a drink and you did not give him water. Had you given him to drink, you would have found him near Me."[11]

God did not send us on mission without equipping us. In addition to his word, he sent us "the power [of the] the Holy Spirit" (Acts 1:8). Christians can therefore rely on the Spirit of God as well as on his word to guide and support them in the task which is theirs in this world. The Qur'an also promises Muslims that God will strengthen them in their lives "by a Spirit emanating from him" (58:22). The teachings of the Sharī'a will direct them in this life and help them to follow the divine will. We thus have all the resources necessary to carry out the mandate we have received from our Creator.

12. Showing Our Gratefulness to Our Creator

The Arabic word for unbelief (*kufr*) comes from the verb *kafara*, which literally means "to cover," "to hide," "to conceal." Muslim theologians explain that unbelievers are those who conceal all the good things they enjoy in this life not recognizing behind the gifts the supreme giver, namely the Creator. Indeed, from our Creator, we receive first our life and then all the other blessings attached to it. In other words, ingratitude is the root cause of unbelief, and unbelievers are basically ungrateful people. This same verb (*kafara*) is also used for God who mercifully "covers" our misdeeds when he forgives our sins instead of punishing us (2:271; 3:193; 4:31; 5:12).

The first two words in the Qur'an are *alhamdu li-llah* (praise be to God). This expression occurs more than thirty times in the Qur'an. It is also the most common response one hears when asking Muslims how they are doing.

---

11. Muslim, *Birr* (Righteousness), 13.

Another Arabic word that expresses gratitude is *shukr*, less common in the Qur'an than *hamd* (praise).

Believers are meant to be grateful for all the blessings they receive from God. But most people are not grateful, according to the Qur'an (2:243; 7:17; 12:28; 27:73). They do not pay attention to all the favors God gives them (10:60; 40:61). God challenges believers about their lack of thankfulness (21:80) and calls them to proclaim, as the Prophet did, their deep gratitude (93:11). God promises to reward his grateful servants by increasing the number of his blessings (14:7). In fact, the bounties of God are too many to count (14:34; 16:18). Among his blessings are those displayed in creation and others disclosed to us in revelation. Muslims are supposed to be people who repent, worship and praise God Almighty (9:112).

In the Bible too, believers are expected to show their gratitude to God for his many blessings, which are displayed in creation and even more so in redemption, that is, in the salvation of humankind achieved through Christ. God's many blessings reflect his infinite love for his human creatures. Our best response to divine love is to reciprocate our heavenly Father's love for us and to love our neighbor as well. Christian love is unique in that it goes beyond what the Torah prescribes, namely to love our neighbor as ourselves (Lev 19:18) – Christ teaches his disciples to love as *he* himself loved them, sacrificially and unconditionally (John 13:34–35). Our good deeds are of no value unless they are motivated by love. The apostle Paul goes so far as to say: "If I give all I possess to the poor and give over my body to hardship that I may boast, but do not have love, I gain nothing" (1 Cor 13:3).

Conclusion

Unconditional Love as a Response to Islamist Violence and Secular Society

As members of the second largest faith community, Muslims have responded in various ways to the threefold civilizational challenge (globalization, Islamism, Christianity) their religion is facing. For many reasons human beings perceive differently the world in which they live. We could group these interactions into two broad categories which reinforce each other. The Muslim community is thus torn by opposing trends which divide it to such a point that some speak of a war within Islam itself. What is common to these trends, whose respective strength is difficult to determine, is that they all take advantage of the new opportunities made available to many of us thanks to groundbreaking information technologies, including social networks.

(1) *Open responses*. An increasing number of Muslims are attracted to universal values (e.g. freedom, democracy, secularity, human rights) which they miss in their own countries because of the political regimes. They attempt to promote these values in their own societies. Some question the traditional teachings of Islam, which have led to violence from the beginnings of Islam until now. Contemporary jihadism is at work in many Islamic and non-Islamic countries. However, an increasing number of Muslims claim they no longer follow the religion of their childhood while others convert in significant number to other religions, including Christianity. Without going that far, other Muslims take a critical approach to Islamic tradition and history, and even to the very foundational texts of the faith (Qur'an, Hadith, Sharī'a). Reformist Muslims, let alone liberals, face very serious difficulties if they live in Islamic lands; some have paid with their lives for their freedom of thought while others end up in Western countries as refugees.

(2) *Defensive responses*. Alarmed by the devastating repercussions of globalization and secularization within the Muslim community, many Muslims feel destabilized in their identity. They feel threatened by an alien civilization that morally corrupts and economically exploits Muslim peoples. Their reaction is to try to protect themselves and to resist this threat. Some escape by finding a shelter in the form of a personal and mystical return to faith (they speak of their experience in terms of conversion). Others commit to fighting the ungodly secularist ideologies and humanist philosophies. These revivalist groups (e.g. the Muslim Brotherhood) are active in non-Muslim countries as well as in Muslim countries that, according to them, are ruled by nominal Muslims. Some politically minded Muslims get involved in politics, which can lead to Islamism, or even jihadism. Jihadist violence targets anything deemed contrary to the interests of the Muslim community, like hegemonic Western nations and their perceived allies, nominal Muslims and Christian communities. This explains the jihadist hostility towards political regimes, Muslim minorities perceived as schismatic groups (e.g. Pakistan, Afghanistan) and Christian communities in Islamic lands.

Each year Open Doors publishes a Global Index showing the top fifty countries where Christians are most persecuted. Here are some comments related to Islamist and jihadist Islam based on the 2021 World Watch List.[1]

- (1) The country that has topped the list (since 2002) is North Korea.[2] This country, whose majority population belongs to traditional religions, is ruled by a communist dictatorship, like China, Laos, and Vietnam. In China, Christians are fiercely persecuted along with other minorities such as the Muslim Uyghurs. As Christians, we must show solidarity with all who are persecuted, including Muslims. Human rights must be defended, without religious or ethnic favoritism, both near and far.

- (2) India is in tenth place on this list, a country often referred to as "the largest democracy in the world." India owes its inclusion in the list to the fact that it is currently governed by the Bharatiya Janata Party (BJP), a Hindu nationalist party that promotes an ethno-nationalist

---

1. Open Doors is an evangelical NGO whose purpose is to support spiritually and materially persecuted Christians and to inform public opinion on the persecution and discrimination against Christians. The estimated number of persecuted Christians worldwide is 340 million: https://www.opendoors.org/en-US/persecution/countries/.

2. In the 2022 Index Afghanistan comes first followed by North Korea.

ideology. Religious nationalism exerts its power in other countries on the list: Bhutan and Myanmar (two Buddhist majority countries), and Nepal (which is Hindu majority). In India it is mainly the Christian and Muslim minorities who are persecuted by Hindu extremists. In Myanmar, the Rohingyas, a Muslim minority group, are persecuted by a nationalist military regime.

(3) Christians are also persecuted in countries ruled by totalitarian regimes (Eritrea, Kazakhstan, Uzbekistan, Tajikistan, and Turkmenistan). These authoritarian regimes persecute all their opponents, Christians as well as Muslims, regardless of their religious or ethnic background.

(4) The list includes two countries of Christian tradition: Colombia and Mexico. These countries suffer systemic corruption due to drug cartels. All those who resist them (especially priests, pastors, and ordinary Christians) fall victim of their organized crimes. It is little consolation that a religious motive is not behind the violence that plagues these countries.

(5) Pakistan comes fifth in the list (behind Afghanistan, Somalia and Libya). The Islamic Republic of Pakistan was founded in 1947 following the partition of India. This partition was intended to give Muslims a country where they would be in the majority. As a result, Hindu Indians also found themselves in a country where they were in the majority. Pakistan's religious foundation partly explains the militancy of extremist groups that persecute Christians and other religious minorities, particularly Shiʻa, Ahmadi Muslims, and Hindus. The anti-blasphemy law, introduced in 1986, is the source of many false accusations against Christians. The high-profile case of Asia Bibi is only one among many.[3] Muslims who courageously fight against obscurantism in Pakistan include the young Malala Yousafzai, who received the Nobel Peace Prize in 2014 for her role

---

3. In 2009 Asia Bibi, a catholic woman of unprivileged background, was unjustly accused of having blasphemed against the Prophet. She was arrested, sentenced to death, jailed for eight years, then acquitted (in 2018) before finally being released. She fled to Canada due to continued death threats. Some of those who stood up for her paid with their lives, including Salman Taseer, the (Muslim) governor of Punjab, and Shahbaz Bhatti, the (Catholic) minister for religious minorities. Both were murdered by extremists in 2011, which did not deter courageous Muslim lawyers from defending her case until she was acquitted.

in defending the right to education of young girls in her country. She almost lost her life in an attack perpetrated by Pakistani extremists.

(6) Nigeria, ninth on the list (behind Iran), holds the sad record for the most Christians killed per country. (The number was 4,761 worldwide in 2020.) This federal country, the largest in Africa (more than 200 million), is divided between the north, where Sharīʿa is the law in twelve States, and the south which has a Christian majority. Boko Haram operates mostly in the northeast of the country, often taking hostages, including schoolchildren. In the "Central Belt" of the country, among the Fulani who are nomadic herders, Muslim extremists regularly attack Christian farmers belonging to other ethnic groups. The religious motive is certainly present in these conflicts, but it is only the tip of the iceberg.

(7) This list of fifty countries includes forty countries where Christians are persecuted because of "Islamic extremism." This extremism is in power in some countries (Iran, Saudi Arabia), but it is most often embodied in very active jihadist individuals or groups, also present in parts of predominantly Christian countries (e.g. Central African Republic, Democratic Republic of Congo, Kenya, Mozambique). This may suggest that it is perhaps not entirely a coincidence if religious violence occurs mainly in predominantly Islamic countries – many are developing countries facing huge challenges. The demographic challenge aggravates all the others. It might be useful to draw up and analyze the list of countries where Muslims may be persecuted by Christians.

(8) Sudan occupies the thirteenth position on the list. However, we must acknowledge and welcome the courageous decision taken on 11 July 2020 by the transitional government. Since that date, the country is no longer governed by Sharīʿa law (promulgated in 1983). As a result, the law punishing apostasy with the death penalty has been abolished, paving the way for religious freedom. But because persecution is most often wielded by family and society, it will unfortunately last until Sudanese mentality and culture have changed.

It thus appears that anti-Christian violence in our time is not the result of a single religion, Islam in this case, since it is also present in countries with Buddhist or Hindu majorities. Religion is not the only cause for persecution as this violence is also found in communist or totalitarian regimes. However, religion is often used as a cover by authoritarian regimes or political groups to justify their murderous ideology.

The main findings of the Open Doors Index largely coincide with the Aid to the Church in Need (ACN) report on religious freedom in the world, published in 2021.[4] According to this very well-documented biannual report, three main reasons are behind the violation of religious freedom, namely authoritarian governments (43 countries; 2.9 billion), Islamist extremism (26 countries; 1.2 billion), and ethno-religious nationalism (4 countries; 1.6 billion).[5] The first two reasons are found combined in eight countries. The report highlights that religious freedom is violated in sixty-two countries, almost one third of the world's countries (31.6 percent) where two-thirds of the world's population lives (67 percent; 5.2 billion). Religious minorities suffer from discrimination in thirty-six countries and from persecution in twenty-six others. Christians are the most persecuted community in the world.[6]

Christians are obviously not the only victims of religious violence. Reformist Muslims and religious or ethnic minorities also suffer to various degrees. Christians with Muslim backgrounds seem to be the prime target of Islamists (Egypt) and nationalist regimes (Algeria). Islamists appeal to texts taken directly from the Qur'an and the Hadith, while nationalist governments resort to the need to preserve "public order" and maintain "social peace."

As the chapter on radical Islam has shown, extremism has many roots, religious and non-religious. We need to fight it at all levels (religious, economic, educational, social, political). This fight must involve all parties concerned, the State as well as ordinary citizens.

In Muslim-minority countries, the best qualified citizens to take the lead in fighting extremism are Christians and Muslims (and Jews). Indeed, these people belong to a dual culture, national and religious. They love their countries and appreciate the cultures despite their criticisms, whether legitimate or not. As believers, they have values that set them apart from the majority of their

---

4. ACN is a Catholic charity whose mission is to support "the faithful wherever they are persecuted, oppressed or in need, through information, prayer and action," http://acninternational.org/.

5. A significant difference between the two documents deserves to be noted. The Index points to Islamic extremism in many countries (e.g. Saudi Arabia, Iran, Pakistan, Qatar, Sudan) where, according to the ACN report, state authoritarianism is the main cause of persecution or discrimination.

6. An Executive Summary (58 pages) of this voluminous report is available on the ACN website, https://rfr.acninternational.org/home/.

agnostic or atheist fellow citizens. They can, therefore, play the role of mediators in "explaining France" (or the UK, or wherever they live) to Muslims who do not feel fully at home in French society. For example, they can highlight all the advantages of a well-understood secularity in order to encourage these Muslims to take full part in the life of this country, without renouncing their religious and cultural distinctiveness. They can also "explain religion" (Islam if they are Muslims, Christianity if they are Christians) to their non-religious fellow citizens to help them understand Islam and Muslims, or Christianity and Christians.

One must strive to understand religion, even in its most controversial aspects, without seeking to excuse what is not excusable. Serving as a bridge between faith communities and the national community, Muslim and Christian citizens will assume the role of reconcilers and peacemakers. This is the specific contribution they can make to prevent radicalization of its members whoever they are: Muslims, Christians, those who have chosen secularism as religion, and people of other faiths or none.

The future of the nations where they live depends on the nations' ability to bring together all their citizens to avoid the polarization of society. Otherwise, it will be only a matter of time before civil war breaks out as partisans of the "big replacement" theory have been predicting for some time. According to these predictions, the native European populations in Western Europe will soon be replaced with foreign migrants from different backgrounds, especially Muslims. Along the way, Christians and Muslims will have many opportunities to bear witness to their faith in a secularized society that has lost its religious and moral landmarks.

Many are now wondering about the collateral victims of the cultural revolution, accelerated by the period of civil unrest in May 1968 in France, with its libertarian slogans like "it's forbidden to forbid." The last few years have been marked by a growing awareness of social ills we did not see coming, or worse, that we tolerated and even excused, in the name of moral liberalism. Among these evils are violence against women and children, sexual harassment, incest, and pedophilia.[7]

Christians have no morality lecture to give on this matter if only because of the sexual abuse scandal within the church. The real dimension of this scandal has been revealed at last thanks to the courage of the victims. This has led the French bishops to take the full measure of this evil and to charge a commission,

---

7. Examples of this awareness include two recently published testimony books: *Le Consentement* by Vanessa Springora (2020), and *La familia grande* by Camille Kouchner (2021).

the CIASE, to investigate these abuses and to write a full report.[8] On 5 October 2021 the commission report was disclosed in a press conference. This 485-page report is a remarkable document in terms of its shocking findings, its wide-ranging investigations and the forty-five recommendations made to the French Catholic bishops.

Every week we learn about very disturbing facts concerning crime and sexual abuse, which speaks volumes about the decadence of our society. It is therefore urgent to unveil the root cause of the evil that is destroying the very fabric of our society.

From a Christian perspective, this evil is deeper than it looks, for it is spiritual first and foremost. Christians understand that turning our backs on our Creator (which used to be known as "sin," an old word we hardly dare pronounce) is the root of all evil. The breaking up of our relationship with our Creator is the root cause of all other break ups: with nature, with others and with oneself. Also, it is up to us Christians, together with Muslims, Jews and everyone else, to contribute to the healing of these ills, each according to their call, with their own skills wherever they are.

Thus, Islamist violence against Christians is present in many countries, including France, the UK and other Western countries. As these countries seek to respond to this violence, Christians have no other choice but to walk in the footsteps of their Lord: "Love your enemies and pray for those who persecute you" (Matt 5:44). Christians in Europe face another challenge of a completely different nature; they have to bear witness to their faith in an increasingly secularized society. This witness is made all the more necessary as the values of society, based on atheistic humanism, are often used to justify alarming libertarian laws.[9]

---

8. This is the Independent Commission on Sexual Abuse in the Church (CIASE), chaired by Mr. Jean-Marc Sauvé (former vice-president of the Council of State), and made up of independent experts in various disciplines. The report (as well as an Executive Summary) is available on the Commission website (www.ciase.fr). In several other countries, Catholic and Anglican bishops have taken similar actions. In May 2021, Nazir Afzal, a very high ranking (Muslim) British judge was appointed by the Catholic Episcopate of England and Wales to head the Commission to investigate sexual abuse in the Catholic church. We would have really liked to see other institutions take such courageous initiatives as sexual abuse seems to have penetrated all areas of social life (art, sport, army, education, administration, etc.).

9. The bill on bioethics (passed on 29 June 2021) is one example of such laws. The article on PMA (Medically Assisted Reproduction) denies the right to have a father to the child born to couples of same-sex women or single women. Besides, children have no right to know who their biological father is and fathers do not have the right to reveal their identity to their biological children.

May God help us to proclaim Christ to our contemporaries, with love, confidence and humility. The prophet Isaiah, in his fourth poem about "the Servant of the Lord," known as "the Suffering Servant," announced that "by his wounds we are healed" (Isa 53:5; cf. Matt 8:17). The arms of Christ, crucified and risen, are wide open. They invite us to receive from his hands, still marked with the scars of the cross, healing from our illnesses and liberation from evil.

Select Bibliography

'Abduh, Muhammad. *Tafsir al-Manar.* 12 vols., 4th ed., edited by M. R. Rida. Cairo: Dar al-Manar, 1954.

Abu Dawud. *Sunan.* 3 vols., translated by Ahmad Hasan. Lahore: Ashraf Publishers, 1988.

Ali, Abdullah Yusuf, trans. *The Holy Qur'an: Translation and Commentary.* Birmingham: Islamic Vision, 1999.

Allam, Mahdi. "The Concept of Forgiveness in the Qur'an." *Islamic Culture* 41, no. 3 (July 1967): 139–53.

Amir-Moezzi, Mohammad Ali. *The Divine Guide in Early Shi'ism: The Sources of Esotericism in Islam*, translated by D. Streight. New York: University of New York Press, 1994.

———. *The Silent Qur'an and the Speaking Qur'an: Scriptural Sources of Islam between History and Fervor*, translated by E. Ormsby. New York: Columbia University Press, 2015.

'Ata ur-Rahim, Muhammad. *Jesus, a Prophet of Islam.* New Delhi: Kitab Bhavan, 2000.

Ateek, Naim. *A Palestinian Theology of Liberation: The Bible, Justice and Palestine-Israel Conflict.* Maryknoll: Orbis, 2017.

Blomberg, Craig. *The Historical Reliability of the Gospels.* Leicester: Inter-Varsity Press, 1987.

Bucaille, Maurice. *The Bible, the Qur'an and Science: The Holy Scriptures Examined in the Light of Modern Knowledge.* Indianapolis: American Trust Publications, 1979.

Bukhari. *Sahih.* 9 vols., translated by Muhammad Muhsen Khan. Beirut: Dar al-'Arabia (Arabic-English ed.), 1985.

Campbell, William. *The Qur'an and the Bible in the Light of History and Science.* Marseilles: Middle East Resources, n.d.

Chapman, Colin. *Christian Zionism and the Restoration of Israel: How Should We Interpret the Scriptures?* Eugene: Cascade Books, 2021.

———. *Cross and Crescent: Responding to the Challenges of Islam.* 3rd ed. Nottingham: IVP, 2007.

———. *Whose Promised Land? The Continuing Conflict over Israel and Palestine.* Oxford: Lion Hudson, 2015.

Cragg, Kenneth. *The Call of Minaret.* Oxford: Oneworld Publications, 2000.

———. *Jesus and the Muslim: An Exploration.* Oxford: Oneworld Publications, 1999.

Deedat, Ahmed. *What the Bible Says about Muhammad.* Birmingham: Islamic Vision, n.d.

———. *Crucifixion or Cruci-fiction?* Durban: Islamic Vision, 1984.

El Karoui, Hakim. *L'islam, une religion française.* Paris: Gallimard, 2018.

El Karoui, Hakim, and Benjamin Hodayé. *Les militants du djihad. Portrait d'une génération*. Paris: Fayard, 2021.
Encyclopedia of Hadith. *Jam'u jawami'i l-ahadithi wa-l-asanid*. Vaduz, Liechtenstein: Thesaurus Islamicus Foundation, 2000. Available online in the original Arabic, http://www.ihsanetwork.org, and in English, http://www.sunnah.com.
Faruqi, Ismail. *Islam and Other Faiths*. Leicester: Islamic Foundation, 1998.
Garrison, David. *A Wind in the House of Islam: How God Is Drawing Muslims around the World to Faith in Jesus Christ*. Monument: WIGTake, 2014.
Ghazali, Abu Hamid. *The Ninety-Nine Beautiful Names of God*. Translated by D. Burrell and N. Dahar. Cambridge: Islamic Texts Society, 1995.
———. *Al-Radd al-Jamil li-ilahiyyat 'Isa bisarihi l-Injil*. Edited and translated by Robert Chidiac, with Introduction, Notes and Commentary, as *Réfutation excellente de la divinité de Jésus-Christ d'après les évangiles*. Paris: PUF, Arabic-French ed., 1939.
Goddard, Hugh. *A History of Christian-Muslim Relations*. Edinburgh: Edinburgh University Press, 2020.
———. *Muslim Perceptions of Christianity*. London: Grey Seal, 1996.
Ibn 'Arabi, Muhyi l-din. *Al-Futuhat al-Makkiyya*. An abridged version edited by Michel Chodkiewicz, *The Meccan Revelations: Selected Texts of Al-Futuhat Al-Makiyya*, translated by William Chittick. New York: Pir Press, 2014.
Ibn Hazm, A. M. *Kitab al-Fisal fi l-Milal wa l-Ahwa' wa l-Nihal*. 3 vols. Cairo: Dar al-Fikr, 1980.
Ibn Majah. *Sunan*. 5 vols., translated by M. T. Ansari. New Delhi: Kitab Bhavan (Arabic-English ed.), 1994.
Ibn Taymiyya, Ahmad. *Al-Jawab al-Sahih liman Baddala Dina l-Masih*. Translated by Thomas F. Michel, with Introduction, Notes and Commentary, *A Muslim Theologian's Response to Christianity*. Delmar: Caravan Books, 1984.
Jubilee Centre. *Immigration and Justice: How Local Churches Can Change the Debate on Immigration in Britain*. Cambridge: Jubilee Centre, 2015.
Juwayni, Abu l-Ma'ali. *Shifa' al-Ghalil fi Bayan ma Waqa'a fi l-Tawrat wa l-Injil mina l-Tabdil*. Edited by Michel Allard, with Notes and Commentary, *Textes apologétiques de Guwayni*. Beirut: Dar al-Mashriq (Arabic-French ed.), 1968.
Kamali, Mohammad Hashim. *Shari'ah Law: An Introduction*. Oxford: Oneworld Publications, 2010.
Kuhn, Michael F. *God Is One: A Christian Defence of Divine Unity in the Muslim Golden Age*. Carlisle: Langham Global Library, 2019.
Kurzman, Charles, ed. *Liberal Islam: A Sourcebook*. Oxford: Oxford University Press, 1998.
Lory, Pierre. "Les signes de la fin des temps dans les traditions sunnites." In *Penser la fin du monde*, edited by Emma Aubin-Boltanski and Claudine Gauthier, 269–80. Paris: CNRS Éditions, 2014.
McAuliffe, Jane Dammen, ed. *Encylopaedia of the Qur'an*, 6 vols. Leiden: Brill, 2001–2006.

Mir-Hosseini, Ziba, Mulki Al-Sharmani, Jana Rumminger, eds. *Men in Charge? Rethinking Authority in Muslim Legal Tradition.* London: Oneworld Publications, 2015.

Moucarry, Chawkat. "The Alien according to the Torah." *Themelios* 14, no. 1 (Oct–Nov 1988): 17–20.

———. *Faith to Faith: Christianity and Islam in Dialogue.* Nottingham: Inter-Varsity Press, 2001. Also published in the USA, *The Prophet and the Messiah: An Arab Christian's Perspective on Islam and Christianity.* Downers Grove: InterVarsity Press, 2001.

———. *The Search for Forgiveness: Pardon and Punishment in Islam and Christianity.* Nottingham: Inter-Varsity Press, 2004.

———. *Two Prayers for Today: The Lord's Prayer and the Fatiha.* Tiruvalla: CSS, 2007.

Muslim, Imam. *Sahih.* 4 vols., translated by Abdul Hamid Siddiqi. New Delhi: Kitab Bhavan, 1977.

Ouardi, Hela. *Les Califes maudits*, vol. 1, *La Déchirure*, vol. 2, *À l'ombre des sabres*, vol. 3, *Meurtre à la mosquée.* Paris: Albin Michel, 2019–2021.

Pohl, Christine. *Making Room: Recovering Hospitality as a Christian Tradition.* Grand Rapids: Eerdmans, 1999.

Qur'an. A bilingual edition of the Qur'an is available online, http://www.quran.com.

Ragg, Londsale, and Laura Ragg, trans. *The Gospel of Barnabas.* Rome: Islamic European Cultural Centre, 1986.

Ramadan, Tariq. *Islam, the West and the Challenges of Modernity.* Leicester: Islamic Foundation, 2009.

Razi, Fakhr-ul-Din. *Al-Tafsir al-Kabir.* 16 vols. Beirut: Dar al-Kutub al-'Ilmiyya, 1990.

Shahrour, Muhammad. *Islam and Humanity: Consequences of a Contemporary Reading.* Berlin: Gerlach Press, 2017.

Sizer, Stephen. *Christian Zionism: Road-Map for Armageddon?* Nottingham: Inter-Varsity Press, 2006.

Spencer, Nick. *Asylum and Immigration: A Christian Perspective on a Polarised Debate.* Milton Keynes: Authentic, 2004.

Langham Literature and its imprints are a ministry of Langham Partnership.

Langham Partnership is a global fellowship working in pursuit of the vision God entrusted to its founder John Stott –

to facilitate the growth of the church in maturity and Christ-likeness through raising the standards of biblical preaching and teaching.

Our vision is to see churches in the Majority World equipped for mission and growing to maturity in Christ through the ministry of pastors and leaders who believe, teach and live by the word of God.

Our mission is to strengthen the ministry of the word of God through:
- nurturing national movements for biblical preaching
- fostering the creation and distribution of evangelical literature
- enhancing evangelical theological education

especially in countries where churches are under-resourced.

Our ministry

Langham Preaching partners with national leaders to nurture indigenous biblical preaching movements for pastors and lay preachers all around the world. With the support of a team of trainers from many countries, a multi-level programme of seminars provides practical training, and is followed by a programme for training local facilitators. Local preachers' groups and national and regional networks ensure continuity and ongoing development, seeking to build vigorous movements committed to Bible exposition.

Langham Literature provides Majority World preachers, scholars and seminary libraries with evangelical books and electronic resources through publishing and distribution, grants and discounts. The programme also fosters the creation of indigenous evangelical books in many languages, through writer's grants, strengthening local evangelical publishing houses, and investment in major regional literature projects, such as one volume Bible commentaries like *The Africa Bible Commentary* and *The South Asia Bible Commentary*.

Langham Scholars provides financial support for evangelical doctoral students from the Majority World so that, when they return home, they may train pastors and other Christian leaders with sound, biblical and theological teaching. This programme equips those who equip others. Langham Scholars also works in partnership with Majority World seminaries in strengthening evangelical theological education. A growing number of Langham Scholars study in high quality doctoral programmes in the Majority World itself. As well as teaching the next generation of pastors, graduated Langham Scholars exercise significant influence through their writing and leadership.

To learn more about Langham Partnership and the work we do visit **langham.org**

www.ingramcontent.com/pod-product-compliance
Lightning Source LLC
Chambersburg PA
CBHW071739150426
43191CB00010B/1632